D0945256

HYPOCRISY AND INTEGRITY

HYPOCRISY
and
INTEGRITY

Machiavelli,

Rousseau,

and

the Ethics

of Politics

RUTH W. GRANT

THE UNIVERSITY OF CHICAGO PRESS
Chicago and London

RUTH WEISSBOURD GRANT is associate professor of political science at Duke University. She is the author of *John Locke's Liberalism* (1987), also published by the University of Chicago Press.

The University of Chicago Press, Chicago 60637
The University of Chicago Press, Ltd., London
© 1997 by The University of Chicago
All rights reserved. Published 1997
Printed in the United States of America

06 05 04 03 02 01 00 99 98 97   1 2 3 4 5

ISBN: 0-226-30582-1 (cloth)

Library of Congress Cataloging-in-Publication Data

Grant, Ruth Weissbourd, 1951–
    Hypocrisy and integrity : Machiavelli, Rousseau, and the ethics of politics / Ruth W. Grant.
      p. cm.
    Includes bibliographical references and index.
    ISBN 0-226-30582-1 (cloth : alk. paper)
    1. Political ethics. 2. Compromise (Ethics) 3. Hypocrisy.
    4. Machiavelli, Niccolò, 1469–1527—Contributions in political science. 5. Rousseau, Jean-Jacques, 1712–1778—Contributions in political science. I. Title.
    JA79.G683   1997
    172—dc21   96-45356
                                            CIP

♾ The paper used in this publication meets the minimum requirements of the American National Standard for Information Sciences–Permanence of Paper for Printed Library Materials, ANSI Z39.48-1984.

To Laura, Joseph, and Anna

CONTENTS

ACKNOWLEDGMENTS

In the course of writing this book, I received many and various gifts which I am very glad to be able to acknowledge here. The National Endowment for the Humanities, the American Council of Learned Societies and the Duke University Arts and Sciences Council were generous in their financial support for this project. Many colleagues and friends have given me the benefit of their learning, their criticisms and their encouragement. I owe a special debt of gratitude to Sanford Kessler and to Michael Gillespie for their careful reading of my drafts and their constant good judgment. Christopher Kelly corrected important errors on more than one occasion and led me to places in Rousseau's work where I might not have travelled otherwise. My students at Duke, particularly all those who served at various times as my research assistants, contributed much more than they realize to my understanding of the issues and (no less importantly) to my ability to complete the project. I would also like to thank Jesamine Jones for her help with the final preparation of the manuscript. Portions of chapters 3–5 originally appeared in an earlier article, "Integrity and Politics: An Alternative Reading of Rousseau," *Political Theory* 22, no. 3 (August 1994): 414–43. © 1994 Sage Publications, Inc. The publisher's permission to reprint this material is gratefully acknowledged.

The debt that I owe to my husband, Stephen Grant, is beyond measure. I wrote this book in the years when our children were young, and it is dedicated to them.

ABBREVIATIONS

Throughout this work, I have referred to readily available English translations. Citations refer to editions in the original language where that was not possible or where it was important to note the author's use of a particular term. Translations from the original-language editions are my own. I have included references to book, part, chapter, or letter numbers where appropriate in addition to page numbers.

While this book was being written, a new English-language edition of Jean-Jacques Rousseau's writings has been in production with pages correlated to the pages of the *Oeuvres complètes* which I have cited. Thus the reader may find it useful to consult *The Collected Writings of Rousseau,* edited by Roger D. Masters and Christopher Kelly, 7 vols. (Hanover, N.H.: University Press of New England, 1990–).

WORKS OF NICCOLÒ MACHIAVELLI

D.   *The Discourses.* Edited with an introduction by Bernard Crick. Translated by Leslie J. Walker (London: Penguin, 1970).

Pr.   *The Prince.* Translated with an introduction by Harvey C. Mansfield, Jr. (Chicago: University of Chicago Press, 1985).

WORKS OF JEAN-JACQUES ROUSSEAU

D'Alembert *Politics and the Arts: Letter to M. D'Alembert on the Theater.* Edited and translated by Allan Bloom (Ithaca, N.Y.: Cornell Univ. Press, 1960).

Confessions *The Confessions.* Translated by J. M. Cohen (London: Penguin, 1953).

Émile *Émile, or On Education.* Translated by Allan Bloom (New York: Basic Books, 1979).

First "Discourse on the Sciences and Arts," in *First and Second Discourses.* Edited by Roger D. Masters. Translated by Roger D. Masters and Judith R. Masters (New York: St. Martin's Press, 1964).

Julie *Julie, ou La Nouvelle Héloïse,* in *O.C.,* II, 5–794.

Mountain "Lettres Écrites de la Montagne," in *O.C.,* III, 683–897.

O.C. *Oeuvres complètes.* Edited by Bernard Gagnebin and Marcel Raymond (Paris: Gallimard, Bibliothèque de la Pléiade, 1959–1969).

Poland *The Government of Poland.* Translated by Wilmoore Kendall (Indianapolis: Bobbs-Merrill, 1972).

Reveries *Reveries of the Solitary Walker.* Translated by Peter France (London: Penguin, 1979).

S.C. *On the Social Contract with Geneva Manuscript and Political Economy.* Edited by Roger D. Masters. Translated by Judith R. Masters (New York: St. Martin's Press, 1978).

Second "On the Origin and Foundations of Inequality among Men." In *First and Second Discourses.* Edited by Roger D. Masters. Translated by Roger D. Masters and Judith R. Masters (New York: St. Martin's Press, 1964).

1

Introduction

"Hypocrite" is an epithet, never a term of praise, and for good reason. Consider the classic hypocritical types: the lecherous priest, the smarmy flattering socialite, the "reform" politician with his hand in the till. What they share is the pretense of virtue, idealism, or sympathetic concern used to further selfish ends. Their victims are the more to be pitied because of the painful betrayal of trust involved in their victimization. When an old woman is persuaded to "invest" her life savings in a phony pension fund we are considerably more outraged than when she loses it all in an ordinary robbery. The "confidence man" (note the term) is a special sort of criminal: his hypocrisy adds insult to injury.

It is a fairly straightforward matter to condemn this sort of hypocrisy. But is hypocrisy always such a bad thing? Consideration of the antihypocrite as the alternative certainly gives one reason to wonder. The antihypocrite too is a classic type.[1] Inflexible in his righteousness and unwilling to countenance any moral lapse, he scarcely recognizes the necessity for compromise. Too often the costs of his efforts to sustain his own purity are borne by others, and hence he ought not to be trusted either. In this respect, the antihypocrite has more in common with the hypocrite than it would seem at first glance.

---

1. Orgon, a character from Molière's *Tartuffe,* and Alceste, from his *The Misanthrope,* are discussed as examples of the type in chapter 3. The Murdstones in Charles Dickens's *David Copperfield* also exemplify the antihypocrite.

It is possible, after all, to be too good. This intuition feeds our suspicion of antihypocrites who appear in the form of political ideologues and religious zealots. The intuition is supported by psychologists who see moral rigidity as indicative of a personality imbalance, usually as evidence of an overweening superego. At best, oversensitivity to hypocrisy and extreme concern for principled consistency are identified as characteristics of adolescent idealism: appropriate for a particular stage of development but meant to be superseded as development progresses.[2] The question is, superseded by what? What ought to be our stance toward principles as adults: should we guide our actions by them or not? Is adolescent idealism to be replaced by mature cynicism? Or are there forms of mature idealism whose characteristics can be identified?

Hypocrisy and antihypocrisy, cynicism and sanctimonious righteousness are not the only possibilities. The alternative we seek is *integrity,* keeping in mind that integrity may take a variety of forms. The person of integrity is one who can be trusted to do the right thing even at some cost to himself. "Doing the right thing" may require compromise; some compromises are certainly possible without compromising oneself. "Doing the right thing" also may require deception, or ethical posturing, or both; some forms of hypocrisy may be perfectly acceptable or even laudable. What we need to know is which kinds of deception, hypocrisy, and compromise are defensible and which are not. What are the ethical alternatives that nonetheless require some sort of departure from a purely principled stance? When is it good to be a little bad? And particularly, when and why is it necessary, when being a little bad, to maintain the appearance of goodness? This book aims to identify the ethical alternatives and to discriminate among them, particularly with a view to the place of hypocrisy in politics.

It is a central claim of this book that hypocrisy and politics are inextricably connected on account of the peculiar character of political relationships. Political relations, ordinarily understood as power relations, can just as readily be conceived as relations of

2. See, for example, Peter Blos, *On Adolescence: A Psychoanalytic Interpretation* (Glencoe, Ill.: Free Press, 1962), 168–97; Erik H. Erikson, *Childhood and Society,* 2d ed. (New York: W. W. Norton, 1963), 263; Erikson, *Identity, Youth and Crisis* (New York: W. W. Norton, 1968), 87–90, 128–35.

dependence. They are dependencies among people who require one another's voluntary cooperation but whose interests are in conflict. In such a situation, trust is required but highly problematic, and the pressures towards hypocrisy are immense. Because political relations are dependencies of this sort, hypocrisy is a regular feature of political life, and the general ethical problem of hypocrisy and integrity is quintessentially a political problem.

Contemporary political theory, however, has been concerned primarily with determining either what principles ought to govern political practice or whether there are principles that can govern political practice at all. It has been relatively unconcerned with the central political problem of how strictly we ought to adhere to whatever political principles we have. Yet this is a problem that regularly confronts political actors with compelling force. Some of the most serious and most frequent political conflicts arise among people who share basic guiding principles but part company over when to take a stand on principle and when to accept a compromise. How can the distinction be made between a legitimate compromise and a sellout, idealism and fanaticism, statesmanship and demagoguery, or moderation and rationalization in defense of the status quo? How can we determine the moral limits of both moderation and moralism in politics?

These are the questions explored here. The investigation proceeds not only through theoretical argumentation but also through the analysis of character types. Ideal types presented in literary and philosophic texts provide the material for a comparison of various sorts of moderates with various sorts of moralists. And while certain criteria emerge for making moral judgments among them, no fixed set of moral rules is elaborated and defended. In fact, part of what is at issue is whether there can be rules for when the rules ought to be bent or broken. Prudence, judgment, and the art of politics coexist in perpetual tension with formal, theoretically grounded, abstract principles. The approach taken here reflects the argument. The elaboration of rules or principles cannot exhaust our exploration of ethical and political issues.

The works of Niccolò Machiavelli, Molière, and Jean-Jacques Rousseau provide the bulk of the material for the discussion, with Rousseau's work given the greatest attention. Certain of Machiavelli's writings are mined as sources in developing and defending the case for hypocrisy in politics. Molière's comedies furnish examples of a wide variety of hypocrites and antihypocrites, as well as the model for the particular type of integrity exemplified by the statesmanlike moderate. In Rousseau's writings, we find a critique of Molière's moderate and an intriguing alternative. Rousseau defends the integrity of the moralist, distinguishing it from the rigid righteousness of the antihypocrite. This Rousseauian ideal of integrity is explored here with a view to its compatibility with prudential political judgment, its relation to Rousseau's understanding of corruption, and, of course, its viability as an ethical alternative.

What the reader will not find here is the direct comparison of Machiavelli and Rousseau that might be expected in a book on hypocrisy and integrity. At first glance, Machiavelli and Rousseau seem to stand at opposite poles on the question of hypocrisy in politics. Machiavelli is as famous for his advocacy of political hypocrisy as Rousseau is renowned for his criticism of it. In *The Prince,* Machiavelli makes the case for the necessity of hypocrisy in politics. Accepting that case might lead either to moral cynicism or to moral purity accompanied by withdrawal from politics. The former is a caricatured version of the Machiavellian alternative, while the latter is a caricature of Rousseau's position. These authors would seem to offer the bipolar alternatives of the hypocrite and the antihypocrite, neither of which is satisfactory, as I have already suggested. Fortunately, our political options are not limited to an unethical pragmatic realism on the one hand and a principled idealism (unethical too in its political irresponsibility) on the other. The situation is considerably more complex, as are the works explored here.

It is particularly difficult to rest satisfied with an interpretation of Rousseau as an antihypocrite or as the polar opposite of Machiavelli. Rousseau, after all, praised Machiavelli, advised the Legislator to use religion to deceive the people, counseled flexibility in applying principles of political right, and, most important, accepted the Machiavellian understanding of the necessarily hypocritical nature of political relationships. This book elaborates an interpretation of Rousseau grounded in an appreciation of the theoretical insights he shares with Machiavelli. Rousseau's position as an antihypocrite is not as simple as it seems, and I argue that an examination of the complexities of his thought yields a new understanding of the ethical alternatives with respect to the problem of hypocrisy and integrity in politics. The question is what political integrity might mean, whether such integrity is possible, and how it might be maintained given the understanding, found both in Machiavelli and in Rousseau, that hypocrisy and deception are endemic to political relationships.

As I have suggested, the argument involves a reevaluation of the relationship between Machiavelli and Rousseau, which has important implications in turn for our understanding of their place in the history of political thought. We can begin with Rousseau's own judgment of Machiavelli's work.[3] In *The Social Contract,* where Rousseau refers to Machiavelli more often than to any other author, he makes his opinion clear. He writes: "While pretending to give lessons to kings, he gave great ones to the people. Machiavelli's *The Prince* is the book of republicans" (*S.C.,* III, vi, 88).[4] For the 1782 edition, Rousseau wrote the following note to this statement:

> Machiavelli was an honorable man and a good citizen; but being attached to the Medici household, he was forced, during the oppression of his homeland, to disguise his love of freedom. The choice of his execrable hero is in itself enough to make manifest his hidden intention; and the contrast between the maxims of his book *The Prince* and those of his *Discourse on Titus Livy* and of his *History of Florence* shows that this profound political theorist [*profond politique*] has had only superficial or corrupt readers until now. The court of Rome has severely forbidden his book. I can well believe it; it is the court that he most clearly depicts. (*S.C.,* III, vi, 88)[5]

3. For Rousseau's knowledge of Machiavelli's writings, see Paolo M. Cucchi, "Rousseau, Lecteur de Machiavel," in *Jean-Jacques Rousseau et son temps: Politique et littérature au XVIIIe siècle,* ed. Michel Launay (Paris: Librairie A. G. Nizet, 1969), 17–35; Yves Lévy, "Machiavel et Rousseau," *Le Contrat Social* 6 (1962): 169–74; and Roger Payot, "Jean-Jacques Rousseau et Machiavel," *Les Études Philosophiques* 26 (1971): 209–23.

4. Rousseau's first explicit reference to Machiavelli is in the *Discours sur l'économie politique,* where he speaks of the "satires" of Machiavelli: the maxims of tyranny, where government and people have different interests and opposing wills, are inscribed in the archives of history and in "les satyres de Machiavel" (*O.C.,* III, 247). Note that here he does not distinguish *The Prince* from the other works. Rousseau also refers to Machiavelli as among the negative examples of modern historians (*Émile,* 239n).

5. "Machiavel étoit un honnête homme et un bon citoyen: mais attaché à la maison de Médicis il étoit forcé dans l'oppression de sa patrie de déguiser son amour pour

Rousseau understood Machiavelli to be a champion of republicanism who had, for political reasons, concealed his views in *The Prince* in a manner calculated to teach republicanism to alert readers. Notwithstanding Rousseau's suggestion to the contrary, this reading was by no means unique. For example, it can be found in the writings of Spinoza, Bayle, and Diderot, who also cites Bacon in agreement on this issue.[6] An alternative reading, however, was available to Rousseau. In 1740, Frederick of Prussia wrote a refutation of *The Prince* called *Anti-Machiavel,* which was edited by Voltaire, who also saw to its publication.[7] The work took Machiavelli's "machiavellianism" seriously and condemned him for his corrupting doctrines. Rousseau's opinion of this work can be found in his letters. He considered the King of Prussia a tyrant without principles or virtue who "began his Machiavellianism by refuting Machiavelli."[8]

Since Rousseau viewed Machiavelli as a fellow republican, most of the surprisingly small literature on their relationship explores the similarities and differences in their republican politics.[9]

la liberté. Le choix seul de son éxecrable Heros manifeste assés son intention secrette et l'opposition des maximes de son Livre du Prince à celles de ses discours sur Tite-Live et de son histoire de Florence demontre que ce profond politique n'a eu jusqu'ici que des Lecteurs superficiels ou corrompus. La Cour de Rome aséverement défendu son livre, je le crois bien; c'est elle qu'il dépeint le plus clairement" (*O.C.,* III, 1480).

6. See Pierre Bayle, *Dictionnaire historique et critique,* 5th ed. (Amsterdam: P. Brunel, 1740); Denis Diderot, *Encyclopédie IV,* vol. 8 of *Oeuvres complètes de Diderot,* ed. John Lough and Jacques Proust (Paris: Hermann, 1976), 3–5; Benedict de Spinoza, *A Political Treatise,* in *The Chief Works of Benedict de Spinoza: "A Theological-Political Treatise" and "A Political Treatise,"* trans. R. H. M. Elwes (New York: Dover, 1951), chap. 5, sec. 7.

7. Frederick of Prussia, *The Refutation of Machiavelli's "Prince" or Anti-Machiavel,* trans. Paul Sonnino (Athens: Ohio University Press, 1981).

8. "Rousseau à Toussaint-Pierre Lenieps," Dec. 4, 1758, *Correspondance complète de Jean-Jacques Rousseau,* ed. R. A. Leigh (Geneva: Institut et Musée Voltaire, 1967), 5:247–48.

9. See Cucchi, "Rousseau, Lecteur de Machiavel"; Yves Lévy, "Les Partis et la démocratie (I)," *Le Contrat Social* 3 (1959): 79–86; Lévy, "Machiavel et Rousseau"; Joseph Masciulli, "The Armed Founder versus the Catonic Hero: Machiavelli and Rousseau on Popular Leadership," *Interpretation* 14 (1986): 265–80; Lionel McKenzie, "Rousseau's Debate with Machiavelli in the *Social Contract,*" *Journal of the History of Ideas* 43 (April–June 1982): 209–28; Payot, "Jean-Jacques Rousseau et Machiavel"; Paule Monique Vernes, "Nicolas Machiavel Chez Jean-Jacques Rousseau: Des leçons aux rois ou des leçons aux peuples?" *Actes du colloque franco-italien de philosophie* (Paris:

Of course, many similarities can be identified: both admired ancient republics, advocated citizen militia, appreciated the political effects of the corruption of virtue, and recognized the role of a Founder or Legislator in establishing republics.[10] The crucial differences between them are variously identified by the commentators, though they do bear a noticeable resemblance: Rousseau is more abstract and utopian, while Machiavelli is more realistic; Machiavelli admired Rome, while Rousseau admired Sparta; Machiavelli stressed the necessity of political violence, particularly at the moment of founding, while Rousseau relied more heavily on the moral excellence of the citizen body; and, perhaps most important, Machiavelli sought to maintain republican liberty through a balance of parties, while Rousseau sought to establish it by eliminating them.[11] But however different their understandings of republican politics, Rousseau certainly approved of what he saw as Machiavelli's republican principles.[12]

With respect to the question of political ethics, this alone does not get us very far.[13] Rousseau admired Machiavelli. But for what exactly did he admire this *profond politique*? Did Rousseau admire Machiavelli's ability to conceal his republicanism in writing *The Prince*? And if he did admire him for writing *The Prince* dishonestly, how is that judgment to be reconciled with Rousseau's own

École Normale d'Instituteur de Nice, 1977): 77–89; Maurizio Viroli, "Republic and Politics in Machiavelli and Rousseau," *History of Political Thought* 10 (autumn 1989): 405–20.

10. Rousseau's "Discours sur la vertu la plus nécessaire aux héros" is also thought to owe a great deal to Machiavelli. See, for example, Lévy, "Machiavel et Rousseau."

11. On this last point particularly, some scholars suggest that Rousseau more or less self-consciously concealed his differences with Machiavelli. See Lévy, "Les Partis et la démocratie (I)," 85; and McKenzie, "Rousseau's Debate with Machiavelli," who suggests that Rousseau may have wished to conceal the extent to which his republicanism represents a departure from the republican tradition.

12. Masciulli and Payot argue that Rousseau could take this position only because he misread Machiavelli.

13. Only Vernes and Viroli discuss this issue in comparing the two, and they disagree. Vernes argues that both Machiavelli and Rousseau believe that politics pursues moral ends with immoral means and that this paradox of politics puts it in opposition to the rational task of philosophy. Vernes, "Des Leçons aux rois ou des leçons aux peuples?" Viroli argues that Rousseau failed to recognize the tragic dimension of politics emphasized by Machiavelli, viz., the irreconcilablity of ethical and political requirements. Viroli, "Republic and Politics," 416 ff.

professed dedication to truthfulness? Rousseau's own motto as an author was "Vitam impendere vero."[14] In the very note quoted above where he described Machiavelli's duplicity as an author, Rousseau praised him as an honorable man and a good citizen (*un honnête homme et un bon citoyen*). This is very interesting and high praise from a man whose philosophy continually exposed the difficulties of being both at the same time.[15] And it raises the possibility that, in this case at least, Machiavelli could be both at the same time only by being deceitful. On the other hand, Rousseau criticized Frederick as a hypocrite. According to Rousseau, his writing also concealed his true political intentions, but in a reprehensible manner.

Rousseau's comments on Machiavelli's *The Prince* and Frederick's refutation of it raise an issue that can be generalized beyond the concern for authorial honesty. Did Rousseau admire Machiavelli in spite of the moral lessons of *The Prince* or, rather, because of them? Moreover, many of the same lessons concerning deceit, manipulation, and expedience in political morality are taught in *The Discourses* as in *The Prince*.[16] The question of political ethics cannot be dismissed—on the contrary, it is only intensified—by the recognition that Rousseau believed *The Prince* to have been written deceptively. I am suggesting that if we take seriously Rousseau's positive judgment of Machiavelli, we may be led to reconsider our assessment of Rousseau. At the least, Rousseau's comments indicate both that his political ethics have a greater pragmatic dimension than is often acknowledged and that he is not a simple antihypocrite.[17] How did Rousseau, who clearly admired Machiavelli, come to terms with the ethical problems of political hypocrisy? The answer to this question should help us to see what Rousseau's alternative political ethics really is.

The reevaluation of the relation between Machiavelli and

---

14. "Dedicate life to truth." See Juvenal, *Satires,* 4:91.

15. See, for example, *Émile,* 40. For a discussion of "honnêteté," see chapter 3.

16. See chapter 2, notes 5 and 6 and accompanying text.

17. For a suggestion of Rousseau's pragmatism see his letter to Mirabeau, 26 July 1767, in which he wrote: "There can never be certitude in natural and political laws except by considering them in the abstract. In a particular government, this certitude necessarily disappears. Because the science of government is only a science of applications of combinations, of exceptions according to the times, the laws, the circumstances." *Correspondance complète de Jean-Jacques Rousseau,* ed. R. A. Leigh (Oxford: The Voltaire Foundation, 1979), 33:242.

Rousseau with respect to the question of political hypocrisy compels us to reconsider the place of these two thinkers in the history of political thought altogether. Two competing accounts of that history give the interpretation of Machiavelli's writings a crucial place. According to Leo Strauss, Machiavelli was the first to break radically with all previous political philosophy.[18] The most important elements of his originality are that he took his bearings from how men are rather than how they ought to be, and that he taught that man can master fortune. Both of these imply a rejection of the ancient conception of nature according to which man has a place in a natural order that determines both his perfection and his limits. Instead, with Machiavelli, political justice is severed from any natural ground. According to Strauss, in these respects Machiavelli stands at the origin of an intellectual tradition leading through Bacon, Hobbes, and Locke that established the ground for contemporary interest-based liberal politics. With self-preservation established as the chief end of human life and political association, "Eventually, we arrive at the view that universal affluence and peace is the necessary and sufficient condition of perfect justice."[19] Rousseau represents the first decisive break with this development. In the name of ancient virtue, Rousseau attacked the modern political philosophy that Machiavelli had set in motion; but Rousseau could not reestablish ancient virtue, having accepted the modern view of man's relation to nature. There remains in Rousseau's thought an unbridgeable chasm between man as a natural being and man as a social and political being. Rousseau must be understood as an alternative to Machiavelli but one who remains firmly within the modern tradition that Machiavelli began.[20]

18. On Machiavelli as a founder who broke decisively with the ancients, see also Harvey C. Mansfield, Jr., *Machiavelli's Virtue* (Chicago: University of Chicago Press, 1996). Other interpreters have also seen Machiavelli as a true innovator in various respects. For a few examples, see Mark Hulliung, *Citizen Machiavelli* (Princeton: Princeton University Press, 1983), 237–57; Sheldon S. Wolin, *Politics and Vision* (1960; reprint, London: George Allen and Unwin, 1961), 199–217.

19. Leo Strauss, "Three Waves of Modernity," in *An Introduction to Political Philosophy: Ten Essays by Leo Strauss,* ed. Hilail Gildin (Detroit: Wayne State University Press, 1989), 89.

20. See Leo Strauss, *Natural Right and History* (Chicago: University of Chicago Press, 1953), 252–94; Strauss, *Ten Essays.* See also Leo Strauss, *Thoughts on Machiavelli* (Chicago: University of Chicago Press, 1984), 294.

According to a competing school of thought originating with
J. G. A. Pocock, Machiavelli was one of a group of Florentine
humanists who attempted to revive an ancient ideal of republican
politics "in which the political nature of man as described by
Aristotle was to receive its fulfillment."[21] Such an attempt was
necessarily problematic since it had to be reconciled with a Christian theological framework that did not admit of the possibility
of secular fulfillment. Machiavelli's work on this problem contributed to a rich legacy of republican thought whose central conceptions included virtue, fortune, and corruption.[22] Rousseau
wrote in the language of republicanism as well and was deeply
indebted to republican thinkers, including Machiavelli, particularly for his conception of republican liberty.[23] Both Machiavelli
and Rousseau can be seen as part of an ongoing civic republican
tradition that stands in opposition to those modern political
thinkers who build their politics around the conception of interest.

A number of important issues are at stake in this controversy,[24]

21. J. G. A. Pocock, *The Machiavellian Moment: Florentine Political Thought and the
Atlantic Republican Tradition* (Princeton: Princeton University Press, 1975), vii.

22. In addition to Pocock, *The Machiavellian Moment,* see Gisela Bok, Quentin
Skinner, and Maurizio Viroli, eds., *Machiavelli and Republicanism* (Cambridge: Cambridge University Press, 1990); Quentin Skinner, *Foundations of Modern Political
Thought,* (Cambridge: Cambridge University Press, 1978), vol. 1, chaps. 5–6; Quentin
Skinner, *Machiavelli* (New York: Hill and Wang, 1981); Maurizio Viroli, *From Politics
to Reason of State: The Acquisition and Transformation of the Language of Politics 1250–
1600* (Cambridge: Cambridge University Press, 1992).

23. See Maurizio Viroli, *Jean-Jacques Rousseau and the "Well-Ordered Society,"* trans.
Derek Hanson (Cambridge: Cambridge University Press, 1988). Viroli argues that
Rousseau used the social contract tradition to explain the legitimacy of political societies and the republican tradition to explain the preservation of a just order and asserts
that these are "unconnected problems" (13). But they are certainly connected at least
in the sense that the grounds of legitimacy might serve to define what means may be
legitimately employed in preserving the society.

For the relation between Machiavelli and Rousseau and their different sorts of
republicanism, see especially Viroli, *Well-Ordered Society,* 168–78. For extensive treatment of Machiavelli's republicanism, see Viroli, *From Politics to Reason of State,* 126–
77.

24. One of the most important is methodological. See J. G. A. Pocock, "Political
Ideas as Historical Events: Political Philosophers as Historical Actors," in *Political Theory and Political Education,* ed. Melvin Richter (Princeton: Princeton University Press,

but of greatest concern here is that each of these tellings of the history of political thought holds different implications for the ethical possibilities for political life in the modern age.[25] According to Strauss's view (briefly stated), modern political philosophy, beginning with Machiavelli's self-conscious rejection of the ancients, grounds politics fundamentally in self-interest or self-preservation and undermines any claims for the naturalness of virtue. Modern philosophic reactions to the politics of self-interest, even critical reactions, have only continued to weaken the foundations of virtue. This would imply that any practical support for virtue in the modern age must draw on premodern elements of the tradition.[26] Alternatively, Pocock's view allows for the presence of two distinct trends within modernity. Interest-based liberalism and civic republicanism have coexisted in various forms throughout modern times. And civic republicanism, which never quite broke from its ancient sources, has functioned as an

---

1980), 139–58; Quentin Skinner, "Meaning and Understanding in the History of Ideas," *History and Theory* 8, no. 1 (1969): 3–53; Leo Strauss, *Persecution and the Art of Writing* (Chicago: University of Chicago Press, 1988), 22–37; Nathan Tarcov, "Quentin Skinner's Method and Machiavelli's *Prince*," *Ethics* 92 (1982): 692–709.

25. Maurizio Viroli wrote:

> The interpretive dilemma seems clear. . . . Did [Machiavelli] dismantle or recover the republican view of politics as the art of instituting and preserving the good political community?
>
> What also seems clear is that the question goes beyond the field of Machiavelli studies. Implicitly or explicitly, we are all using the supposedly Machiavellian understanding of politics as games of power, convenience and self-interest which are to be discussed in the language of empirical science. If we discovered that Machiavelli had actually told us a completely different story, that politics pertains only to the preservation of a community of men grounded on justice and the common good we might be tempted to reconsider our mental habits concerning politics. An accurate historical understanding of Machiavelli's language could produce an interesting theoretical account, one which would, as is often the case, have its own moral.

Maurizio Viroli, "Machiavelli and the Republican Idea of Politics," in Gisela Bok et al., *Machiavelli and Republicanism,* 144.

26. "The theoretical crisis [of liberal democracy] does not necessarily lead to a practical crisis. . . . [A]bove all, liberal democracy, in contradistinction to communism and fascism, derives powerful support from a way of thinking which cannot be called modern at all: the premodern thought of our western tradition." Strauss, *Ten Essays*, 98.

active alternative to Lockean liberalism and early modern capitalism, especially in the English-speaking world.[27] According to this
view, we can find in civic republicanism a modern alternative
that includes a viable conception of civic virtue.

Both Strauss's interpretation and Pocock's are called into question in certain respects by the analysis presented here. I argue,
contrary to Strauss, that Machiavelli and Rousseau share considerable common ground in opposition to the liberalism that develops from the works of Hobbes and Locke. I also argue, contrary
to Pocock, that the concept of civic republicanism is not what
they share. Strauss's interpretation obscures similarities between
Machiavelli and Rousseau as well as dissimilarities between
Machiavelli and certain later modern philosophers.[28] Pocock's interpretation distorts what those similarities and dissimilarities are.
Neither of the standard interpretations fully accommodates the
importance of hypocrisy for either Machiavelli's or Rousseau's
understanding of the relation between morality and politics.

In what follows, I do not return to the Strauss/Pocock controversy directly, although the relation between Machiavelli, Rousseau, and early modern liberalism remains a strong secondary
theme. I have introduced the interpretive controversy here both
to situate my own analysis and to indicate that that analysis opens
up a different perspective on the alternative understandings of
political morality available within modern thought.

What, then, do Machiavelli and Rousseau have in common
that is revealed in their understandings of political hypocrisy? In
the first instance, they share an understanding of political depen-

---

27. See Pocock, *The Machiavellian Moment*, viii–ix; J. G. A. Pocock, "Machiavelli, Harrington and English Political Ideologies in the Eighteenth Century," *William
and Mary Quarterly* 22 (Oct. 1965): 549–83. See also Joyce Appleby, *Liberalism and
Republicanism in the Historical Imagination* (Cambridge: Harvard University Press, 1992),
135–39.

28. The relation between Machiavelli and Hobbes is particularly interesting. New
evidence of Machiavelli's influence on Hobbes is provided in Noel B. Reynolds and
Arlene W. Saxonhouse, eds., *Three Discourses: A Critical Modern Edition of Newly Identified Work of the Young Hobbes* (Chicago: University of Chicago Press, 1995), pt. 3. See
also Leo Strauss, preface to American edition of *The Political Philosophy of Hobbes: Its
Basis and Its Genesis,* trans. Elsa M. Sinclair (1936; reprint, Chicago: University of
Chicago Press, 1952), xv–xvi. While both stress similarities between Machiavelli and
Hobbes, both also suggest a difference between them precisely on the question of the
need for duplicity.

dence and of the inevitability of hypocrisy associated with that dependence. Machiavelli and Rousseau are theorists of dependence. Politics is characterized by relationships of mutual need among parties with conflicting interests. To enlist the support of the other party requires flattery, manipulation, and a pretense of concern for his needs. The Machiavellian ruler seeks to ensure that he will be the manipulator and not the manipulated by acquiring enough power to secure his autonomy—to rely on his "own arms." Rousseau's major political prescription is also "avoid personal dependence," but he would add "avoid power," since, in his view, it too is a form of dependence.

Equally important, Machiavelli and Rousseau share an appreciation of the strength of vanity, pride, and ambition as political forces irreducible to calculations of interest, and consequently they share an abiding pessimism concerning the prospects for rational solutions to political problems. Liberalism envisions politics at its best as a rational process for adjudicating competing claims of interest. Both Machiavelli and Rousseau emphasize the importance in politics of passions that are independent of interests and that are amenable to control by force, fraud, or symbolic manipulations, but not by reason alone, or even predominantly. Rousseau particularly makes us aware of the frequency with which reason is perverted into rationalization that only serves a hypocritical complacency.

Finally, in the works of both authors, the analysis of political hypocrisy reflects a more general understanding of the place of morality in politics altogether. Neither author understands evil as a matter of mere ignorance or error which could be significantly alleviated with the progress of enlightenment. The pressures toward evil are present not only in the political passions of vanity, pride, and ambition but in the very structure of political relationships. Yet at the same time, the rhetoric of morality is also embedded in political relationships. Political discourse always has a moral component. This dimension of public life shows its power in political and religious rhetoric and symbol. And in public life, as in private life, "Hypocrisy is the homage vice pays to virtue."[29]

29. François, duc de la Rochefoucauld, *Maximes et réflexions diverses* (Librairie Larousse, 1972), no. 218. In "Observations de Jean-Jacques Rousseau de Genève sur la réponse qui a été faite à son discours" (*O.C.*, III, 49–51), Rousseau attacks the maxim that hypocrisy is the homage vice pays to virtue. See also "Lettre à M. Grimm"

Machiavelli and Rousseau appreciate the necessity of political hypocrisy,[30] which is to say, they appreciate the importance of appeals to genuine public moral principles. Hypocrisy requires moral pretense, and that pretense is necessary because politics cannot be conducted solely through bargaining among competing particular interests. To argue that political hypocrisy is necessary is thus to argue that moral cynicism as a public principle is impossible. Ironically, the frequency of hypocrisy in politics testifies to the strength of the moral impulse in public life.

By attending to Machiavelli's and Rousseau's understandings of the place of hypocrisy in political life, we come to see their opposition to the modern liberal project in a somewhat different light than that cast by the civic republicanism thesis. The politics of interest and the politics of virtue do not exhaust the possibilities.[31] Neither author is optimistic about the practical possibilities for a community of honest and virtuous citizens. More important for contemporary politics, neither are they optimistic about the prospects for a politics based on the controlled competition of private interests. On the contrary, one finds here the theoretical grounds for serious doubts as to the viability of open, honest, rational politics aimed at the fair adjudication of competing interests. Their insight serves as a caution against liberalism's overly optimistic attempt to overcome the inevitable irrationalities of political life.[32]

(*O.C.,* III, 60). But in his "Préface de *Narcisse,*" Rousseau praises the positive effects of the public simulacrum of virtue (*O.C.,* II, 971 ff.).

30. Contrast Viroli, *From Politics to Reason of State,* 417–18. Viroli is correct in a certain sense that the rulers will not be deceptive in Rousseau's ideal republic. But Rousseau's ideal is, in important respects, a trans- or supra-political vision made possible only by overcoming the usual character of political relations. Moreover, certain sorts of deception are essential tools even for the ideal ruler. See the section of chapter 4 entitled, "Rousseau's Political Ethics: Beneficial Manipulation."

31. See Mansfield, Jr., *Machiavelli's Virtue,* xv, where Mansfield distinguishes Machiavelli from both civic republicanism and bourgeois liberalism. And contrast Lévy, "Machiavel et Rousseau," and Lévy, "Les Partis et la démocratie," where he traces Rousseau's differences with Machiavelli on the role of parties in a republic to their differences regarding virtue and interest. Again, Rousseau's optimism regarding civic virtue must be viewed in the light of the utopian character of his republican vision and his deep pessimism concerning the historical possibilities.

32. Of course, Machiavelli could not have developed his ideas as a critique of liberalism; he was responding to the humanism of his own time. Hulliung, *Citizen Machiavelli,* 219–29; Victoria Kahn, "*Virtù* and the Example of Agathocles in Machia-

Because liberal regimes have made extraordinary claims along these lines, they have been particularly susceptible to charges of hypocrisy.[33] These charges take several forms, beginning with the straightforward claim that liberal regimes have not lived up to their principles—they have never actually achieved the promise of liberty, justice, and equality for all. The invocation of these principles, it is alleged, has a hypocritical ring in light of both the historical record and contemporary practice. The allegation of hypocrisy deepens with the claim, defended throughout Karl Marx's writings, that the principles themselves are merely part of the systematic apparatus of oppression. They allow the ruling class to believe that they act justly while serving as a smoke screen for the advancement of their interests. In this view, liberal ideology altogether is a hypocritical rationalization for capitalism. Lastly, the citizen of a liberal regime comes to be understood as a certain kind of hypocrite, the bourgeois. The bourgeois is alienated and inauthentic, never himself, never in public life what he would privately wish to be. Subjected to the pressures of modern life in commercial, liberal societies, he must create a phony self to satisfy his anxious concern to be pleasing, acceptable, or respectable in the eyes of others.[34]

How does it come to pass that the citizen of the regime most committed to honesty, openness, and the independence of the rational individual comes to seem the epitome of hypocrisy?[35] There is evident irony in that. And the irony is only partly explained by noting the high expectations created by liberalism in the first place. Most important, it is an irony that cannot be understood from within the tradition of liberal political thought itself. In other words, the liberal tradition in political thought obscures the problem that is the focus of this study—a problem that

---

velli's *Prince,"* in *Machiavelli and the Discourse of Literature,* ed. Albert Russell Ascoli and Victoria Kahn (Ithaca, N.Y.: Cornell University Press, 1993).

33. See Judith Shklar, *Ordinary Vices* (Cambridge, Mass.: Belknap Press, 1984), chap. 2.

34. For a literary example of this critique, see Arthur Miller's play *Death of a Salesman;* for a sociological comment, see David Reisman's analysis of the "other-directed" type in *The Lonely Crowd* (1950; reprint, New Haven, Conn.: Yale University Press, 1961).

35. Alexis de Tocqueville makes many suggestive observations related to this question. See, for example, *Democracy in America,* trans. George Lawrence, ed. J. P. Mayer (Garden City, N.Y.: Doubleday and Co., 1969), vol. 1, pt. 2, chap. 7, p. 257.

is acutely brought to the fore in the work of Machiavelli and Rousseau.

This study remains focused throughout on the ethical/political problems of hypocrisy and integrity. It explores what they are, the forms they take, why they appear when they do, and the political implications of identifying their characteristics in one way rather than another. The historical issue of the place of Machiavelli and Rousseau in the history of ideas, and consequently of the ethical alternatives available within modern thought, remains a subtext. My alternative perspective on their place in the tradition is suggested by, rather than fully developed as, the argument of the book. Instead, the book argues for an appreciation of the problematic character of any attempt to conduct politics honestly and rationally—an appreciation that Machiavelli and Rousseau shared. Without that appreciation, it becomes too easy to condemn hypocrisy wherever we find it. And if it is true that an honest politics is beyond reach, it is critically important not to condemn all dishonesty, but rather to distinguish with some subtlety what sorts of dishonesty ought to be condemned. The elaboration and critique of Rousseau's thought can help us to make precisely those distinctions.

The book begins with an examination of the case for the necessity of political hypocrisy, which draws on Machiavelli's writings (chapter 2), and proceeds to a consideration of the sorts of integrity that are nonetheless possible in politics. This consideration involves a comparison of Molière and Rousseau, who are critics of hypocrisy with very different understandings both of what it is and of the alternative to it. Two types of integrity emerge from the analysis: the moderate, represented as the ideal in Molière's works, and the moralist, represented as the ideal in Rousseau's writings. In the eyes of the moralist, the moderate appears to be a complacent hypocrite; in the eyes of the moderate, the moralist appears to be a self-righteous one. But each is mistaken about the other. There are two genuine possibilities for integrity, grounded in different moral and psychological premises. Comparing these alternative types, along with their hypocritical counterparts, allows us to identify the criterion for making crucial ethical distinctions among them (chapter 3). Rousseau's ideal is given additional consideration in order to respond to the criticism that his concern for individual moral purity leads either to fanaticism or to withdrawal from public life. I explore how his ideal of integrity accommodates prudential compromise as well as certain forms of deception. Prudential flexibility remains compatible with integrity so long as political compromise flows from judgment of the circumstances and not from the corrupting pressures of dependence (chapter 4). Dependence leads us to care for how we appear in the eyes of others and to experience envy, vanity, resentment, and a myriad of corrupting passions associated with *amour-propre*.[36] The fragility of integrity arises from the interaction between dependence and *amour-propre*, which is always the mechanism of corruption. Thus integrity can be maintained and hypocrisy prevented only when dependence and its usual effects can be avoided. Paradoxically, Rousseau justifies deceptive manipulation when it is used to conceal the dependency characteristic of political relations and thereby to suppress the most destructive forms of *amour-propre* (chapter 5). The book concludes with an assessment of the ethical alternatives and with reflections on the implications of this analysis for the conduct of contemporary liberal politics (chapter 6).

---

36. This term, which could be translated as "self-love," is contrasted throughout Rousseau's works with *amour de soi,* which could also be translated "self-love." The latter is a natural sentiment belonging to all human beings, even in isolation from others. It is a positive self-concern that leads us to care for our own well-being. The former is a relative passion involving comparison with others, and thus it can become a destructive form of self-concern, such as when we take pleasure in another's failure because it enhances our own position relative to him. Both terms will remain untranslated here throughout. See chapter 5, note 1. See also *Émile,* 483, n. 17.

2

Machiavelli and the Case for Hypocrisy

INTRODUCTION

The argument in favor of political hypocrisy is that in politics there is no viable alternative to it. This is a claim concerning the nature of politics rather than the moral status of hypocrisy. If it can be shown that political aims cannot be met honestly, then no further moral justification for hypocritical behavior is needed. To condemn hypocrisy would be to condemn politics altogether.[1] When hypocrisy is defended as not only necessary for the conduct of politics but also as the preferred alternative, a moral claim is introduced. This preference also depends on the premise that honest politics is not always possible. Where the only alternatives are force and fraud, fraud has a certain moral appeal. The argument for hypocrisy, whether as simply necessary or as the preferred alternative, depends on a critique of the possibility of honest political relations. And this depends in turn on a certain understanding of the character of political relations per se.

Machiavelli makes his case for hypocrisy as part of the more general case for the necessity of deception in political life. He describes three kinds of deception. The simplest deceits are the cunning tricks, like those described as "glorious fraud," that allow you to outwit an enemy, for example, by a ruse that leads him

---

1. This is a legitimate position, and an individual might decide to shun political life because a political life cannot be a moral life. But this does not help to answer the question how politics ought to be conducted by those who will be conducting it.

to believe that you are stronger than you are (*D.*, III, 40).[2] This sort of deception presents no obvious ethical problem. The second sort is making promises or contracts you have no intention of honoring when it is no longer in your interest to do so (*Pr.*, chap. 18). This sort of fraud always includes an element of hypocrisy since, at a minimum, it requires the pretense of trustworthiness. And lastly, Machiavelli recommends the use of "true" hypocrisy, which requires cultivating the appearance of moral goodness, virtue, or religiosity while actually seeking to further one's own ends, or even for the sake of furthering one's own ends (*Pr.*, chap. 18). Much of what Machiavelli has to say about the necessity of deceit and fraud altogether applies to the special case of hypocrisy as well.

Machiavelli's defense of deception of all kinds is part of his still more general case for the necessity of abandoning conventional moral constraints in politics and learning instead "to be able not to be good, and to use this and not use it according to necessity" (*Pr.*, chap. 15, p. 61). But what is the foundation for Machiavelli's claim that it is necessary to feign virtue at the same time that it is necessary to abandon it as a constraint on behavior? Why not abandon the appearance of goodness along with the reality? Why not honest knavery rather than the hypocritical kind? In addition to the argument for the necessity of immoral behavior generally and of deception particularly, a special case must be made for the necessity of moral pretense.

The discussion that follows explores the case for hypocrisy by analyzing Machiavelli's response to these questions. It identifies the particular characteristics of political relationships that require hypocritical behavior and the premises for Machiavelli's claim that it is indeed required in politics. His argument, as it turns out, is very similar to the case that can be made for social hypocrisy in the form of manners. Considering manners, it is easier to see both why hypocrisy might be necessary and how it might be defended. The discussion then takes up the strongest challenges to Machiavelli's case for hypocrisy in politics and develops a Machiavellian reply to them. One major implication of this con-

2. Note that Machiavelli says here that "immoral" types of deception cannot be considered glorious. A similar distinction is made in chapter 8 of *The Prince* with reference to Agathocles. Note also *The Discourses*, where Machiavelli comments that fraud is less blameworthy the better it is concealed (*D.*, II, 13).

troversy, if Machiavelli is correct, is that, although democracies officially justify themselves as the most honest and rational, least hypocritical form of government, politics in modern democracies is in fact particularly apt to be conducted hypocritically.

The Necessity of Political Hypocrisy

Machiavelli makes his case for hypocrisy in a section of *The Prince* that is devoted to the prince's relations with subjects and friends ("con sudditi o con li amici," *Pr.,* chap. 15). This section immediately follows the section of the work that is devoted to offense and defense in war.[3] It might be supposed that the distinction between the two sections is that between foreign affairs and domestic affairs, but that supposition would be a mistake. Instead, Machiavelli is distinguishing relations between enemies from relations between potential supporters, internal and external. This interpretation depends on understanding *amici* (translated as "friends") as equivalent to "allies" and as distinct from private, true friendship. Machiavelli frequently uses the term *amici* in discussing relations between allies.[4] He also makes it clear that true friendships are possible, based on "greatness and nobility of spirit," but that these are rare and cannot be taken as models for the prince's relations (*Pr.,* chap. 17, p. 66). When Machiavelli embarks on his discussion of the prince's relations with "subjects and friends" after concluding his treatment of "offense and defense," the distinction he is making is between politics and warfare. Thus the subject of hypocrisy arises when Machiavelli considers political relations. It is not necessary to be hypocritical with one's enemies, nor would it be necessary with one's true friends; hypocrisy is necessary in that area in between where false "friends" make mutually useful arrangements, that is, in international diplomacy as well as in domestic politics.

Political relationships, unlike either true friendships or open

3. Two chapters in *The Prince* begin with the assertion that Machiavelli is turning to a new subject, i.e., one that "remains" to be discussed. The first is chapter 12, which begins the section on offense and defense. The second is chapter 15, which begins the section on the prince's relations with subjects and friends.

4. See, for example, *Machiavelli's The Prince: A Bilingual Edition,* trans. and ed. Mark Musa (New York: St. Martin's Press, 1964), chap. 19, p. 150, and chap. 21, p. 186.

enmities, require hypocrisy because they are relationships of dependence among people with conflicting interests. Even a very powerful prince, for example, will find himself at various times in need of allies and supporters. His dependence on them makes it necessary for him to flatter them and to appear to be trustworthy. He needs their voluntary cooperation because he is not in a position to coerce their compliance. Yet he cannot simply expect that their cooperation will be forthcoming, because their interests do not coincide with his own and no altruistic motive is at work. Only a very foolish prince would rely on lifelong loyalties, true friendships, or trust. Political alliances are not like family ties: politics is about creating useful partnerships with people whose aims overlap, but do not coincide with, your own—with people who are ultimately your competitors. The same logic applies with respect to the people as a whole, who might throw their support to your competitors. Rulers depend on the support of the people and must cultivate that support since it cannot be reliably secured on the basis of either force or friendship. The people must be persuaded that the ruler seeks to secure their interests as well as his own where the two are not coincident. And so, politicians must employ rhetoric, flattery, and deception in order to build alliances and gain support. Political relations are relations of dependence as much as they are power relations. And it is dependence that breeds manipulation and hypocrisy.

For this reason, hypocrisy is necessary in every polity inasmuch as it arises out of the character of political relationships per se and not out of the character of the regime. Machiavelli praises the politic use of hypocrisy by the governors of republics no less than by princes.[5] The Romans successfully used religious pretense to secure the cooperation of the people and the dedication of their soldiers in situations where cooperation and loyalty would not otherwise have been forthcoming. Examples include Numa's pretended consultations with a nymph to lend authority to his

5. I do not claim that Machiavelli's advice regarding the government of principalities and republics is the same in every respect, but it is the same in this respect. The relation between *The Prince* and *The Discourses* is a disputed issue in Machiavelli scholarship. See, for example, Hans Baron, "The *Principe* and the Puzzle of the Date of the *Discorsi*," *Bibliothèque d'Humanisme et Renaissance* 18 (1956): 405–28; Strauss, *Thoughts,* chap. 1; David Wootton, introduction to *Machiavelli: Selected Political Writings* (Indianapolis: Hackett Publishing Co., 1994), xxiii–xxv.

laws, the justification of the return of the tribunate to the nobles as a means of pacifying angry gods, and the use of oracles to convince Roman soldiers to withstand a siege. Machiavelli makes it clear that it would have been very difficult to secure these political aims without the use of religious hypocrisy. A straightforward appeal to the interests of the plebeians and the soldiers certainly would not have sufficed (*D.*, I, 11–15; III, 33).

Machiavelli recommends fraud for republics in their dealings with allies as well (*D.*, II, 13). Rome was exemplary in befriending some of her neighbors in order to subdue the others, only to betray the original alliance when she had become strong enough to have no further need of it. Fraud works better than force for princes and republics who seek to rise from a humble position. Machiavelli writes, "And what princes have to do at the outset of their career, republics also must do until such time as they become powerful and can rely on force alone" (*D.*, II, 13, p. 311). In times of weakness or dependence, hypocrisy is the preferred mode of conducting politics for republics as well as for principalities.[6]

My claim here is that this behavior is necessitated by the nature of political relations understood as relations of dependence. This would seem to imply that Machiavellian ethics are a specifically political ethics—that is, that instead of applying a predetermined set of moral rules to politics as to every other human activity or relation, Machiavelli generates a set of rules for political activity that are justified by the unique character of that activity.[7] Machiavelli scholars differ on this issue, and there is evidence to support both views.[8] The same section of *The Prince* that most directly

6. Note also Machiavelli's recommendations regarding manipulating elections (*D.*, I, 48).

7. This is a matter of general interest in thinking about professional ethics. Machiavelli could be thought of as developing a professional ethics for politicians. When we speak of professional ethics, we do not always clarify whether we mean (1) the application of ethical principles that have some independent foundation to situations that most often arise in a particular profession, or (2) the ethical rules demanded by the nature of that particular professional activity. There is clearly a great deal of difference between the two.

8. See Hanna Fenichel Pitkin, *Fortune Is a Woman* (Berkeley: University of California Press, 1984), 5; Sheldon S. Wolin, *Politics and Vision* (1960; reprint, London: George Allen and Unwin, 1961), 224–28. See also Martin Fleisher, "Trust and Deceit in Machiavelli's Comedies," *Journal of the History of Ideas* 27, no. 3 (July 1966): 365–

develops Machiavelli's moral prescriptions from the nature of politics begins with a chapter titled "Of Those Things for Which Men and Especially Princes are Praised or Blamed," indicating that what follows applies to all men and not exclusively to princes.

This title also suggests a resolution of the issue. Machiavelli's rules apply especially to politics, but they do not apply exclusively to politics. Machiavelli does derive particular ethical rules from the character of politics. The logic of the analysis is to derive the moral rules from the requirements of political relations understood as relations of dependence or mutual need among people with conflicting interests. The same logic would apply to nonpolitical relationships whenever they share these particular qualities. There is a "politics" of business, of relations between the sexes, et cetera.

But this does not mean that Machiavelli believed that best friends, children, husbands, wives, or lovers ought to be treated as if they were foreign powers or members of opposing factions. Conversely, political ethics need not be identical to the ethics of private relationships. Dishonesty and betrayal in particular are more offensive in relationships that presuppose trust than in others. Despite the story that Americans tell their children on George Washington's birthday, we do not really expect that our leaders will never tell a lie, and I doubt that we would be simply proud of our leaders if they were scrupulously honest when it cost us something. We tell our children that Washington was an honest child, not because we do not want our leaders to lie to us, but because we do not want our children to lie to us. Private relationships are not the same as political ones.

Machiavelli gives ethical advice that applies particularly to political relations because it is derived from an analysis of those relations. In this important sense, Machiavelli articulates a specifically political ethics. This must be qualified with the observation that his advice *does* apply outside the political sphere whenever private relations most resemble political ones. This is why Machiavelli's play *Mandragola,* a private family drama, also teaches political lessons, as we will see below.

---

80. Fleisher argues that Machiavelli's depiction of family life in his comedies offers no private morality to distinguish it from political life (379). He also offers a useful but brief survey of earlier scholarly opinion according to which Machiavelli separates public and private, or political and moral realms (367).

Thus far I have argued that the case for hypocrisy in Machiavelli's writings is that hypocrisy is necessary in political relationships where neither force nor friendship can be relied on to secure cooperation. Hypocrisy is essentially a part of the art of persuasion, and persuasion is a preeminently political art. But there is a second premise to Machiavelli's argument: he justifies hypocrisy on the basis of certain characteristics of human nature as well as on the basis of the characteristics of political relations. He repeatedly asserts that his defense of hypocrisy, and of immorality generally, is supported by the observation that men are not good (*Pr.*, chaps. 15, 18). In what respect does this observation serve as a justification? Machiavelli is certainly not the first to notice that many people in public life are not exemplars of moral virtue. But not all observers conclude from this that politicians ought to abandon virtue when their political situation requires the judicious use of vice.

Machiavelli justifies immoral behavior, in the first place, as a means of self-defense. "For a man who wants to make a profession of good in all regards must come to ruin among so many who are not good" (*Pr.*, chap. 15, p. 61). The same point is developed more fully in the chapter of *The Prince* that deals specifically with hypocrisy, and especially with breaking agreements (*Pr.*, chap. 18). Faithlessness is described as compulsory for princes because it is necessary to maintain their rule, and so the prince is advised to break his promises when they no longer serve his interests. Machiavelli is explicit about his premise: "And if all men were good, this teaching would not be good; but because they are wicked and do not observe faith with you, you also do not have to observe faith with them" (*Pr.*, chap. 18, p. 69). This is Machiavelli's "golden rule": do unto others as you can expect them to do unto you. Faithlessness is a matter of self-defense in a world of faithless men. The prince must play the role of the fox who, unlike the lion, can recognize snares and defend himself against them (*Pr.*, chap. 18, pp. 69–70).

But to prevent yourself from falling victim to deceivers does not require deception on your part; it requires only distrust. Machiavelli's position, as he develops it in *The Prince,* goes far beyond the minimal claims of a defensive necessity for hypocrisy. The best foxes do not merely avoid snares, they set them, like Severus, "a very astute fox" (*Pr.*, chap. 19, p. 79). Moreover, success in breaking agreements requires the cultivation of the appearance of trustworthiness; it requires a more general hypocrisy. Alexander VI and Ferdinand the Catholic were great deceivers because they knew how to use the appearance of honesty, humanity, mercy, and especially religion to color their self-aggrandizing deceptions in virtuous hues (*Pr.,* chap. 18). Machiavelli's defense of this behavior is certainly not clearly and directly linked to his observation that many people are not good.

Instead, Machiavelli treats hypocrisy and deceit as one type of tool that the prince might use to further his aims. The prince can fight with laws or with force. To fight with laws, the human way, is insufficient, so the prince must also use force, the way of beasts. The relevant beasts are the lion and the fox, strength and deception.[9] Surprisingly, this classification puts the way of the fox (deceit and its accompanying hypocrisy) in the category of fighting with force (*Pr.,* chap. 18).[10] Deceit is good if it works to overcome opposition and to achieve political aims, and Machiavelli assures us that it is likely to work; there will always be dupes aplenty. In a sense, the gullibility of human beings justifies hypocritical tactics more than does their general dishonesty. The latter would serve as a justification only if a person had no moral obligation to be better than others are likely to be, which is a position that would be difficult to defend persuasively.

Nonetheless, the necessity of a certain sort of hypocrisy does seem to follow from the premise that men are not good. If hypocrisy means the failure to live up to professed moral standards, then politics certainly will always be hypocritical.[11] Moral principles

9. The relations between strength and deception and between force and fraud are complicated. As indicated above, Machiavelli suggests that deception is especially useful where strength is lacking. On the other hand, the Roman use of religious deceits seems to have been backed by force so that one wonders whether the Romans were afraid of breaking their oaths or afraid of human punishments. See, for example, *D.,* I, 15.

10. Contrast Cicero, *De Officiis,* I, 13, 41. "There are two ways a man may wrong another, by force or by fraud. A man may be as violent as a lion or as crafty as a fox. Both are quite inhuman kinds of behaviour, but fraud is the more odious. Particularly to be deplored is the hypocrisy of those who under the guise of respectability practise the worst acts of deception." Cicero, *On Moral Obligation,* trans. John Higginbotham (Berkeley: University of California Press, 1967), 54. Note also that Machiavelli speaks of two ways of fighting, not two ways of committing injustices.

11. Shakespeare's *Measure for Measure* treats the necessity of hypocrisy in politics in this way.

cannot be fully realized in practice. Rulers and subjects can be just and good only in imaginary republics (*Pr.,* chap. 15). In the real world, men are often not good, but moral standards must be publicly defended nonetheless. Consequently, every government is susceptible to the charge of hypocrisy—and so is every individual.

Yet therein lies the difficulty: apparently, to define hypocrisy as the failure to practice what one preaches is overinclusive. It allows no distinction between hypocrisy and moral weakness. To profess principles that one has no intention of following is hypocrisy; to be unable to live up to our best expectations of ourselves is not hypocrisy but human nature. The observation that men are not always good, that there will always be a gap between the real and the ideal, is a recognition of inevitable human weakness but not a justification for hypocritical behavior.

There is, finally, a more serious case for the necessity of political hypocrisy. It is grounded in the recognition of natural human weakness and the limitations of political reality that follow from it. In a world where men are not good, those who attempt to adhere strictly to moral standards in their political actions may find that the consequences are far worse in ethical terms than they would have been had they allowed themselves the use of immoral political means. Thus immoral political actions are justified when, and only when, moral ones would be worse in their effects. An assassination that prevents a war could be justified in this way, for example.

According to Sheldon Wolin, this is essentially Machiavelli's position.[12] Max Weber makes a similar case for abandoning strict adherence to moral standards in politics, basing it on the recognition that men are not good.[13] He develops a distinction between the ethic of ultimate ends and the ethic of responsibility. Although finally the two ethics may supplement each other in a mature individual, Weber is far more critical of the former than

---

12. Wolin, *Politics and Vision,* 220–24.

13. "Politics as a Vocation," in *From Max Weber: Essays in Sociology,* ed. and trans. H. H. Gerth and C. Wright Mills (New York: Oxford University Press, 1958), 115–28. Note that Weber's argument is not only an argument for moral flexibility and against utopianism but also an argument for a distinctive political ethic. Because violence is the decisive means in politics, the Christian ethic does not apply. Politics requires its own ethics.

of the latter. The latter is the true political ethic, and the true political man possesses the "knowledge of tragedy with which all action, but especially political action, is truly interwoven" (117). He "takes account of precisely the average deficiencies of people" (121), and he takes responsibility for the consequences of his actions. In contrast, the man who pursues an ethic of ultimate ends in politics blames the world, the stupidity of other men, or God's will if his well-intentioned action leads to bad results. He is concerned only to preserve the "flame of pure intentions" (121), and his political actions can have only exemplary value at best. Weber condemns this sort of politics as morally irresponsible.

Yet the alternative to it can only be defended on ethical grounds if impure political means are used only when no viable alternative exists and if the aims that are served by them are ethically defensible. Wolin and Weber would ultimately have to rest their case on this. Of course, the absence of other alternatives and the ethical status of the aim are as critical for a defense of hypocrisy as they are for the defense of any other questionably moral political means. The case for hypocrisy begins with the claim for its necessity. Rulers must cultivate a reputation for virtue while doing whatever is necessary, because that reputation is itself equally necessary. Publicly cynical politics will not work; it is the lion without the fox. Politics requires deceit, and particularly deceit about moral principles; it is particularly important for the prince, for example, not to be always religious but to appear to be so (*Pr.*, chap. 18). The prince must be willing not only to use the bad whenever necessary but to appear to be good while he does so. Hypocrisy is effective, while honest knavery would not be. Principles or moral ideals in politics seem to be the sort of thing that we cannot live with or without; we can neither adhere to them strictly nor simply abandon them.

But Machiavelli's case for hypocrisy and for unethical conduct in politics generally is not precisely the case that I have just outlined. Machiavelli certainly never explicitly states that unethical action in politics is justified if and only if, first, there is no effective available alternative and, second, the action has a morally justifiable aim. This "if and only if" proposition is a minimalist justification for deviations from accepted moral principles in politics. *The Prince* is written in such a way that it has invited the maximalist, "Machiavellian" interpretation according to which any wickedness is justified so long as it maintains the power of the prince. In fact, Machiavelli's writings are full of ambiguities and puzzles that make it extremely difficult to discern his principles of justification. The religious hypocrisy of the Romans, for example, might be distinguished from the hypocrisy of Severus because the former could be said to serve the public good while the latter is a self-serving fraud and betrayal of trust. But Machiavelli does not make this distinction clearly. Moreover, even in the case of the Roman Republic, one might question the identification of the imperialistic aims of Roman politics with the public good. As an additional example, consider the ambiguities of Machiavelli's discussion of Agathocles (*Pr.,* chap. 8). Although Machiavelli claims that Agathocles' success could not bring him glory on account of his wickedness, he describes Agathocles' deeds in a manner difficult to distinguish from the deeds of those he praises elsewhere, referring to his *virtù* and greatness of spirit along with his criminality.

Commentators have struggled with difficulties such as these, attempting to discern the criteria that inform Machiavelli's judgments. Interpretations include those I have identified as "minimalist" and "maximalist"; the argument that action is justified when it maintains the state, but not when it aims simply at the personal aggrandizement of the prince;[14] that action may be praiseworthy when it strengthens republics which would not be praiseworthy when used to destroy them and establish principalities in their stead;[15] and that *The Prince* was written for particular political purposes that allow us to discount the advice it contains as an indicator of Machiavelli's political ethics.[16]

With respect to hypocrisy in particular, Machiavelli's advice is that both princes and republics should not shy away from

14. See, for example, Allan H. Gilbert, *Machiavelli's "Prince" and Its Forerunners* (Durham, N.C.: Duke University Press, 1938), 132–39.

15. David Wootton develops this position in explaining the discussion of Agathocles. *Machiavelli, Selected Political Writings,* xxi–xxii. For a discussion of the variety of interpretations of Agathocles, see Victoria Kahn, "*Virtù* and the Example of Agathocles in Machiavelli's *Prince,*" in *Machiavelli and the Discourse of Literature,* ed. Albert Russell Ascoli and Victoria Kahn (Ithaca, N.Y.: Cornell University Press, 1993), 201–8. See also note 2 above.

16. See, for example, Mary Dietz, "Trapping the Prince: Machiavelli and the Politics of Deception," *American Political Science Review* 80, no. 3 (Sept. 1986): 777–800, and, of course, Rousseau, in a different vein, as we saw.

breaking faith, from appealing to religion to gain support for political enterprises, or from attempting to maintain the reputation for virtue while abandoning the practice of the virtues when it is necessary to do so. But this necessity is not quite of the "minimalist" kind. Machiavelli does not recommend abandoning the virtues only in extreme and rare cases where adhering to them will necessarily result in political failure. Instead, Machiavelli recognizes that certain of the virtues, as they are customarily understood, are not actually as good as they seem to be. Liberality and mercy are prime examples (*Pr.,* chaps. 16, 17). The prince who is "liberal" actually takes from the many to give to the few; his liberality is in fact rapacity. Similarly, mercy may be cruel: a failure to destroy swiftly a few dangerous leaders may allow continuing disorder and cruelty among the people. To *be* liberal and merciful in the usual sense is in fact only to *seem* liberal and merciful. This is a sort of hypocrisy that Machiavelli does not endorse. Instead, he urges the prince to feign the virtues for which princes are ordinarily praised while practicing *virtù.*[17]

However one reads Machiavelli's ethical position and whether or not his position is persuasive in the end, his argument exposes the premises of all claims for the ethical necessity and practical inevitability of hypocrisy in politics. Hypocrisy will arise in relations of mutual dependence among people with conflicting interests who cannot be relied on to adhere to moral prescriptions. The nature of political relations, along with the morally retrograde character of humanity, dictate hypocritical behavior. They also justify it. The alternatives to hypocrisy are force, on the one hand, and honesty, on the other. Force can hardly be defended as a morally superior alternative, and besides, it is not a viable alternative for the weak. Hypocrisy, deception, and manipulation must be their weapons.[18]

Honesty would appear to be the ethical option, but if it is the case that honest politics is a utopian ideal and that hypocrisy is the inevitable consequence of the nature of political relations, the attempt to remain honest and to adhere strictly to stated moral

---

17. It is not always possible to do both simultaneously. In such cases, good princes must be willing to accept a reputation for illiberality or cruelty, for example (*Pr.,* chaps. 16, 17).

18. One would expect, for example, the most highly developed "feminine wiles" where women are most subservient.

principles is bound to end in political failure. This complicates the ethical situation considerably, because the ethical purist also has a responsibility for the political failure produced by his moral rigidity. The ethical purist, however, fails to accept this responsibility, and thus he compromises the very purity he is so intent on maintaining. While he pretends to a concern for others, he is actually more concerned with the preservation of his own righteousness. Thus the antihypocrite is also a kind of hypocrite, and in that sense, too, hypocrisy in politics is unavoidable. We actually have the choice, not between honesty and hypocrisy, but between different forms of hypocrisy. And it certainly can be argued plausibly that to insist on moral purity in spite of the consequences is a more dangerous form of hypocrisy than to accept the fact that some deceit, some compromises of one's principles, or some deviation from established moral norms is necessary.

This case for hypocrisy in politics ought to be applicable wherever hypocrisy is prevalent, and not only in politics. Indeed, if we consider as an example the little hypocrisies of social life, we find that the case for manners resembles the Machiavellian argument, particularly in its premises. In both instances, hypocrisy is defended in public relations of authority and dependency, rather than intimate and equal relations. And in both instances, the defense of hypocrisy follows from a rather pessimistic view of natural human impulses and, consequently, of the possibilities for public happiness. However, in the case of manners, perhaps the ethical dimension of the defense of hypocrisy is more readily apparent than it is in Machiavelli's defense of hypocrisy in politics.

Manners do not always appear to be hypocritical strictly speaking. They often involve little "white lies," but lying is a much broader category than hypocrisy, and they rarely require a pretense of belief in a particular principle or ethic. But there is a kinship between social manners and more serious hypocritical behavior that lies in the pretense of sympathetic concern or respect for others—a kind of pretense of virtue—that manners express. Manners are insincere or "phony." People are not treated according to their individual merits or their just deserts, nor according to one's true feelings toward them as individuals, but according to conventional forms.

This is precisely the advantage of manners: they are formalities. They allow civil public relations between people who are not friends, and delineate the boundary between public and private. By abandoning the usual formalities, people signal to one another that their interaction is a personal one. Conversely, by conforming to conventional expectations for public behavior, that is, by playing a specified role, people enjoy the enormous advantage of concealing themselves from those they have no particular reason to trust. Because formalities standardize behavior, they provide the additional convenience that every interaction need not be negotiated anew.

One price for these advantages is diminished independence, a fact of which most adolescents are acutely aware. Civility is a restraint, and in more than one respect. In the first place, people are motivated to conform to social conventions out of a concern for the opinion of others, and to care for one's reputation is to surrender a degree of autonomy. It may also involve concealing certain things from public view, or hypocrisy, to protect one's reputation. Thus does dependence breed hypocrisy in social as well as political relations.

Civility requires another form of restraint: the willingness to accept small slights or incivilities on the part of others. To be too scrupulous about justice produces unnecessary conflicts, and to treat people with the respect implied by good manners is often to treat them as better than they are. In this sense, manners, like political hypocrisy, are necessitated by the moral shortcomings of human beings. John Locke appreciated the ways in which civility can be understood as restraining dangerous and powerful passions. A revolutionary and a liberal, he nonetheless advised that children be taught to tolerate injustice as well as to care about their own reputation. He sought to moderate their pride so that they would not be too touchy on points of honor, too quick to avenge insults, too eager to right every wrong. His education also aimed to moderate their wish to dominate others, replacing it with the desire to be freely esteemed by them, even though that desire involves dependence on general opinion.[19] A little injustice and a little dependence are a small price to pay for social peace. Social, like political, hypocrisy can be justified when it serves a value deemed more important than honesty (e.g., kindness or

19. See Nathan Tarcov, *Locke's Education for Liberty* (Chicago: University of Chicago Press, 1984), 137–41, 181.

stability). And the case for social hypocrisy includes the thought
that social harmony would be very difficult to achieve without
it.[20]

The defense of manners is ordinarily conservative, as is the
defense of hypocrisy generally to the extent that it rests on a pessimistic assessment of the possibilities for human goodness. The
restraints of civility are taken by Edmund Burke, for example, as
emblematic of, and essential supports for, the restraints of civilization altogether. According to Burke, the opinions rooted in chiv-
alry, though they are "illusions," make "power gentle and obedience liberal." They are the "decent drapery of life" that "cover
the defects of our naked shivering nature."[21] The case for social
hypocrisy rests on the premise that human beings in the raw are
none too attractive.

Burke argued that without the illusions that support a system
of social formalities, without the civilizing restraints represented
by manners, people will feel free to use what power they have
in their own interests.

> On this scheme of things, a king is but a man, a queen is but a woman;
> a woman is but an animal, and an animal not of the highest order.
> All homage paid to the sex in general as such . . . is to be regarded
> as romance and folly. . . . The murder of a king, or a queen, or a
> bishop, or a father are only common homicide; and if the people are
> by any chance or in any way gainers by it, a sort of homicide much
> the most pardonable.[22]

Treating people as respectable on account of their position and
regardless of whether they personally merit respect is part of the

20. This is the crux of the exchange between Alceste and Philinte in the opening
scene of Molière's play *The Misanthrope*. To Alceste's charge that the manners of the
day demand praise for the worthy and the unworthy alike, Philinte replies: "Wouldn't
the social fabric come undone if we were wholly frank with everyone?" The play is
interesting only because each character has a point: Alceste is right that his society is
built on insincere flattery, influence, and corruption; Philinte is right that common
courtesies are no great evil. As in political life, in social life one needs a sense of
proportion in these things and a means of distinguishing innocent hypocrisies from
serious ones. Jean Baptiste Poquelin de Molière, *"The Misanthrope" and "Tartuffe,"*
trans. Richard Wilbur (New York: Harcourt, Brace and World, 1965).

21. Edmund Burke, *Reflections on the Revolution in France,* ed. H. D. Mahoney
(New York: Macmillan Publishing Co., 1955), 86–91.

22. Burke, *Reflections,* 87.

hypocritical pretense of manners and a form of hypocrisy that supports social order.

Manners regulate relations between the powerful and the powerless. For this reason, they will be most elaborate in the most rigidly hierarchical societies.[23] They express deference and delineate class and status. When the weak defer to the strong, they acknowledge the legitimacy of their subordination. When the strong defer to the weak, as in courtesies toward women and the elderly, they show respect by refraining from asserting their strength. Courtesies such as these can be defended as a form of protection for the weak against the raw use of power, but they are certainly also an indication of subordinate status. It is not accidental that revolutionaries and social reformers are sensitive to social forms such as modes of address, exposing their symbolic content by insisting on instituting new ones, e.g., citizen, Ms., and comrade. While egalitarian societies will generate their own systems of manners, the fact that manners are far more elaborate in hierarchical societies is yet another indication of the link between hypocrisy and dependence.

Apparently, the case for social hypocrisy has much in common with the case for political hypocrisy. Manners operate not between enemies or intimate friends but in the public realm, where friendly interaction must be maintained among nonfriends. Manners are supported by our psychological dependence on the good opinion of others. They also reflect dependence in the hierarchical system of social status. They are defensible to the extent that they provide social goods that could not be provided if strict honesty were the rule. They prevent conflict by treating people who are not good or respectable as if they were and by supporting habitual restraints on self-interested behavior.

Hypocrisy, social and political, cannot be altogether eliminated. It is necessitated by the natural and ineradicable moral shortcomings of human beings; it functions as an alternative to force in public relationships; and it is also a necessary concomitant of relationships of dependence among people who are not intimate. It is therefore a preeminently political phenomenon.

23. See Alexis de Tocqueville, *Democracy in America*, trans. George Lawrence, ed. J. P. Mayer (Garden City, N.Y.: Doubleday and Co., 1969), 616–27. While it is true that manners are more elaborate in hierarchical societies, no amount of egalitarianism will do away with them.

But the suggestion that it is natural for people to act hypocritically in political life is not necessarily an endorsement for all such actions. Some sorts of hypocrisy might be tolerable and even beneficial and others not. Political hypocrisy might be treated as an unfortunate necessity or encouraged as clever strategy. We need to know whether distinctions can be made between the hypocritical "sellout" and the legitimate compromise, the demagogue and the statesman, simple cruel treachery and the exercise of *virtù*. In *Tartuffe,* Molière gives Cléante a speech detailing the criteria by which to distinguish true religion from false piety. We need such a list for making the crucial distinctions in politics, keeping in mind that in politics, unlike in religion, there seems to be a place for some hypocrisy.

But before approaching this task, the case against hypocrisy must be given its due. The effort to make ethical distinctions among various sorts of hypocritical behavior is only necessary if hypocrisy of some sort is truly necessary. As we have seen, the case for hypocrisy depends on this claim. Contrariwise, the case against political hypocrisy is an argument for the possibility of honest politics. That possibility deserves the full consideration it has not yet received.

THE POSSIBILITY OF HONEST POLITICS

The necessity of political hypocrisy can be challenged in a variety of ways. First, it could be argued that hypocrisy may be an effective political tool, but it is not an unavoidable necessity. When ethical action in politics entails some sacrifice of political success, that sacrifice must be made. Political acts must be judged by the same moral standards as any other. Second, it could be argued that the political community need not be construed as a composite of mutually dependent but fundamentally hostile forces. In a healthy and harmonious polity, hypocrisy would not be necessary. Last, one might concede that politics takes place among mutually dependent conflicting groups but argue that the conflict can be managed honestly. Only this last position challenges the Machiavellian case on its own terms. The first two, which will be treated only briefly here, are tainted with utopianism.

The first case against hypocrisy in politics rests on a denial that politics constitutes some sort of special ethical realm. Moral rules, this critic might argue, do not change as political realities change, and the demands of personal moral consistency are paramount. St. Augustine's *Against Lying* exemplifies this position and contrasts starkly with Machiavelli's treatment of lying.[24] Defending lying, Machiavelli implicitly judges the Christian ethical standard from the point of view of its effect on politics. In contrast, Augustine argues that, because lying is a sin, it cannot be justified even when used by pious spies in their efforts to snare heretics. He judges political actions according to their conformity to Christian precepts, and consequently argues that the political goal in this case must be sacrificed to ethical imperatives.[25]

The argument can be extended to include the further claim that only by taking this approach can there be any hope of improving political life. Machiavellian "realism," from this perspective, appears to be merely defeatism. The goal ought to be to encourage people to act in the public realm in accordance with their private moral convictions. If enough individuals were to insist on maintaining their own morality in all their actions, the state would be unable to prosecute immoral projects. Politics can be better than it has been because people can be better than they have been. We need not resign ourselves to the moral shortcomings and defective nature of humankind.

But unless and until this idealistic vision is fulfilled, this position will remain problematic. First, to the extent that the political actor is responsible for the consequences of his actions, his moral claim is compromised when evil triumphs as the result of his attempts to maintain his personal moral purity. Second, this position concedes Machiavelli's fundamental point: hypocrisy is often necessary to achieve certain political aims. The real disagreement here is over whether political aims are the most important ones; that is, whether political goals ought to be sacrificed for nonpolitical moral reasons.

The second challenge to the claim that hypocrisy is necessary

24. St. Augustine, "Against Lying," in *Saint Augustine: Treatises on Various Subjects,* ed. Roy J. Deferrari (New York: Fathers of the Church, Inc., 1952), 125–79.

25. Augustine's position is not exhausted by the argument he presents in "Against Lying," and it is considerably more nuanced and complex than this one piece would indicate. There are elements of pragmatism and flexibility in his thought that have been developed by contemporary theologians. Nonetheless, Christianity as he understands it always supplies the standards according to which political actions are to be judged.

questions the characterization of political relationships that is its ground. Those who argue for hypocrisy see its necessity particularly in relationships that combine dependency and conflict and thus stand somewhere in between friendships and settled enmities. Those who argue against it also tend to argue that politics is at its best when it takes place in a community that most resembles a church, an extended family, or, at a minimum, a group of potential friends; that is, in a homogenous and harmonious moral community whose members are tied by affection as well as interest.

In this regard, Rousseau offers an appropriate contrast to Machiavelli. His criticism of the hypocrisy of his contemporary world and his positive vision of a harmonious political community are two sides of the same coin. Rousseau depicts small communities in *The Social Contract* and elsewhere where hypocrisy is not required because the personal dependence associated with inequality does not exist and the conflict of particular wills has been replaced by universal subordination to the general will.[26] But Rousseau's vision is utopian. Again, this second challenge, like the first, fundamentally concedes the point. Politics as we know it necessitates hypocrisy; in order to eliminate political hypocrisy, one would have to create a community where the "political" character of politics has been eliminated as well.[27]

Lastly, there is an alternative challenge that is the most difficult of the three to overcome from a Machiavellian perspective and consequently the most revealing. Unlike the first two, it begins from the same premises that ground Machiavelli's argument for political hypocrisy: viz., that politics is a matter of managing inev-

---

26. Though it is not quite correct to say that hypocrisy has no place even here. See the section of chapter 4 entitled "Rousseau's Political Ethics: Beneficial Manipulation."

27. Consider the analogy: Machiavelli is to Rousseau as Aristotle is to Plato. Both Rousseau and Plato develop utopian visions of unified politics, or of communities that overcome the "political" character of politics. Aristotle and Machiavelli think in terms of balancing competing forces in societies permanently divided between rich and poor, nobles, people, and soldiers, and so on. See Lévy, "Machiavel et Rousseau," 173.

See also Alexander Hamilton, John Jay, and James Madison, *The Federalist Papers,* ed. Clinton Rossiter (New York: New American Library, 1961), no. 10, for one explanation for why even a very small and very homogeneous community cannot be small enough or homogenous enough to overcome the political character of politics.

itable group conflict short of war and that human beings are fundamentally selfish and therefore untrustworthy. The argument here is that selfishness itself, and even a doctrine of selfishness, can provide the conditions for the honest negotiation of differences. Public moral pretense can be replaced by a kind of public cynicism, hypocrisy can give way to honesty, and negotiating can take the place of "politicking." Conditions of mutual dependence among people with conflicting interests are conditions not for hypocritical manipulation (as Machiavelli would have it) but for trade.

Essentially, this claim for the possibility of honest politics is grounded in the model of the economic rationality of the market applied to politics. That trade is an alternative to hypocrisy is made abundantly clear in Adam Smith's discussion. Human beings possess a unique "propensity to truck, barter, and exchange one thing for another." But,

> [w]hen an animal wants to obtain something either of a man or of another animal, it has no other means of persuasion but to gain the favour of those whose service it requires. A puppy fawns upon its dam, and a spaniel endeavours by a thousand attractions to engage the attention of its master who is at dinner, when it wants to be fed by him. Man sometimes uses the same arts with his brethren, and when he has not other means of engaging them to act according to his inclinations, endeavours by every servile and fawning attention to obtain their good will.[28]

Fawning and flattery work reasonably well for animals who, as adults, are naturally independent and rarely have need of the services of other creatures. But these techniques would be terribly inefficient for human beings whose dependence on others is so much greater. The human capacity to trade becomes essential because no one could possibly make his own needs a matter of personal concern to all those on whom he must depend for their satisfaction. Consequently, we trade in order to

> obtain from one another the far greater part of those good offices which we stand in need of. It is not from the benevolence of the butcher, the brewer, or the baker that we expect our dinner but from

28. Adam Smith, *The Wealth of Nations,* ed. Edwin Cannan (Chicago: University of Chicago Press, 1976), bk. 1, chap. 2, p. 18.

their regard to their own interest. We address ourselves, not to their humanity but to their self-love, and never talk to them of our own necessities but of their advantages.[29]

This famous statement is often regarded as an admission of the moral bankruptcy of market relations, and there is certainly something to this. Markets depend on self-interest, which is reliable, rather than on virtue, which is not. But the context of the passage suggests that the observation might be viewed as the grounds for a moral defense of the market, rather than as a condemnation of it. When people depend on the benevolence of their fellows or on their virtue, they are essentially in the position of beggars. And nothing creates greater pressures toward flattery, manipulation, and hypocrisy. These behaviors flourish in rigidly hierarchical aristocratic societies characterized by economic dependency. If aristocratic economic relations are the alternative to market relations, then the latter might represent a moral advance.

In other words, Smith might agree with Rousseau's compelling condemnation of the morally corrupting effects of economic dependence. Rousseau writes,

> having formerly been free and independent, behold man, due to a multitude of new needs, subjected so to speak to all of nature and especially to his fellow men, whose slave he becomes in a sense even in becoming their master; rich, he needs their services; poor, he needs their help; and mediocrity cannot enable him to do without them. He must therefore incessantly seek to interest them in his fate, and to make them find their own profit, in fact or in appearance, in working for his. This makes him deceitful and sly with some, imperious and harsh with others, and makes it necessary for him to abuse all those whom he needs when he cannot make them fear him and does not find his interest in serving them usefully. (*Second,* 156)

Economic dependence is the source of hypocritical manipulation particularly as well as of moral corruption more generally. Precisely for this reason, a Smithian might argue, market relations have a moral advantage.

The partners to a trade have no ongoing relation of personal dependence. They are brought together by the momentary coincidence of their needs. Their exchange is facilitated, rather than

29. Ibid.

hampered, by straightforward, honest communication of their desires. Participants in economic markets enter the market in a position determined only by the resources they bring to it. And all are governed equally by market forces and the compelling rationality of the laws of economic exchange. Openly selfish calculation replaces the loyalty, duty, and care of master-servant or patron-client relations, but it also replaces sycophancy and arbitrariness. Moreover, commercial relations have the additional moral advantage that they promote toleration without, at the same time, encouraging hypocrisy. One needn't pretend to like one's trading partner, or even to have anything at all in common with him, in order to join with him in economic society. Toleration is possible precisely on the grounds of mutually acknowledged self-interestedness requiring no hypocritical pretense of mutual concern, respect, or commonality.

If it is possible to reconcile differing economic interests through honestly negotiated trades, then perhaps honest politics is also a real possibility. Honesty in politics was one of the aspirations of modern democratic republicanism in the eighteenth century. The favoritism, corruption, and manipulation characteristic of European monarchies were to be replaced by open, honest, and rational deliberations in legislatures where a variety of interests were equitably represented. Representatives of differing interests, each needing the cooperation of at least some of the others, would secure that cooperation either through trading and negotiation or, ideally, through a rational deliberative process. Public deliberation at its best would require representatives to weigh policy alternatives according to rational criteria and to adjudicate the claims of competing interests to reach an informed choice consonant with the public good.[30] Representatives would have no need to conceal their true interests in order to satisfy them, or at least to have a fair shot at their satisfaction, because, in a democratic republic, representatives would speak for the legitimate interests of some portion of the society. Political hypocrisy, zealous partisanship, and demagoguery may have been characteristic of a political system where representatives fought for the illegitimate interests of artificial classes seeking to maintain

30. Ruth W. Grant, *John Locke's Liberalism* (Chicago: University of Chicago Press, 1987), 188–92.

their advantages, but they are not characteristic of politics per se. When personal dependence on a political patron has been rendered obsolete, when all enter the political arena on an equal footing, political conflicts can be rationally resolved through open and honest negotiation of differences.

This vision of honest politics and the argument for its possibility is not exclusively a phenomenon of the eighteenth century. There are a number of versions of the essential claim.[31] All of them include a striking combination of optimism and cynicism. Optimistically, they hold forth the hope that politics can be purged substantially of its irrationality. But this hope is grounded in the cynical premise that self-interest is the bedrock of human motivation that will prevail over benevolence, principle, or virtue whenever there is a tension between them.[32] This particular combination of optimism and cynicism is quite apparent in the foreign policy doctrine of realpolitik, which is one version of the case for honest politics, and so I will use it to illustrate.

Realpolitik contains a cynical descriptive element as well as an optimistic prescriptive one.[33] Descriptively, according to this view, nations must and do act on the basis of their interests. At best, ethical considerations in foreign policy are merely a sentimental veneer over the hard realities of international politics; at worst, they can mislead nations into undertaking disastrous crusades. In the end, ethical considerations can be no more than

31. One contemporary version is rational choice theory. As compared to the eighteenth-century version, it emphasizes negotiation over deliberation in politics since it is directly derived from the economic model and therefore operates with an exclusively instrumental understanding of rationality. William Riker, one of the founders of this approach to political science, fully understands that negotiation too can be manipulative, though he does not analyze this manipulation as hypocritical or as posing ethical dilemmas for political actors. See William H. Riker, *The Art of Political Manipulation* (New Haven, Conn.: Yale University Press, 1986).

32. This is the combination characteristic of Hobbes's thought and the one that makes it so difficult to separate the descriptive from the prescriptive elements in *Leviathan*.

33. In the contemporary literature of realist theory in international relations, the descriptive and prescriptive elements are combined in various ways by different authors. Kenneth Waltz, a neo-realist, comes closest to articulating "descriptive realpolitik," while the prescriptive argument can be found in the work of the classical realist, Hans Morgenthau. See Hans J. Morgenthau, *Politics among Nations: The Struggle for Power and Peace* (New York: Alfred A. Knopf, 1948), and Kenneth N. Waltz, *Man, the State and War: A Theoretical Analysis* (New York: Columbia University Press, 1959).

hypocritical pretense, because they will be abandoned necessarily whenever national interests are at stake. To some, this suggests a prescriptive claim; i.e., that in making foreign policy decisions, it is best to cultivate a cynical attitude and pursue the national interest unapologetically. Only by taking this approach will nations be protected from miscalculations of their security, from unwise involvements in international conflicts, and from a host of other errors that a moral sentimentality can produce. We would be better off if we operated honestly on the basis of what we know about the hard realities of international relations. It is far better to forgo the veneer of ethical public rhetoric and to forthrightly acknowledge the true selfish basis of foreign relations. Thus a more rational, peaceful, and humane politics can be achieved in part through an openly cynical political rhetoric.

Adherents of the realpolitik approach frequently cite Machiavelli as its first modern proponent,[34] but this is a mistake in one important respect. While Machiavelli may agree with the descriptive claim, he certainly rejects the prescriptive one. Machiavelli *recommends* hypocrisy. He advises the prince to clothe his use of vice in a mantle of public virtue. And, although an adherent of the descriptive claim of realpolitik would certainly accept the tactical use of hypocrisy in certain circumstances, Machiavelli's recommendation is far more comprehensive.[35] The actions of states take place within a particular moral horizon and are always subject to ethical judgment. Rulers must attend to the way their actions will appear, they must speak a moral language, and they should exploit the opportunities to advance their aims that public moral discourse offers. In other words, politics may be either hyp-

34. In fact, Machiavelli is described in this way both by realists and nonrealists. See, for example, Raymond Aron, *Peace and War: A Theory of International Relations,* trans. Richard Howard and Annette Baker Fox (Garden City, N.Y.: Doubleday and Co., 1966), 3, 58, 133, 298, 609, 783; Charles R. Beitz, *Political Theory and International Relations* (Princeton: Princeton University Press, 1979), 21–23; Edward Hallett Carr, *The Twenty Years' Crisis, 1919–1939: An Introduction to the Study of International Relations* (London: Macmillan and Co., Ltd., 1940), 63–64, 81–84, 102, 144, 194; Stephen Forde, "Varieties of Realism: Thucydides and Machiavelli," *Journal of Politics* 54, no. 2 (May 1992): 372–93; Morgenthau, *Politics among Nations,* 169; Waltz, *Man, the State and War,* 211–16; and Kenneth N. Waltz, *Theory of International Politics* (Reading, Mass.: Addison-Wesley, 1979), 116–17.

35. It would be hard to imagine any adherent of "realpolitik" praising the hypocrisy of Ferdinand, King of Spain, as Machiavelli does (*Pr.,* chaps. 18, 21).

ocritical or moral but not frankly self-interested. Machiavelli
never imagines the possibility of a political community acting
without public appeals to standards of virtue and vice, and he
never recommends educating the people to look only to their
interests. He would reject as impossible the notion that cynicism
ever could become a public doctrine.

From a Machiavellian standpoint, "realists," economic and
political are, in fact, unrealistic to the extent that they do not
recognize the importance of the forces at work beyond self-
interest that make a politics of simple rational calculation impossible. What are those other forces? What would be a Machiavellian
critique of the claims for honest politics? We need to understand
why the conception of politics as the negotiation of mutually
beneficial trades between competing interests will never be an
exhaustive description or, consequently, the basis for a viable prescription. We need to understand why political deliberation will
always include persuasion, sometimes honest and sometimes not,
on the basis of appeals to principles and shared ethical concerns.

A Machiavellian Critique of the Possibility of Honest Politics

For a variety of reasons, neither the argument for economic honesty nor the argument for political honesty has managed to silence
the skeptics. Liberal democratic societies with market economies
have not fulfilled the hopes of those who believed that such societies might minimize public hypocrisy, though public hypocrisy
certainly takes an entirely different form than it did in aristocratic
Europe. In addition to the testimony of experience, there are two
primary theoretical grounds for continued skepticism. First, the
type of equality embedded in market relations and in liberal democratic political relations is not sufficient to overcome dependence, and dependence remains the major source of pressure toward hypocritical and manipulative behavior.

Second, there are moral and psychological forces inevitably
linked to political discourse which, by their very nature, are not
susceptible to direct negotiation and compromise of the kind that
can take place among competing economic interests. Honor and
the pride associated with it is an obvious example. The boundary
of a person's honor is defined by the point at which he will not

yield for any price. Machiavelli's *Mandragola* will be used to illustrate this point. The play reveals why it is that, in politics, there are times when the mutually desirable outcome cannot be achieved by a straightforward exchange of benefits, but only through deception and manipulation.

Let us begin with the first point, that greater egalitarianism in economics and in politics cannot overcome the destructive moral effects of dependence. The critique of the claims for the possibility of honesty in economic exchange proceeds by exposing the elements of dependence that remain among trading partners. It is true that, in a free market situation, a trade will occur only voluntarily and when it is beneficial to both parties. Nonetheless, because it is always advantageous to increase the frequency of such occasions, any given individual will constantly have the need to persuade others to want whatever it is that he has to offer in trade. In this respect, the seller depends on the buyer or potential buyers. This dependence provides the impetus for advertising and, of course, for false advertising, which can range from adept manipulation of people's desires to outright fraud of the kind that is ordinarily controlled by law. Or consider the effects of the dependence between seller and buyer when the "seller" is a person looking to sell his particular combination of skills and personal attributes to a potential employer. He attempts to "sell himself," and a similar dynamic continues to operate so long as retaining his job requires continued consciousness of the need to please the boss. These illustrations merely suggest the outlines of an argument that has been fully articulated by critics of contemporary consumer capitalism for many years now. Advanced capitalist economies are said to generate and manipulate false needs in a way that produces a wide variety of deceptions, manipulation, and vices. By no means the least of these deceptions is that we are led to see ourselves as independent agents of choice when we are actually chained to a set of dependencies crucial to the maintenance of the economic system.[36]

In short, it is not at all obvious that the justification for market relations offered by Smith can serve as a sufficient reply to the

---

36. The argument is made most famously by Karl Marx and Friedrich Engels, "Manifesto of the Communist Party," in *The Marx-Engels Reader,* ed. Robert C. Tucker, 2d ed. (New York: W. W. Norton, 1978), 484–91.

critique of economic dependence developed by Rousseau. In fact, in modern bourgeois societies the tendency for economic interdependence to produce hypocrisy may be exacerbated rather than alleviated. The attempt to ground society in nothing more than calculations of individual selfish interest gives rise to a kind of paradox: the more selfish each man is, the more he needs things that others can supply, but the less he truly cares for other people. If it is only his selfishness that ties him to others in society, the virtues of sociability that are required to maintain society will always be a sham. According to Arthur Melzer, this is the lesson we learn from Rousseau's critique of the modern experiment initiated by Hobbes and Locke:

> The egoistic individual is forced by his very selfishness to appear just and benevolent toward others—so that they will help him—but because he is selfish, he never sincerely desires to be this way for its own sake. The same thing that makes him need to appear moral—his selfishness—makes him dislike being moral. In short, among selfish but mutually dependent human beings, it is necessarily bad to *be* what it is necessarily good to *seem* . . . and this is why it becomes psychologically necessary that all men become phonies, actors, role players, and hypocrites. . . . In sum, the modern commercial republic, generating sociability from selfishness, necessarily creates a society of smiling enemies, where each individual pretends to care about others precisely because he cares only about himself.[37]

A greater egalitarianism in economic relations cannot overcome dependence sufficiently to remove the impetus to hypocritical behavior; quite the contrary.

The same can be said for political egalitarianism. Or rather, the point has even greater force with respect to politics. Egalitarianism in politics simply substitutes a new web of shifting dependencies for the more fixed dependencies of hierarchical social orders. Democratic politicians, unable to take their support for granted and subject to frequent elections, must continually cultivate the public as well as actual and potential coalition partners. It would be difficult to imagine a less autonomous actor than a

---

37. Arthur M. Melzer, "Rousseau and the Modern Cult of Sincerity," in *The Legacy of Rousseau,* ed. Clifford Orwin and Nathan Tarcov (Chicago: University of Chicago Press, 1997), 282.

politician in a democracy. In order to achieve anything at all in a democracy, political actors need the cooperation of a great many other people. And they need to be able to count on that cooperation over time by cultivating trust and loyalty. The language of democratic politics requires "You can count on me" and "I know I can count on your support." Politics, even or especially in a democracy, takes place among people embedded in relationships of dependence.

Dependence breeds opportunities for hypocritical manipulation, but it does not in itself necessitate hypocrisy. The "Smithian" argument, after all, is that people who are interdependent, rather than economically self-sufficient, can negotiate trades that are mutually beneficial in a straightforward and honest fashion. But this argument cannot be applied readily to politics because politics differs from economics in one crucial respect. Politics necessarily involves matters that are not negotiable in the manner of interests: trust, loyalty, pride, honor, vanity, ambition, moral belief, etc.[38] Machiavelli's play *Mandragola* is illustrative here. An analysis of the play reveals why it is that, so long as these psychological and ethical elements are inseparable from politics, there will also be political hypocrisy.

In this play, Callimaco, a young gentleman, returns from Paris to Florence after hearing of the extraordinary beauty and manners of a Florentine woman, Lucrezia. He becomes obsessed with his desire for her. Lucrezia, described as "most honest" and "fit to govern a kingdom," is married to a wealthy and very stupid older man, Nicia. Nicia and Lucrezia have been married six years but are childless. Callimaco seeks to exploit in some way their desperate desire for a child in order to further his own aims. He enlists the help of Ligurio, a former marriage broker and a parasite, who is acquainted with Nicia. Ligurio promises to pursue a plot that will bring Callimaco successfully to Lucrezia's bed within 24 hours.

At Ligurio's direction, Callimaco, posing as a doctor trained in France, tells Nicia that he can make a potion of mandrake root

38. It is difficult to know what the "noneconomic" elements in politics ought to be called. Some are status issues, some ethical issues, some are called "identity" issues in contemporary political discourse. See, for example, Charles Taylor, *Multiculturalism and "The Politics of Recognition"* (Princeton: Princeton University Press, 1992), 37–44.

(mandragola) that will cure his wife's sterility. But, the first man to lie with her after she drinks the potion will surely die. Nicia must find some other man to take his place on the night she takes the potion. They plot to kidnap a vagabond off the street (who, unbeknownst to Nicia, will be none other than Callimaco in disguise) to perform this office. They decide to enlist Lucrezia's mother and her confessor, both known to be corrupt, to get Lucrezia to agree. Frate Timoteo, bribed, succeeds in persuading Lucrezia that to spend one night with a stranger will be no sin and will fulfill her duty to her husband. Callimaco, disguised as a street musician, is kidnapped by Ligurio, Nicia, the Frate, and his own servant, all also disguised. Nicia himself, suspecting nothing, takes Callimaco to Lucrezia.

In the night, Callimaco makes himself known to Lucrezia, and professes his love for her. She accepts him as her permanent lover, realizing that her husband's trust in the "doctor" can be used to gain continuing access to the house for Callimaco. She takes the position that this turn of events must have been the will of God. In the morning, all the characters gather at the church beaming with happiness: Nicia will have his son; Lucrezia and Callimaco will have each other; Frate Timoteo will have his money; and Ligurio will have rewards from Callimaco as well as the satisfaction of having brought all this to pass.

Not only are all the characters better off than they were at the beginning of the play, we are led to believe that, in a certain sense, justice has been done. The marriage of Nicia and Lucrezia is a mismatch. He doesn't deserve her, and she deserves better. Ligurio, the former marriage broker and mastermind of the plot, is motivated by the desire to rectify this situation.[39] He remarks,

> I don't believe there's a stupider man in the world than this fellow [Nicia], yet how fortune has favored him! He's rich, he has a beautiful wife, wise, well-mannered, and fit to govern a kingdom. It seems to me that proverb on marriages which says "God makes men and they pair themselves off!" is rarely proven true. Because one often sees that

39. He explicitly states that he does not pursue the plot only for profit. Niccolò Machiavelli, *Mandragola,* trans. Mera J. Flaumenhaft (Prospect Heights, Ill.: Waveland Press, 1981), act 1, scene 3, p. 18. All citations to plays refer to act, scene, and page number unless otherwise noted.

it's the lot of a well-qualified man to end up with a beast, and vice-versa, of a prudent woman to have a madman. (1.3.17)

It proves possible to remedy this injustice in a way that benefits all parties.

Why, then, is it impossible to reach this remedy through a negotiated solution? It would clearly be another comedy, and a modern one at that, if Ligurio were to act as mediator in a negotiation between Callimaco, Nicia, and Lucrezia. But *why* is this a comic suggestion, not to be taken seriously? After all, Nicia wants a son and is willing to be cuckolded to get one,[40] Callimaco wants Lucrezia, and Lucrezia both wants a child and prefers a young lover. A rational solution is available. Why can it be achieved only through deceit and hypocrisy? If we can answer this question in the context of the play, perhaps we will be able to make the case for the necessity of hypocrisy more generally.

Actually, in principle, there is more than one solution to the problem of the play. The rational and moral approach would have been for Callimaco to have remained in Paris in the first place[41] or to decide to seek the favors of an eligible Italian lady. But the problem of the play is set by the fact that Callimaco is stricken with love, which is depicted as an overpowering passion leading to the greatest irrationalities.[42] He cannot simply return to Paris or seek satisfaction elsewhere. Alternatively, as Callimaco suggests, he may be led to satisfy his desires through "bestial, cruel, nefarious" means (1.3.17).[43] Where the rational and lawful approach proper to man will not do, the way of beasts remains. But the beasts include the fox as well as the lion (*Pr.,* chap. 18, p. 69). And once again, when these are the only practicable alternatives, Machiavelli portrays fraud, the way of the fox, as the preferred course of action.

---

40. Worse than that, he is willing to commit murder. He believes that the "stranger" will die.

41. His servant suggests that this might have been his advice (1.1.13).

42. See the song that ends act 1, p. 19.

43. The suggestion is often made that the play is a satire on the rape of the Roman Lucretia. Machiavelli discusses the political importance of that event in *The Discourses* (*D.,* III, 2, 5, 26). See Mera J. Flaumenhaft, "The Comic Remedy: Machiavelli's *Mandragola,*" *Interpretation* 7, no. 2 (1978): 37–47; Hanna Fenichel Pitkin, *Fortune Is a Woman* (Berkeley: University of California Press, 1984), 47–48; Arlene Saxonhouse, *Women in the History of Political Thought* (New York: Praeger, 1985), 168–69.

In this case, the fraud is required because Nicia's sense of honor, Lucrezia's religion, and the laws and conventions of Florence present insuperable obstacles to an openly negotiated arrangement.[44] The legal obstacle is evaded simply through secrecy, and this could have been accomplished equally well with a secret negotiation. But even a secret negotiation would have foundered on Nicia's honor and Lucrezia's religiosity. These obstacles can be overcome only through fraud. Nicia's sense of honor and Lucrezia's moral sensibilities must be given their due.[45] Nicia, initially resistant to the plot, agrees after assurances that kings, princes and lords have done the same (2.6.25–26). Lucrezia, a deeply religious woman, remains extremely reluctant to the end, but she does allow herself to be persuaded to cooperate. She is unwilling to resist the combined authority of her mother and the priest, and she has no reply to the series of specious arguments the priest devises to convince her that Biblical precedents and theological doctrines support the morality of their proposal (3.11.35–36). Without the priest's hypocritical use of religion, there is simply no way for the plot to proceed, no way to secure Lucrezia's cooperation.[46] She could never be persuaded to abandon her moral scruples outright, but she can be manipulated through rationalizations that allow her to continue to believe in her own righteousness.

In this situation, to ask why hypocrisy is necessary is to ask why law, religion, and honor—or public morality altogether—are necessary. A negotiated solution on the basis of interest alone would be possible only among totally cynical people. Machia-

44. Most commentators interested in the political lessons of *Mandragola* discuss only why fraud is preferable to force. They do not consider the question raised here—why fraud can succeed where honesty cannot. See Flaumenhaft, "Comic Remedy," 38; Martin Fleisher, "Trust and Deceit in Machiavelli's Comedies," *Journal of the History of Ideas* 27, no. 3 (July 1966): 374–78; Theodore A. Sumberg, "*La Mandragola:* An Interpretation," *Journal of Politics* 23, no. 2 (May 1961): 322.

45. See chapter 5, text accompanying notes 22–25. Rousseau and Machiavelli share an appreciation for the power of honor as a motivating force independent of interest and often even against self-interest.

46. Despite the crucial role of the priest in the play, Machiavelli does not simply endorse his behavior by any means. The audience is meant to understand that the priest is corrupt and that his hypocrisy is an element of his corruption. Machiavelli distinguishes among forms of hypocrisy; they are not all equally venal nor equally justifiable.

velli's argument for the necessity of hypocrisy depends on the impossibility of conducting social relations in an openly cynical fashion. He explains how the moral dimension of public life can be effectively manipulated for political purposes, but he assumes that public life always will have a moral dimension of great political significance.

It seems a fair assumption, almost self–evident. A political community cannot exist without some shared morality and some common standard for honor or respectability. Public discourse is conducted in moral terms, and that shared language is itself part of the constitution of any particular public. Common interests or mutually interdependent interests are not enough to create lasting bonds between people. Common religion, common myths and traditions, shared historical experience—these are the sorts of things that define distinct particular communities and bind their members to one another.

In a double sense, those bonds are not rational. They do not result from rational calculations of utility, but instead are affective attachments formed, for the most part, long before we reach the age of reason. Moreover, they are irrational in that, while human beings do need to belong to particular societies, there is generally little reason why any given society deserves an individual's allegiance any more than any other in which he might have found himself. We are attached to our communities because they are ours, and not necessarily because they are the best or the most useful to us. A public doctrine that acknowledged this arbitrariness and encouraged people to act on the basis of interest alone would undermine the attachments necessary to sustain communal life.[47]

Of course, commonly accepted public moral standards are necessary not only to serve as a basis for common bonds but because moral behavior is necessary. All conflicts are not conflicts of interest, and all conflicts of interest are not readily negotiable. In *Mandragola,* it is fortuitous that the conflict has a mutually beneficial resolution. And it should be recalled that the conflict arises in the first place only because Callimaco is overcome with the

---

47. Because there is no international community in this sense, "realpolitik" is a more plausible doctrine for international relations than it would be if applied to domestic politics.

strength of his desire to have what belongs to someone else. Love, vengeance, and ambition are passions that cannot always be satisfied through peaceful negotiation, nor even through deceit. Society is impossible without moral constraints on selfish desires. Moreover, moral constraints do not simply go against the grain. They find powerful psychological support in the fact that, by and large, people want to be thought of as good. More important, they want to think of themselves as good. For all these reasons, public cynicism is an impossibility.

So long as there are public moral standards, there will be, and sometimes even should be, hypocritical manipulation of them. There will be hypocrisy if only because there is necessarily a gap between the real and the ideal. Human beings cannot always practice what they preach. There will be hypocrisy too whenever there are justifiable exceptions to the rules and a simultaneous need to maintain public commitments to the rules. Most important, there will be hypocrisy because it works in situations where neither force nor honesty is a viable alternative. This is the lesson of *Mandragola*. Even in a case where a negotiated solution serving both justice and the interests of all parties is possible in principle, the desired outcome often can be reached only through deception, manipulation, and hypocrisy because of the importance of public moral standards and of certain kinds of psychological forces. Hypocrisy is an extremely useful tool when you depend on the cooperation of others to further your aims. You must persuade them not only that it is in their interest to cooperate, but that you can be trusted, that the action you propose is the right thing to do, and that their reputation will be secure. In politics, simple, rational, honest negotiation on the basis of interest alone cannot replace either "politicking" or moral suasion.

At this point, an objection could be raised to drawing general conclusions about the nature of politics from a play written about private, domestic affairs. But the play holds many indications that it was meant to carry political messages, such as the implicit reference to the rape of Lucretia.[48] Explicitly, the play is about how to lead others in the direction you wish them to go and how to avoid being misled or tricked by them in turn. The play is replete

48. See note 43.

with military metaphors (e.g., 2.9). It exposes the dangers of trusting too much in authorities who speak a little Latin (1.3.18; 2.2). Commentators have argued that the play is an expression of Machiavelli's political views in a number of ways, ranging from demonstrating the thematic similarities between the play and the political works to analyzing the plot as a direct allegory of a Machiavellian conspiracy.[49]

For the purposes of explaining the necessity of hypocrisy in politics, what matters most is that the relationships among the characters in the play resemble political relationships. For example, Callimaco and Nicia are neither friends nor enemies. Enemies have conflicting interests, but they do not depend on one another, and there is no question of trust between them. Friends depend on one another and share their interests so that bonds of trust can be formed between them. Political relations are relations of conflicting interests, like enmities, but between people who depend on one another, like friendships. This describes the relation between Callimaco and Nicia. Though these people have conflicting interests, they belong to the same community. They must take account of its legal and moral constraints even if only ultimately to circumvent them for the sake of the satisfaction of their selfish desires. Callimaco needs Nicia's cooperation to get what Nicia would not give him voluntarily. He cultivates Nicia's trust, but he is not trustworthy, and he deceives Nicia into giving him what he wants.

In contrast, there is one truly private moment described in the play, and it is, significantly, the moment when the pretense is dropped. Callimaco, telling Ligurio about his night with Lucrezia, reports:

> I stayed with a troubled mind until three o'clock, and although I took great pleasure in it, it didn't seem good to me. But then I made myself known to her, and made her understand the love I bore for her, and how easily, on account of her husband's simplicity, we could live happily without any scandal, promising her, whenever God did otherwise with him, to take her for my wife. (5.4.52)

---

49. See Fleisher for the former and Sumberg for the latter. Pitkin sees some political parallels but does not view *Mandragola* as just another version of *The Prince*. Pitkin, *Fortune Is a Woman*, 30–31, 46, 101.

Callimaco wants more than the satisfaction of his desire. He wants to be chosen in turn by the one he has chosen, and as himself. Making himself known to Lucrezia, he also makes himself vulnerable. Lucrezia could have rejected him and exposed the whole plot. By accepting him, a bond of trust is established between them. Each trusts the other to maintain the secrecy of their relationship.

It is the only instance of trust in the play where the trust is justifiable, either because these two care for each other or because their interests are identical. In all the other relations of the play, those who are trusting are deceived as a result.[50] In political relationships, one must beware of trusting others. Political relationships are not true friendships. The contrast between the rather touching moment Callimaco describes between Lucrezia and himself and the deceitful, exploitative relations among the other characters in the play is stark and instructive.

What we learn about politics is that, because society requires trust but men are not trustworthy, deceit is inevitable. And because society requires morality but men are not always moral, hypocrisy is inevitable. Machiavelli does not embrace the public cynicism of the political "realists." That political negotiation could be conducted honestly, publicly, rationally, and on the basis of interest alone, as if it were indistinguishable from economic negotiation, is not a realistic possibility. Political discourse will always include appeals to pride, honor, ambition, religion, loyalty, morals, and principles. I do not mean to suggest that such appeals are necessarily either irrational or dishonest, but only that, first, they cannot be explained by the understanding of rational politics that defines rationality as the calculation of maximum utility and second, that they create opportunities for hypocritical manipulation. Attempts to "rationalize" politics tend to give too little weight both to irrational passions that are not reducible to interests and to the moral structures whose purpose it is to constrain those same passions. Machiavelli does not make these mistakes, and consequently he gives full recognition to the importance of hypocrisy in political life.

50. I disagree here with both Fleisher and Sumberg, who do not distinguish this case from the others. It could be argued that Callimaco's trust in Ligurio is justified, but also that Ligurio is genuinely interested in seeing Callimaco succeed for his own reasons.

Though political hypocrisy in many of its forms is morally reprehensible and politically dangerous, its necessity indicates something positive nonetheless. Hypocrisy only occurs where people try to appear better than they are. The pretense is only necessary where people need to be thought of as good and to think of themselves as good. Where there is political hypocrisy, there is a public moral standard and a significant moral impulse. The necessity of hypocrisy in politics is one indication of the enduring strength of that impulse in human life.

THE PARADOX OF DEMOCRACY

One of the important moral claims for democratic politics is that, in democracies, politics can be conducted openly and without manipulation. The facts and the arguments will be put before the public or a representative body, and a decision will be made. Ideally, each individual will choose on the basis of his own best judgment and each individual's choice will carry equal weight. Where independence and equality are valued, as they are in democracies, hypocrisy will be derided as a vice and secrecy will always be suspect. In contrast, in hereditary monarchies and aristocracies, it was possible to lead one's life as a court flatterer or social parasite. Hypocrisy was not considered the greatest of vices. Largely because modern politics is democratic politics, modern political discourse is very often a matter of charges and countercharges of hypocrisy.[51]

But if Machiavelli is correct that hypocrisy arises from the dependence inherent in political relationships, one would expect to find a great deal of hypocrisy in democracies. Democratic politicians, particularly in pluralist societies, find themselves most in need of supporters and coalition partners. Their need for "coalition building" and "building a base" is merely the democratic form of the prince's need for allies and supportive subjects. It is widely recognized that hypocrisy arises as a useful tool, particularly for the weaker party, in relations of dependence.[52] Demo-

---

51. Shklar, *Ordinary Vices*, 67–78.

52. Examples could range from Charles Dickens's portrayal of Uriah Heep to Friedrich Nietzsche's contrast between the truthfulness of the noble and the deception, self-deception, and *ressentiment* of slave morality (see, e.g., *On the Genealogy of Morals*, First Essay, paras. 5 and 10).

cratic politicians, because they can act in the end only by securing majority support, are far more dependent than politicians in inegalitarian regimes.[53]

This is the paradox of democracy. Because democracies uphold an egalitarian ideal, they will loathe hypocrisy. But on account of their very egalitarianism, they will continue to generate it. And, of course, this adds an additional layer of hypocrisy. Hypocritical politicians are hypocritical once; if they also pretend to uphold an ideal of honest political dealing, they are hypocritical twice. Machiavelli would have been skeptical of the democratic hope that politics could be conducted through an open deliberative process to reach a reasonable accommodation among competing interests. His work stands as a challenge to the high hopes of any attempt to rationalize political life, whether in the form of Enlightenment liberalism or in the form of contemporary efforts to construe politics in the light of economic rationality. Similarly, his thought provides insight into the difficulties confronting efforts to expand the sphere of rational public discourse in liberal democracies in the hope of producing a nonmanipulative politics.

To eliminate manipulation and hypocrisy from politics would require, not more egalitarianism, but more autonomy for democratic politicians. But it is precisely because politicians depend on supporters and coalition partners to achieve their ends and because they remain beholden to them for their support that they can be held accountable and the system can maintain its democratic character. Alternatively, one could attempt to diminish hypocrisy by diminishing moral discourse in politics altogether, but this also has its obvious disadvantages. So long as the political community is composed of people with genuine differences, with overlapping but never coincident interests, the attempt to forge

53. Of course, political hypocrisy exists in all kinds of regimes, though its characteristics vary. An interesting comparison could be made, for instance, between democratic and totalitarian political hypocrisy.

The relation between dependency and hypocrisy could be empirically verified in democratic politics. One would expect, for example, to find more extreme rhetoric from factions who are so weak that they cannot expect to secure a majority but can maintain their minority status by holding onto their electoral base. One would also expect more "hypocritical" rhetoric from stronger factions who have the possibility of forging a winning coalition. The stronger party is not necessarily the most autonomous or least dependent.

a consensus will involve the essentially political art of persuasion, the necessity to compromise, and the pressure toward hypocrisy.

CONCLUSIONS

The issue of hypocrisy in politics comes to the fore when political relations are understood not as power relations but as relations of dependence. Machiavelli, so often understood as a theorist of "power politics," rests his case for hypocrisy in politics precisely on this view. The necessity for hypocrisy arises whenever potential competitors depend on one another. And politics itself is understood as the situation where potential competitors depend on one another.

Machiavelli's aim in politics is not so much to maximize power as it is to minimize dependence. The goal of the prince is to secure a position where he is beholden to no one and relies on his "own arms." The search for autonomy is not the same as the search for unlimited power. The distinction between dependence and autonomy emerges as the distinction that governs Machiavelli's analysis in *The Prince* and *The Discourses* and unifies his thought.[54] Machiavelli admires those qualities in princes and republics that enhance their autonomy. For example, Machiavelli's ideal type is defined by his lack of constancy. There is no fixed principle or fixed character trait that constrains his ability to respond to his circumstances. In this sense, he lacks integrity, because integrity that requires constancy limits autonomous action. But in another sense, Machiavelli recognizes the value of integrity. He admires men who cannot be bought, again because they retain their autonomy. Similarly, Machiavelli conceives of hypocrisy as a tool that can be adopted without psychological threat to the autonomy of its user. His hypocrite is fully self–conscious and calculating, in contrast to the fawning, sycophantic sort of hypocrite. The dependence that necessitates his hypocrisy is political and not psychological. Machiavelli thus justifies the political use of hypocrisy both because it is necessitated by the peculiarities of political relationships and because it is not a sign of personal weakness.

54. See Pitkin, *Fortune Is a Woman*, 7 ff. Pitkin ties this distinction to Machiavelli's ambivalence about manhood.

Rousseau is also a theorist of dependence. He accepts the Machiavellian notion that the particular sort of dependence implicit in political relationships is the source of hypocrisy and corruption. But, in Machiavelli's view, politics takes place in divided communities among people with divided souls, among "so many who are not good." Unlike Machiavelli, Rousseau argues from the premise of the natural unity and goodness of the self, and he develops an ideal of a unified political community. We turn to Rousseau's thought to explore the possibility that, despite the inevitable pressures toward political hypocrisy, there is an alternative to the self-conscious manipulator of principles held up as a model by Machiavelli.

3

Molière, Rousseau, and the Ideal of Integrity

INTRODUCTION

On the subject of political hypocrisy, the works of Jean-Jacques Rousseau seem to present the starkest possible contrast to those of Machiavelli. Machiavelli teaches princes to cultivate the art of hypocritical behavior. He admires the masters of deceit. Rousseau presents hypocritical behavior, though not itself the source of all evil, as the first effect of that inequality which is the source of all evil in human affairs (*Second,* 156). Where there is hypocrisy, human beings have been corrupted. Much of Rousseau's writing is devoted to developing portraits of innocence, virtue, and integrity that form the counterpoints to his scathing critique of the corruption, flattery, and hypocrisy that infected the social and political life of his age.

This is the dominant and familiar image of Rousseau. But, as is so often the case in Rousseau's work, an opposing strain complicates the matter considerably while enhancing its interest. Rousseau, as we have seen, admires Machiavelli; Rousseau's great Legislator deceives the people by using religion for political purposes; and Rousseau himself is willing to make political compromises that seem to violate his principles, such as recommending the continuation of serfdom in Poland.[1] These are a few indications that Rousseau's condemnation of hypocrisy is not a simple one. Is he a critic of hypocrisy in politics, a teacher of political duplicity, or both?

In order to answer this question, we must understand what

---

1. Compare *S.C.,* II, vii, and *S.C.,* III, vi, with *Poland,* chap. 6.

Rousseau is for as well as what he is against. His critique of hypocrisy and corruption cannot be separated from his admiration for a particular kind of integrity. There are varieties of integrity, as well as varieties of hypocrisy and duplicity. Rousseau's commitment to a distinctive ideal of integrity governs his judgments concerning which kinds of hypocrisy are most contemptible and which kinds of duplicity might be acceptable.

I have chosen to speak of "integrity" rather than "authenticity" in characterizing the quality that Rousseau sets in opposition to hypocrisy. In doing so, I depart from the common usage for several reasons. Most important, the vocabulary of integrity is closer to Rousseau's own. His common terms include *probité, vertue, droiture, integrité,* and *honnêteté.*[2] He does not use *authenticité* and *authentique(s)* at all in the *First* or *Second Discourse,* in the *Confessions,* in the *Reveries of the Solitary Walker,* or in *The Government of Poland.* The terms are used twice in *The Social Contract,* three times in *Émile,* and five times in the *Letters Written from the Mountain.* In each case, the clear sense is to characterize an act as genuine or original as opposed to counterfeit (e.g., authentic documents, authentic miracles, or an authentic act of the general will).[3]

In French usage, *authenticité* did not acquire its association with sincerity or its quality as an attribute of the self until long after Rousseau's death.[4] Thus the use of the term "authenticity" to describe the central focus of Rousseau's work colors interpretation of that work with reflections of developments in continental philosophy that postdate Rousseau, notably romanticism and existentialism. Rousseau is certainly one of the sources of these developments, but his own work contains a distinctive moralism that is obscured by an emphasis on authenticity.[5] One can be

2. Rousseau's use of this term is discussed below. See text accompanying notes 68–74.

3. *O.C.,* III, 374, 425, 736, 756, 845, 852, 887; *O.C.,* IV, 611, 615.

4. See *Le Grand Robert de la langue française,* 2d ed., 9 vols. (Paris: Dictionnaires Le Robert, 1985), 1:715–16.

5. See Marshall Berman, *The Politics of Authenticity: Radical Individualism and the Emergence of Modern Society* (New York: Atheneum, 1970). Berman writes: "But the choice of the word [authenticity] was rather arbitrary; so many others might have done as well. 'Identity,' 'autonomy,' 'individuality,' 'self-development,' 'self-realization' . . ." (xv). The use of these other terms distorts in the same way as the use of "authenticity." See, for example, Irving Babbitt, *Rousseau and Romanticism* (Boston:

authentically many things, including authentically dishonest.[6] Authenticity's only command is "be yourself." But Rousseau seeks goodness. His terminology is precisely one of honesty, uprightness, and faithful performance of duty. The use of authenticity as a substitute for Rousseau's terms conceals the moral content of this vocabulary and thus attributes a greater subjectivity to Rousseau's thought than is implied by his own words.

To recapture Rousseau's moralism while remaining true to his usage, one could characterize his ideal in terms of virtue rather than integrity. Carol Blum has pursued this alternative in her account of the way in which Rousseau's concept of virtue became "the language of politics in the French Revolution." According to Blum, Rousseau understands virtue not as the painful self-overcoming of a divided soul but as a pleasure for a soul unified

---

Houghton Mifflin, 1919). My point is supported by Charles Taylor, *The Malaise of Modernity* (Concord, Ontario: Anansi Press, 1991), 27–28.

Jean Starobinski's analysis also obscures the moral content of Rousseau's thought. He employs the morally neutral terms "transparency" and "obstruction" to describe the governing problem of Rousseau's work, viz., the attempt to overcome the rift between appearance and reality by achieving immediate, rather than mediated relationships. He is led to conclude, for example, that "the law of authenticity" does not require Rousseau to tell the truth in writing his autobiography. *Jean-Jacques Rousseau: Transparency and Obstruction,* trans. Arthur Goldhammer (Chicago: University of Chicago Press, 1988), 198–99. But this is not Rousseau's opinion. See *Reveries,* Fourth Walk, and the discussion of it in the section in chapter 4 entitled, "Rousseau's Personal Ethics: Acceptable Lies." My position contrasts also with that of Alessandro Ferrara's *Modernity and Authenticity: A Study of the Social and Ethical Thought of Jean-Jacques Rousseau* (Albany: State University of New York Press, 1993). He argues that Rousseau's ethic of authenticity is at the core of his thought and that it requires us to choose for our feelings and against our ethical principles when those feelings are central to our identity (25–27, 105). He provides a useful discussion of the differences between authenticity, sincerity, intimacy, and autonomy (86–91).

6. Diderot's portrait of Rameau's nephew is a good example. He *is* a sycophant and manipulator—an artist of hypocrisy. To be himself is to develop his talent for manipulation, however vile. In short, he is an authentic hypocrite and a character whom Rousseau could never admire. Denis Diderot, *Rameau's Nephew and D'Alembert's Dream,* trans. Leonard Tancock (New York: Penguin Books, 1966). See also note 60.

To the extent that authentic means original or natural, Rousseau would deny the possibility of authentic dishonesty on account of his view of the natural goodness of man. But if one rejects that premise, authentic dishonesty is not in principle impossible or by definition incorrect.

and unconflicted.[7] Virtue, in Rousseau's usage, does require suffering the painful and conflictual demands of duty in some instances.[8] Blum fails, however, to recognize that Rousseau's use of
the term "virtue" is ambiguous, and so, although Blum correctly
identifies the combination of goodness and wholeness as characteristic of the Rousseauian ideal, "integrity" expresses that particular ideal combination better than "virtue." Integrity comes
closer to an accurate English term for Rousseau's ideal while remaining true to his usage.[9]

Recognizing the centrality of Rousseau's concept of integrity
allows for a more coherent interpretation of his thought than the
alternative terminologies provide in several important respects.
First, it reveals the common foundation for Rousseau's praise of
apparently opposing human possibilities. For example, if the distinction between virtue and vice is thought to govern Rousseau's
writings, it becomes difficult to explain his praise of the natural
man, for whom this distinction has no meaning. If authenticity/
artificiality is taken as the governing distinction, it is difficult to
explain Rousseau's praise of the citizen. The Rousseauian citizen
is certainly not authentic, since he is the product of artifice and
convention and is even described as denatured (*Émile*, 40). But
it is not so difficult to see the citizen as a fulfillment of the Rousseauian ideal if that ideal is defined in terms of integrity. Integrity
includes both morality and wholeness or unity, and it opposes
corruption and conflict or alienation. The citizen is a man of
integrity because he combines unity and moral virtue. The natural man is a man of integrity because he combines unity and moral
innocence. In this latter sense, integrity *is* the authentic condition
of man according to Rousseau. Why would it be desirable to
be authentic? Only because, in Rousseau's view, the authentic
individual has integrity. It is not that Rousseau does not value
authenticity but that the distinction between integrity and cor-

7. Carol Blum, *Rousseau and the Republic of Virtue: The Language of Politics in the
French Revolution* (Ithaca, N.Y.: Cornell University Press, 1986), 49, 64–67. Blum's
treatment of Rousseau resembles Hannah Arendt's in many respects. See Hannah
Arendt, *On Revolution* (New York: Viking, 1965), 70–76.

8. See note 44.

9. "Integrity" has an additional advantage in that the term is used to describe
qualities of character more than attributes of action. "Virtue" is more ambiguous in
this regard.

ruption takes precedence over that between authenticity and artificiality in his thought.

Second, when Rousseau is viewed as an advocate of integrity,
an interpretation of his work emerges that can incorporate his
more pragmatic political writing—writing that is often given insufficient consideration. While Rousseau sometimes speaks with
a moralistic voice, announcing absolute, universalistic principles
and insisting on rigid adherence to them, there is nonetheless a
surprising degree of flexibility in his political judgments. He is
noteworthy for his sensitivity to historical and natural conditions
in his recommendations for applying political principles in practice.[10] He modifies his educational recommendations to suit the
different temperaments of different children (Émile, 35, 192). He
is aware that the best is not possible at every time and in every
place and for every individual. Rousseau's conception of integrity
allows for both the purity and the pragmatism, reconciling to
some extent the abstract, universalistic, moralistic, and revolutionary elements in his thought with the historical, particularistic,
politically practical, and even conservative ones. In contrast,
where Rousseau is interpreted either as an advocate of authenticity or as a champion of virtue, this more politic side of his work
tends to be ignored, and he appears to promote an indefensibly
rigid moral purity whose political consequence is either revolutionary fanaticism or withdrawal.[11]

Without doubt, the strain of moralism in Rousseau's writings
has dangerous political implications. But fanaticism and withdrawal from public life do not exhaust the possibilities for a Rousseauian political ethic. And this is the third reason that this interpretation focuses on the conception of integrity: it permits an
alternative assessment of the political implications of Rousseau's
work. Integrity implies neither the subjectivity nor the moral rigidity attributed to Rousseau's thought by those who see authenticity or virtue at its core. Consequently, its political consequences are more positive. We are led to consider what types of
political flexibility and political compromises are consistent with

    10. D'Alembert, 65, 107, 110; Émile, 464; S.C., III, viii, 44–155.
    11. See Arendt and Blum on fanaticism. See Arthur M. Melzer, The Natural Good-
ness of Man (Chicago: University of Chicago Press, 1990), 253–61, and Judith Shklar,
Men and Citizens: A Study of Rousseau's Social Theory (Cambridge: Cambridge University Press, 1969), 58–59, 88, 159 on withdrawal.

integrity in Rousseau's view and what types are not. The picture that emerges is a complex and interesting mix of purity and pragmatism. Rousseau's thought contains a political ethic that stands as an alternative both to the simply pragmatic complacent moderation he attacks and to the essentially antipolitical moralism for which he is sometimes attacked.

The chapters that follow explore Rousseau's conception of integrity and the political ethic it entails. The discussion begins in this chapter with an analysis of Rousseau's ideal of integrity in comparison to the ethical alternatives to it. Rousseau understands integrity as purity, and the man of integrity emerges as an uncompromising moralist. This characterization is then reassessed by exploring the grounds for Rousseau's defense of certain sorts of compromises, lies, and political manipulations. As it turns out, prudence and integrity are not incompatible (chapter 4). Finally, the discussion turns to the question of why Rousseau's ideal is so rarely actualized. Rousseau's understanding of the process of corruption is examined along with the implications of his ethical posture for individuals living in corrupted times. In defending his ideal of integrity, Rousseau supports the sort of moral fortitude necessary to resist corrupted politics. Rousseau's ideal is neither a fanatic nor a misanthrope, but a person capable of making flexible political judgments and certainly more likely to resist fanatical political movements than to collaborate with them (chapter 5).

Molière and Rousseau:
The Ethical Alternatives

In the *Letter to M. D'Alembert on His Article, "Geneva,"* Rousseau distinguishes himself from another of the great French critics of hypocrisy, Molière.[12] Molière and Rousseau were connoisseurs of the varieties of political and social hypocrisy, severe critics of certain of its forms, and strikingly opposed to each other in their criticisms. Molière admires as a true gentleman the very type that

---

12. Although separated by roughly a century, Molière and Rousseau share in a tradition of French thought whose dominant themes include every aspect of the problem of hypocrisy, including sincerity in religion; flattery, influence, and power; society as a theater of masked role-players; and the corrupting effects of vanity and self-interest in public life. See Henri Peyré, *Literature and Sincerity* (New Haven, Conn.: Yale University Press, 1963), 45–78. See also E. J. Hundert, "A Satire of Self-Disclosure: From

Rousseau condemns as a hypocrite. Molière admires the politic moderate. Rousseau defends a moralistic, but impolitic, type and even presents himself as a model of that type.

Developing the contrast between Molière and Rousseau should accomplish several aims. It should clarify Rousseau's status as a critic of hypocrisy, a status that I have already indicated is problematic. It will also allow identification of the qualities that he admires and defends. More important, the contrast between Molière and Rousseau puts before us the best alternative responses to the ethical question that guides this study and invites us to critically evaluate them. The case for political moderation is set against the case for uncompromising moralism.[13] Each is a plausible response to the question, "What are the moral limits of political compromise?" How serious must we be about our commitments to stated ideals?

Framed in this way, the question presupposes a continuum of degrees of fidelity to principle; political actors might be always, sometimes, or never faithful to their moral commitments. This suggests that we might attempt to respond to the problem by adopting what, for the sake of brevity, I will call the "Aristotelean" scheme and seek to identify the mean along this continuum.[14] At one extreme would be the con man or the "Machiavellian." He is thoroughly unprincipled, a hypocrite, and probably a cynic. At the other extreme would be the righteous fanatic, the man who is rigidly principled. Midway between these two vices would be the virtue with respect to "principledness." It is the virtue of the statesman, combining seriousness about principles with a realistic view of the limitations on their full realization in practice.

But on further reflection, as I argue here, this way of conceptualizing the moral possibilities turns out to be more misleading

---

Hegel through Rameau to the Augustans," *Journal of the History of Ideas* 27 (1986): 235–48.

13. "Idealism" has a more positive contemporary connotation than "moralism," which suggests formality and stuffiness to modern ears. On the other hand, "moralism," unlike "idealism," does not imply that a person is unrealistic. Rousseau's moralism is a contested issue in Rousseau scholarship, so the term is more appropriate here.

14. Jay Newman uses this scheme as the basis for his discussion in *Fanatics and Hypocrites* (Buffalo, N.Y.: Prometheus Books, 1986). The discussion here is not meant to be a comment in any respect on Aristotle's actual treatment of the virtues of truthfulness and friendliness in *Nichomachean Ethics,* bk. 4.

than illuminating. This is so, first, because the righteous man too can be a kind of hypocrite; righteousness and hypocrisy do not stand as opposing extremes. Second, the "virtuous statesman" who applies his principles with moderation often turns out to be merely too tolerant of injustice, and therefore also a kind of hypocrite. What is praised as moderation may be nothing more than a mask for complacency. Vice with respect to hypocrisy is possible at each point along the spectrum: cynical hypocrisy, complacent hypocrisy, and righteous hypocrisy. The "Aristotelean" scheme, composed of two extreme types, each a kind of vice, plus one virtuous mean, is thus inadequate. In other words, the simple three-part typology (cynical hypocrite, statesman, righteous fanatic) does not exhaust the possibilities.

Consequently, I abandon the "Aristotelean" scheme and instead develop a different conception of the ethical alternatives, taking the various forms of hypocrisy into account, although the cynical, hypocritical con man is given little consideration.[15] The new conceptual scheme includes four alternative types, two of them moderate and two of them moralistic. In each case, one of the two is a hypocrite while the other is a man of integrity. On the moderate side, the complacent hypocrite is distinguished from the true statesman, while on the moralistic side, the righteous hypocrite is distinguished from the truly righteous man.[16]

Looking for the virtue with respect to principle in politics, we thus find that we must choose between two virtuous types: the

15. This is because there is no positive type of which he is the degenerate form. The con man is a morally simple case; he has chosen to be bad, accepting the same standards of morality as those who choose otherwise. In other words, the case of the con man does not present the problems of defining the standards that are presented by the other types. Consider Machiavelli's discussion in *The Prince*. It is very different to say that sometimes bad behavior can be justified than it is to say that your behavior is the model of the good. Machiavelli always speaks in the former terms.

16. The "Aristotelean" scheme is a linear picture:

Faithful to principle

too little — moderately — too much

cynic   statesman   fanatic

The ethical alternatives I consider can be diagrammed as a two-by-two matrix:

	Moderation	*Moralism*
Integrity	statesman	moralist
Hypocrisy	complacent hypocrite	righteous hypocrite

statesmanlike politic moderate and the righteous moralist. The differences between them are not differences of degree but differences in kind. Just as there is more than one kind of hypocrisy, there is more than one kind of integrity as well. The politic moderate and the uncompromising moralist are both attractive, and there is a plausible ethical justification for the behavior of each of them. Rousseau, in criticizing Molière, makes the case for the moralist over the moderate on the basis of a certain understanding of integrity. Is his case sound? And what are its political implications? We begin by examining the target of his attack, that is, the position he sets up as a foil for his own.

Tartuffe is a play in which Molière directly addresses the theme of hypocrisy present in so many of his works. In this play, a religious hypocrite, Tartuffe, manages to persuade the head of a prosperous household, Orgon, of his sincere piety. Gradually, he increases his power over him. Tartuffe nearly succeeds in securing all of Orgon's property and his daughter in marriage. Orgon finally sees Tartuffe for what he is when Elmire, Orgon's wife, convinces him that the "pious" Tartuffe has been making advances toward her. But only the King's intervention at the last moment restores Orgon's household and brings Tartuffe to justice.

At first glance, the hypothetical "Aristotelean" scheme for categorizing the ethical possibilities with respect to hypocrisy appears to correspond to Molière's presentation in *Tartuffe*. Tartuffe is the hypocritical con man at one extreme. Orgon, the man he dupes, stands at the other extreme as the righteous fanatic, imposing his severe moral standards with extreme rigidity. (Mme Pernelle, his mother, shares this characteristic.) Cléante, Elmire, and Dorine represent the virtuous mean. They are the moderates, attempting to revive the political health of this domestic kingdom by restoring common sense and humane sensibilities.[17] But a closer look at Orgon in particular reveals the weakness of the conceptual scheme. According to this scheme, hypocrisy and righteousness are best understood as opposites. Orgon's righteousness, however, is better understood not as the opposite of hypocrisy but as a form of it.

Orgon does not share Tartuffe's cynical attitude toward princi-

---

17. Cléante is Orgon's brother-in-law, Elmire is his wife, and Dorine is a house-servant.

ple,[18] but he does share with Tartuffe the use of principle for self-serving ends, and with such an effective mask that he even deceives himself. Orgon uses his newfound religiosity to enhance his authority over the members of his household. He begins by imposing strict constraints on their social pleasures in the name of moral rectitude. In this he resembles a male version of the coquette-turned-prude described by Dorine in the opening scene. Unable to join in the fun any longer, he spitefully tries to deny it to anyone else.[19] As the play progresses, the abuses of his authority become more severe as he reneges on his promise concerning his daughter's marriage and finally disinherits his son. Orgon's type of righteous hypocrisy is foreshadowed in the opening scene by Molière's portrait of his mother, who is blissfully unaware that she indulges in the behavior she censures in others and is cruel to her servant while criticizing others for unchristian behavior.[20]

Orgon is a tyrant, and his righteousness is in the service of his tyranny. It is a particularly inhumane tyranny because Orgon must adhere rigidly to the principles which he believes justify his new assertion of his authority. He cannot allow himself to make exceptions for those closest to him on the basis of natural affection or kindness. There is no place for mercy in the censorious religious attitude he has adopted from Tartuffe and no possibility of the pleasure a more secure ruler might take in granting it. Proud of his otherworldliness, Orgon brags, "My mother, children, brother and wife could die, and I'd not feel a single moment's pain" (1.5).[21] In another example of his inhumanity, Orgon steels himself to resist his daughter's pleas when he orders her to marry Tartuffe, saying to himself, "Be firm, my soul. No human weakness now," while saying to her, "The more you loathe the man

---

18. Martin Turnell describes Tartuffe as self-deceived in *The Classical Moment: Studies of Corneille, Molière, and Racine* (New York: New Directions, 1946), 62–63. I find this implausible. He is portrayed as a professional schemer. See Richard Wilbur's introduction to *Tartuffe* in Jean Baptiste Poquelin de Molière, *"The Misanthrope" and "Tartuffe,"* trans. Richard Wilbur. (New York: Harcourt, Brace and World, 1965), 159.

19. See Richard Wilbur's introduction to *Tartuffe*, p. 161, and *The Misanthrope*, 3.5.

20. As in *The Misanthrope*, the opening scene is a true introduction to the play.

21. All quotations from *Tartuffe* and *The Misanthrope* are taken from the Richard Wilbur translation.

and dread him, the more ennobling it will be to wed him. Marry Tartuffe, and mortify your flesh!'' (4.3).

Orgon enhances his own authority while he appears to seek the benefit of those he rules; his hypocrisy is evident. But it is not evident to him. Orgon is an unselfconscious hypocrite. This might seem a paradoxical notion, yet the claim that there are hypocrites all along the "spectrum," that the con man is not the only kind of hypocrite, depends on the premise that unselfconscious hypocrisy is an intelligible possibility. A hypocrite is a person who pretends to be morally better than he is for the sake of some advantage to himself. But can a person be unaware that he is pretending? This is the phenomenon of self-deception that is readily recognizable, for example, in the alcoholic who can neither acknowledge his alcoholism nor acknowledge that he is not acknowledging it.

Granting that a person may be ignorant of his own pretense, there is a further troubling question, particularly in the case of hypocrisy: is this ignorance tantamount to innocence? Is the unselfconscious hypocrite still morally culpable for his hypocrisy? The first inclination might be to excuse Orgon, since he himself apparently believes sincerely that he is acting piously. He does not appear to be a hypocrite in any pejorative sense; rather, he has been duped, and Tartuffe seems the true villain of the piece. Alternatively, Orgon's self-deception might be seen as actually increasing his culpability in a certain sense. He should have known better. He is not merely ignorant, but willfully blind. All the evidence is put before him, and he either selectively perceives it or disavows it (see, for example, 1.4). His blindness itself is self-serving. To acknowledge the truth about Tartuffe might require Orgon to acknowledge truths about himself that he would rather deny.[22]

Orgon is a hypocrite, but he is not like Tartuffe. Tartuffe knows himself for what he is, and he uses hypocrisy deliberately to further his tyrannical designs. It takes an unusually bold man

22. See Herbert Fingarette, *Self-Deception* (London: Routledge and Kegan Paul, 1969); Mike W. Martin, *Self-Deception and Morality* (Lawrence: University Press of Kansas, 1986), 44–52; Mike W. Martin, ed., *Self-Deception and Self-Understanding: New Essays in Philosophy and Psychology* (Lawrence: University Press of Kansas, 1985). Fingarette has an interesting discussion of whether Arsinoé in *The Misanthrope* is a cynical, self-conscious hypocrite or a self-deceived one (54–58).

to do this, and Orgon is a coward. Whereas Tartuffe is culpable for the criminal effects of his actions and for the intent to deceive, Orgon is culpable for the criminal effects of his actions and for his cowardice. Cowardly tyranny is much easier than the bold kind, which is why Orgon is at least as important for understanding hypocrisy as is Tartuffe.

Understanding Orgon as a hypocrite reveals why con men are never lacking for victims and why the victims too are often culpable, particularly in politics. Tartuffe uses Orgon in obvious ways, but Orgon uses Tartuffe as well. Tartuffe provides him with a justification for breaking his agreements and getting what he wants.[23] People want to satisfy tyrannical desires but still think of themselves as good, and the sort of hypocritical righteousness illustrated by Orgon is one way they do it.

This type of hypocrite is certainly both more common and more dangerous than the consciously manipulative "phony" or con man. He can be found among leaders as well as followers. Ideological demagogues, for example, may be self-conscious "Tartuffes," but they also may be as self-deceived as their followers. The danger lies in the difficulty of exposing this sort of fraud. People can be swept up by a religious or political zeal that covers their selfish aims with an altruistic appearance. Such people often become so smug, sanctimonious, and self-satisfied that they cannot recognize reality.

Molière dramatizes this possibility throughout the play but gives it a particularly pointed and hilarious treatment when Orgon, finally aware of Tartuffe's true aims, confronts his disbelieving mother (5.3). She behaves exactly as he did before his eyes were opened. In reply to his "I saw it, saw it, saw it with my eyes," she remarks, "Appearances can deceive, we cannot always judge by what we see."[24] And her remark is true, of course, as a general statement, which only increases Orgon's frustration in trying to get her to overcome her blindness to the par-

---

23. For example, Orgon allows Tartuffe to ease his conscience about concealing certain documents (5.1). Tartuffe tries this technique with Elmire, arguing that adultery is not a sin if no one knows about it. See Turnell, *The Classical Moment,* 74, on the critique of Jesuitical casuistry, "la devotion aisie."

24. "Je l'ai vu, dis-je, vu, de mes propres yeux vu," and her reply—"Mon Dieu! le plus souvent l'apparence déçoit: Il ne faut pas toujours juger sur ce qu'on voit."

ticulars of this situation.[25] Impenetrable blindness of this kind can result from political commitments as easily as from religious ones when those commitments serve unconsciously as rationalizations for personal aggrandizement in whatever form.

To speak of these characters in political terms does no injustice to the play despite its domestic setting. The play is clearly meant to address religious hypocrisy as a political problem. Even Martin Turnell, who sees the writers of the Classical Age as devoid of reformist spirit, attributes a political message to *Tartuffe.* The king must protect the community as a whole from the fraud of "les dévots." Molière gives the king this role in the final scene of the play, which is rather ironic since the actual king failed to withstand their pressure. The play received an immediate hostile reaction, and the Archbishop of Paris ruled that attendance at a performance would result in excommunication. As a result, there were no public performances of *Tartuffe* for five years. With *Tartuffe,* Molière picked a fight and got one.[26]

But the discussion here suggests that the political problem that concerned Molière is not susceptible to such a simple solution as might be provided by an alert and forceful monarch. A good deal may be learned from this play about the danger of demagoguery, both in its appeal to ordinary, decent people and in its power to transform them. The unselfconscious hypocrisy of those who have been duped is as great a political danger as the self-conscious manipulations of the con man.

The unselfconscious, righteous hypocrite is distinguished by one other characteristic: he appears as an antihypocrite. He displays his sense of moral superiority with his willingness to expose the moral failures of others. Molière presents Alceste in *The Misanthrope* as the epitome of the righteous antihypocrite.[27] This is both character study and social commentary since the flattery and hypocrisy of salon society (the direct target of Alceste's attack) is

25. Molière plays with the hypocritical uses of the truth. Hypocrites are not always lying. See W. G. Moore, *Molière: A New Criticism* (1949; reprint, Garden City, N.Y.: Doubleday and Co., 1962), 63–64, on Tartuffe's confession of guilt (3.6).

26. See Turnell, *The Classical Moment,* 44, 58–60, 77; W. D. Howarth, *Molière: A Playwright and His Audience* (Cambridge: Cambridge University Press, 1982), 195.

27. See Judith Shklar, *Ordinary Vices* (Cambridge, Mass.: Belknap Press, 1984), 45–86, for a critique of the antihypocrite.

clearly associated in the play with a system of patronage, petty lawsuits, and political influence. Hypocrisy and flattery necessarily grease the wheels in a system run on influence rather than merit. Like *Tartuffe, The Misanthrope* has a political dimension that forms the backdrop for the private setting of the play.[28]

Alceste is constantly enraged at the hypocrisy and insincerity of those around him. He is disgusted by the way his contemporaries flatter one another indiscriminately. But he appears equally lacking in discrimination in his condemnation of others. For example, he appears unable to see clearly the differences so obvious to the audience between his friend Philinte and the fops surrounding Célimène, the woman he is courting. Alceste is full of indignation; feeling that he does not get his just deserts, he rails against the standards of his age and claims a right to rage against the injustices he suffers (1.1, 5.1).

This posture as indignant, righteous critic is self-serving in that it allows Alceste to feel superior to those around him at the same time that it allows him to avoid taking responsibility for his situation. In his eyes, a defeat is not his failure, but simply a confirmation of the corrupt character of his environment. Alceste is an adolescent type,[29] and a modern version of this story might cast him as the high school intellectual trying to compete with the sports heroes for the affections of the cheerleader. A protective coating of hostility and pride hides his true feelings of inadequacy and jealousy. He too is playing a role—the role of the critical outsider. Célimène understands this, though her remarks are unduly harsh:[30]

> Indeed, he's so in love with contradiction,
> He'll turn against his most profound conviction,

---

28. Alceste himself has been interpreted as a prototype of the modern reformer, trying to live up to a standard superior to those of society but unaware that his attempt is a "consequence of self-interest and vanity." Moore, *Molière: A New Criticism,* 124–26.

29. This observation forms the basis for Cavell's excellent discussion. Stanley Cavell, "A Cover Letter to Molière's *Misanthrope,*" *Themes Out of School: Effects and Causes* (Chicago: University of Chicago Press, 1984).

30. Wilbur's translation makes them sound even harsher than the original: "L'honneur de contredire a pour lui tant de charmes, Qu'il prend contre lui-même assez souvent les armes; Et ses vrais sentiments sont combattus par lui, Aussitôt qu'il les voit dans la bouche d'autrui."

And with a furious eloquence deplore it,
If only someone else is speaking for it. (2.5)

Alceste wishes to be distinguished, and by a true standard of merit. Unfortunately, he also wishes to be distinguished by Célimène, a woman who represents all that he abhors about his society. This is the conflict that leads him unknowingly to a hypocritical use of his antihypocritical stance.[31]

Alceste, like Orgon, is severe, rigid, indiscriminate, blind to his own faults, indignant, and, like Orgon, a hypocrite. Whereas righteousness first appeared as the opposite of hypocrisy, it now appears as a form of hypocrisy. The extremes of the "Aristotelean" scheme collapse into varieties of the same category: the cynical manipulator of principles and the proud self-righteous man are both hypocrites, though one is deliberately so and the other unselfconsciously so.

A closer look at the man in the middle, the moderate statesmanlike type, collapses the scheme altogether. The man who applies his principles with moderation and flexibility, who finds it easy to compromise and to make exceptions according to the circumstances, can be truly admirable. But he can also be so easygoing that he becomes too accepting of injustices, too willing to compromise his principles so as to avoid provoking confrontations that might disturb his comfort. And all the while he retains his image of himself as a principled and moral man. Complacency is a form of hypocrisy. A comparison of the "moderates" in *Tartuffe* with those in *The Misanthrope* should clarify the distinction between true moral moderation and hypocritical complacency.

In *Tartuffe,* the moderate characters are presented in an entirely positive light, though they are not above resorting to deception, conspiracy, and tricks to expose Tartuffe for what he really is and restore justice to the household. Elmire, Dorine, and Cléante each reveal different aspects of what is appealing in the politic moderate. Elmire is characterized by a gentle morality (4.3) and politic discretion.[32] She is a moral woman, but she is not moralistic. She prefers to politely and quietly discourage improper ad-

---

31. See Lionel Gossmann, *Men and Masks* (Baltimore: Johns Hopkins University Press, 1963), 76–80.

32. Compare Philinte's speech in favor of *vertu traitable* (malleable, or flexible, virtue) in *The Misanthrope* 1.1.

vances rather than to fly into a rage about them. She works to overcome Tartuffe's influence in upsetting her daughter's marriage plans by handling things privately. She cuts a deal with Tartuffe, blackmailing him, in a sense, with his attempt to seduce her. She will remain quiet about it if he agrees to endorse the marriage of Valère and Mariane (3.3). Her mission accomplished, she shows no desire for revenge against Tartuffe and no desire to humiliate her husband. She contrasts sharply with her enraged and indignant son, Damis, who would vindicate his "rights" regardless of the consequences. Dorine, a servant, seeks to calm Damis's rage and get him to be practical. On the other hand, she seeks to arouse Mariane from her passive reaction to her father's authority, and so she moderates both extremes. Forming a conspiratorial faction, she too schemes behind the scenes (2.4). But she is also quite outspoken and shows no deference to Orgon's authority so long as he is behaving in a manner unworthy of authority. Dorine is not fooled by appearances and is not governed by concern over how she appears to others.

Her good sense is a peasant version of the good sense of the worldly and sophisticated Cléante. He also knows better than to judge by appearances. In fact, he knows without seeing, characterizing Tartuffe and his effects on Orgon perfectly even before having met him (1.5). Orgon, on the other hand, is so enslaved to appearances that he actually has to see Tartuffe seduce his wife before he will believe it (4.3). Cléante also cares little for how he appears to others but instead recommends a life guided by conscience (1.5, 4.1). He is able to distinguish between the mask and the face, between false and genuine piety. Sharing Elmire's gentle morality and Dorine's measured attitude, he is able to counsel Orgon at the end of the play to calm his indignation, refrain from rushing to extremes again, and forgive Tartuffe (5.1, 5.7).

These three characters are all able to act effectively because they understand the practical limitations inherent in the situation and because they are not carried away by a passionate response to injustice, though they see it for what it is. Cléante in particular stands apart from the action as an observer who intercedes on behalf of others. All three of them are less concerned with exposing injustice to public view or with "making a statement" than they are with rectifying the situation. They are good judges of character—measured, tolerant, forgiving, and dispassionate.

These qualities are shared by Philinte, the central moderate character in *The Misanthrope,* but in his case, it is not clear that they are virtues. Philinte is phlegmatic, in sharp contrast to the indignant posturing of his friend Alceste. In general, he is aware of the social and political hypocrisies around him but takes a complacent attitude toward them, either because they are inconsequential or because he sees no real possibility for changing the situation for the better. Philinte accepts the flattery characteristic of the social relations of his day. He knows the ways of the world and he plays the game. Molière portrays him as a moderate, easygoing, sociable fellow. And Philinte's attitude does seem rather innocent in the context of the play. Social courtesies, the little hypocrisies of manners, are really not great evils. The problem is that Philinte's attitude is not easy to distinguish from complacency toward significant social injustice.

Whereas Cléante's politic moderation is clearly in the service of justice, as he attempts to keep Orgon faithful to his contracts, Philinte's is not. And whereas Cléante's concern is for justice rather than reputation, Philinte's motivation is more ambiguous. For example, he is willing to use influence in Alceste's legal case if that is necessary to secure a favorable result for his friend, and he voices his concern for Alceste's reputation (1.1, 5.1). Moreover, while Orgon's self-righteousness is clearly in the service of injustice, Alceste remains attractive precisely because, whatever our suspicions regarding the motivations for his critical posture, the criticisms themselves are generally just.[33] *Tartuffe* and *The Misanthrope* can each be read as critical satires of righteous hypocrisy and censorious moralism, but the latter can also be read as a corrective of the perspective of the former. At the very least, it raises serious doubts as to whether a philosophic distance, i.e., a realistic and moderate attitude, suffices to ensure social justice.

Rousseau sharpens the critique of the moderate type in his discussion of *The Misanthrope* in the *Letter to D'Alembert.* Rousseau says of Philinte that he is

---

33. Molière makes sure that the audience recognizes this. See Eliante's speech (4.1). Cavell, in ''A Cover Letter,'' tries to explain why Alceste is such a compelling character and why we care so much about his critical attitude.

one of those gentle, moderate people who always find that everything is fine because it is in their interest that nothing be better, . . . who, with a well-lined pocket, find it quite disagreeable that some declaim in favor of the poor; who, their own doors well secured, would see the whole of humankind robbed, plundered, slain, and massacred without complaining, given that God has endowed them with a most meritorious gentleness with which they are able to support the misfortunes of others. (*D'Alembert,* 39)

Rousseau remarks:

I know of no greater enemy of man than everybody's friend who, always charmed by everything, constantly encourages the vicious, and who, by his culpable complacency, flatters the vices out of which are born all the disorders of society. (*D'Alembert,* 38)

In short, in Rousseau's view, the Philintes of the world are also hypocrites. They play their roles in a corrupt society that is riddled with injustice, but because they conform to the morality expected of men in their position, they rest secure in the conviction of their own decency. Like the righteous antihypocrite, these men too are smug and self-satisfied. And, as in the case of the righteous antihypocrite, their hypocrisy is unselfconscious.

It seems now that there are hypocritical types all along the spectrum suggested by an "Aristotelean" sort of scheme; it is necessary to reformulate the alternatives. We began by asking what ought to be our stance toward our political principles—how seriously should we take them as guides for political action? Either we should take them very seriously indeed, as Alceste would have it, or we should adjust according to the realities of the situation, as Philinte recommends. If Philinte and Alceste represent the competing alternatives, the choice seems to be between two smug and hypocritical types. So far, these two characters have been presented only in a negative light, but each of them can also be seen in a positive light. Unlike Tartuffe, Alceste and Philinte can each make a plausible claim to be the model for the truly just man: Alceste because he upholds moral principles regardless of the consequences and Philinte because his actions produce beneficial social consequences.

An improved version of Alceste and an improved version of Philinte should also be included among the alternatives. There is, after all, a true moralism that can be distinguished from the self-righteous attitude described thus far, and there is also a truly moderate, decent pragmatism that can be distinguished from conventional complacency. We have seen Cléante, Elmire, and Dorine as positive examples of political moderation, but we have yet to develop the positive moralistic type, the "improved Alceste."

Rousseau sketches an improved version of Alceste in the *Letter to D'Alembert*. We begin with that sketch and then expand the analysis to include Rousseau's depictions of various human types in his other works. What are the characteristics of a principled integrity, according to Rousseau? And why does he reject the possibility that one might find those characteristics in an urbane and moderate man?

Rousseau's Ideal of Integrity

Rousseau offers a characterization of Alceste as he believes Molière ought to have portrayed him (*D'Alembert,* 36–45). According to Rousseau, the character of the true misanthrope is set by his dominant passion, a hatred of vice and love of virtue. This passion produces five major effects that distinguish Rousseau's version of Alceste from Molière's. First, Alceste ought to have been portrayed as disinterested, enraged at every injustice he sees directed at others but calm when injustice directly affects him. He knows men too well to expect anything other than abuse from them in response to his frank defense of virtue. Consequently, he is not easily offended and is without vengeance, his second distinguishing characteristic. Third, Alceste ought to have been depicted as proud but without vanity. Fourth, Alceste always ought to speak the truth, even if the truth offends.[34]

> For if one permits oneself the first circumspection and the first alteration of the truth, where is the sufficient reason for stopping before one becomes false as a courtier? (*D'Alembert,* 43)

Last, Alceste knows that it is better to lose a just cause than to act badly. For example, he would never consider talking to the

---

34. But see *Reveries,* Fourth Walk, in which Rousseau discusses the requirements of truthfulness in relation to the requirements of justice. See also the section of chapter 4 entitled, "Rousseau's Personal Ethics: Acceptable Lies."

judge about his pending lawsuit, as Philinte urges him to do. This characteristic, in Rousseau's view, distinguishes him, perhaps most of all, from the *homme du monde,* the Philinte type.[35] He cares more for the preservation of his own integrity than for the consequences of his actions for his own well-being, and consequently, he cannot be corrupted.

Why does Molière fail to portray the misanthrope in this light? Because he must please his audience. The theater cannot promote morality, because the portrait of the moral man will not be pleasing to people with corrupted tastes.[36] The best it can do is to promote worldliness:

> [I]n that it causes the practice and the principles of society to be preferred to exact probity; in that it makes wisdom consist in a certain mean between vice and virtue; in that, to the great relief of the audience, it persuades them that to be a decent man [*honnête homme*] it suffices not to be a complete villain. (45)[37]

This is precisely the moral stance of Philinte. Molière, as a playwright, can be no better than Philinte and can only encourage "Philintism" in his audience. Although Rousseau characterizes Molière personally as an *honnête homme,* as a playwright, he must be an *homme du monde.*[38] The truth must be sacrificed in order to win the approval of the audience. It is this desire to please that is corrupting, and the theater must always please. Rousseau's entire discussion of *The Misanthrope* is meant to condemn this easygoing attitude toward principle that results from the corrupting effects of vanity, of the desire for applause and approval. That discussion is a condensation of his general argument against the theater, and his argument against the theater is a condensation of his critique of society itself.

35. For a discussion of the significance of this distinction for Rousseau's analysis, see the section of this chapter entitled, "Evaluating the Alternatives: Moralist or Moderate?"

36. See *Émile,* 112–16, for a similar argument regarding why fables cannot teach virtue to children.

37. In an already corrupted society, the theater can have limited benefit precisely because, by employing vanity, it promotes "the practice and principles of society" as against complete villainy. It cannot, however, promote true virtue. See Rousseau's "Préface de *Narcisse,*" *O.C.,* II, 971–74.

38. *Lettre à M. D'Alembert sur son article Genève, O.C.,* V, 35–36. The statement can be found in the English version at *D'Alembert,* 38.

There are, of course, forms of public entertainment of which Rousseau approves. Toward the end of the *Letter to D'Alembert,* for example, he describes various public festivals suitable to the Genevan republic, festivals conducted in the open air, often with an element of spontaneity, in which the "audience" and the "performers" are one and the same. These festivals nourish a spirit of common fellowship and pride and contrast starkly with Parisian theater, which nourishes only vanity.[39] Again, this contrast is a microcosm of the contrast between Genevan and Parisian society altogether. A corrupt society is one in which social life resembles theater. People assume roles in order to please others, and vanity leads them to abandon both virtue and truth.

Rousseau distinguishes himself from the playwrights precisely by his willingness to speak the truth regardless of the hostility his writings might inspire. He clearly identifies himself as an author with his own version of the misanthrope, and his contemporaries often made the same identification.[40] Rousseau portrays himself exactly as he argues Alceste should be portrayed; as disinterested, truthful, neither vain nor vengeful, and consequently, incorrupt-

---

39. See *D'Alembert,* 125–37. On the Greek theater as a special case, see *D'Alembert,* 77–79. For the distinction between pride and vanity and its political importance, see *Projet de constitution pour la Corse, O.C.,* III, 937–38; see also chapter 5, text accompanying note 28.

Elizabeth Wingrove argues that there is no authenticity in the Genevan spectacles Rousseau approves, because playing sexual roles as Rousseau understands them is a form of theatricality. Her analysis tends to collapse any significant distinction between Paris and Geneva, a distinction Rousseau would insist on maintaining even if he granted her main point. He would judge between forms of theatricality on the basis of their effects on *amour-propre.* Elizabeth Wingrove, "Sexual Performance as Political Performance in the *Lettre à D'Alembert sur les spectacles,*" *Political Theory* 23 (1995): 585–616.

Tracy Strong argues that Rousseau fails to see the potential of theater to transform the audience. Tracy Strong, *The Idea of Political Theory: Reflections on the Self in Political Time and Space* (Notre Dame, Ind.: University of Notre Dame Press, 1990), chap. 2, especially p. 61. Rousseau certainly believes theater can change an audience for the worse; the question is whether people will applaud plays that challenge their self-satisfaction as well as those that flatter their vanity. For a powerful analysis of the way in which *The Misanthrope* does exactly that, see Cavell, "A Cover Letter," 97–105.

40. In fact, they did before he did, although they identify him with the Alceste of Molière's play, of course. See M. LeCat, "Refutation of the Observations of Jean-Jacques Rousseau of Geneva," in *Collected Writings of Rousseau,* trans. Roger D. Masters and Christopher Kelly (Hanover, N.H.: University Press of New England, 1992), 2:58.

ible. He defends writing this work despite his friendship with
D'Alembert by introducing in the preface a central principle of
the argument to come, saying: "consideration [for the feelings
of a friend and the obligations of friendship] outweighs duty
only for those for whom all morality consists in appearances"
(*D'Alembert,* 3).[41] Several passages in Rousseau's discussion of
Alceste cannot fail to remind any reader of the *Confessions* of
Rousseau himself. "If a false woman betray him, unworthy
friends dishonor him, or weak friends abandon him, he must suf-
fer it without a murmur. He knows men" (*D'Alembert,* 40). And,
arguing that Molière had to temper Alceste's righteousness in order to make him tolerable in society at all, Rousseau remarks that
"It is the author's interest to make him ridiculous but not mad;
and that is how he would appear to the eyes of the public if he
were entirely wise" (*D'Alembert,* 45).

In a note, worth quoting at length, Rousseau attributes to
himself all the qualities that he had earlier ascribed to the "improved" Alceste.

> If my writings inspire me with some pride, it is for the purity of inten-
> tion which dictates them, it is for the disinterestedness for which few
> authors have given me the example. . . . Never did personal views
> soil the desire to be useful to others which put the pen in my hand
> and I have almost always written against my own interest. *Vitam im-
> pendere vero:* this is the motto I have chosen. . . . Love of the public
> good is the only passion which causes me to speak to the public; I
> can then forget myself, and if someone offends me, I keep quiet about
> him for fear that anger make me unjust. . . . Holy and pure truth to
> whom I have consecrated my life, never will my passions soil the
> sincere love which I have for thee; neither interest nor fear can corrupt
> the homage that I am wont to offer to thee and my pen will refuse
> thee only what it fears to accord to vengeance. (*D'Alembert,* 131–32)

Rousseau's self-description is identical to his description of the
man of integrity. He offers this depiction of himself as an author
as a model for our admiration.

And it is precisely Rousseau's aim as an author to alter the
objects of our admiration and to improve our moral judgments.
In the *Confessions,* Rousseau clearly casts his reader as the judge,

---

41. Compare chapter 4, note 27 and accompanying text.

and clearly wishes him to abandon the customary standards of judgment. Mme de Warens or the Savoyard Vicar, for example, fall far short if measured against conventional moral standards but are highly esteemed by Rousseau. In *Émile,* the reader is invited to imagine the world around him as seen through the eyes of a young man raised with natural tastes. How does an elegant dinner party appear compared to a peasant supper when we judge as Émile judges (*Émile,* 190–92, 344–55)?[42] Rousseau's writings, if they were effective, would purify and naturalize moral judgment rather than corrupt it. He can succeed in this where the playwright cannot, because his success does not depend on flattering our already corrupted tastes. The contest between Philinte and Alceste as models, as Rousseau sees it, is equivalent to a contest between Molière and Rousseau over which of them deserves to be the poet who educates the moral opinions of a people.

That Rousseau understood this effort to revise moral judgment as a highly political undertaking is forcefully argued by Christopher Kelly:

> Rousseau's goal in a number of his works was to change the objects of his corrupt contemporaries' esteem by describing ways of life the emulation of which would allow people to survive the age of corruption in which they lived.[43]

The poet functions as does the legislator, creating heroes who can guide the imagination and direct the processes of imitation that are fundamental for social life. If Rousseau is correct that the dominant passion of social man is *amour-propre* (*Second,* 148–49, 155–56), then the formation of the objects of that passion determines the character of society. If men in society are necessarily dependent on the approval of those around them, then the quality of the public's judgments is critical. The Spartans, for example, are defended against the corrupting effects of the theater by the purity of their opinions; they simply would not find it attractive enough to attend (*D'Alembert,* 67).

Rousseau tries to revise our opinion of what is admirable in people. Thus far, we have relied on his discussion of Alceste and

42. See also *Émile,* 247–49.
43. Christopher Kelly, "Reading Lives: Rousseau on the Political Importance of the Hero" (University of Maryland, 1990), 28–29.

Philinte to establish what it is that Rousseau admires. But the number of competing alternative models in Rousseau's work requires at least a cursory glance beyond the *Letter to D'Alembert*. Rousseau offers as models Spartan and Genevan citizens, male and female, as well as his misanthrope and himself as an author. The Savoyard Vicar, Mme de Warens, Sophie, and Émile, among others, might be added to the list. Moreover, what Rousseau admires in men must be distinguished from what he admires in women. A variety of human types are depicted favorably in Rousseau's writings. The question is whether, despite this variety, they share the component characteristics of integrity.

Rousseau's positive examples are of two kinds. First, there are those who remain uncorrupted, either because they are innocent (Émile and Sophie) or because they are virtuous (the Spartan or Genevan).[44] These are utopian models, meant to express the distance between what is real and what is possible and to show men what they could be.[45] Their juxtaposition starkly poses the alternative, man or citizen, and the portraits seem to be overdrawn in order to emphasize their opposition. They are fictional portraits, but true nonetheless in that they each illustrate a genuine possibility.[46] The second type includes those living individuals who retain a measure of integrity despite their sophistication and their participation in the real world of corrupt contemporary society. This group includes Mme de Warens, the Savoyard Vicar, and Rousseau himself.[47] Some of the obvious problematic inconsistencies of Rousseau's judgments appear when statements

44. Virtue in the sense of self-overcoming is actually as lacking in the Spartan as it is in the young Émile. And, at the very end of his education, Émile does need to develop virtue because his attachment to Sophie can conflict with his duty (*Émile*, 38–41, 443–49).

45. Judith Shklar, *Men and Citizens: A Study of Rousseau's Social Theory* (Cambridge: Cambridge University Press, 1969), 3.

46. See Ann Hartle, *The Modern Self in Rousseau's "Confessions": A Reply to St. Augustine* (Notre Dame, Ind.: University of Notre Dame Press, 1983), 9–24. Hartle makes a similar claim about Rousseau's self-portrait in the *Confessions*. On the relation of fiction and truth, see also *Émile*, 34, 50–51, and Rousseau's discussion of lying in *Reveries*, Fourth Walk. This last is discussed extensively in chapter 4.

47. According to Rousseau's discussion in the *First Discourse*, *probité* and *vertu* are the qualities that are destroyed by the progress of the arts and letters. Book 8 of the *Confessions* shows Jean-Jacques as he struggles to retain his virtue despite his new renown in the literary world. In other words, his life at this period is an example of the conflict he depicted in the *First Discourse*.

applying to members of one group are set beside statements which apply to members of the other. For example, Rousseau's praise for Sophie as a female ideal and his admiration of Mme de Warens seem difficult to reconcile. Or, Rousseau condemns Molière's plays as morally corrupting for Genevans at the same time that he confesses that he himself has never willingly missed a performance—and this admission immediately precedes his self-characterization as among the least corrupt of men quoted above (*D'Alembert*, 131–32). But what is striking about Rousseau's exemplary characters is the extent to which, despite the differences between them, they are appealing because of the important characteristics they share.

It would not be difficult to show that these characteristics include the five Rousseau ascribed to the "improved" Alceste in the *Letter to D'Alembert*. Consider the following characterization of Mme de Warens:

> She loathed duplicity and lying; she was just, equitable, humane, disinterested, true to her word, her friends, and what she recognized as her duties, incapable of hatred or vengeance, and she did not even imagine that there was the slightest merit in being forgiving.[48]

This description applies equally well to Sophie. In a section titled "Sophie; or the Woman," Rousseau describes the female ideal— a woman raised according to her nature (*Émile*, 357–406). She is modest; her dominant passion is a love of virtue; she cares little for status (*Émile*, 386, 391, 396–97). Like the women of Sparta, she is physically robust and morally superior. As a lover of virtue, she will love only virtuous men (*Émile*, 366, 393). The greatest difference between this ideal type and Mme de Warens is that the latter lacks judgment and is easily led astray, while the former has acquired through a proper education a discerning judgment that renders her incorruptible (*Émile*, 387–89, 398, 407).[49] Real people make mistakes, though those with integrity commit no crimes (*Confessions*, 190). While initially it might seem odd to describe the Spartan *citoyenne*, Sophie, and Mme de Warens as

48. Jean-Jacques Rousseau, *Les Confessions*, *O.C.*, I, bk. 5, p. 199.
49. Rousseau stresses that there is nothing unusual about Émile or Sophie. Anyone with the proper upbringing could approach the ideal. The faults of his nonfictional positive characters may be attributed to poor education and upbringing (*Émile*, 52, 393).

versions of the same ideal type, their similarities are readily apparent when they are compared to their shared opposite, the Parisian coquette. While the coquette is preoccupied with manipulations to secure personal advantage and status, Rousseau's ideal women seem totally lacking in such self-concern.[50]

Rousseau's ideal men are portrayed as candid, independent, without affectation, and respectful of others regardless of status. The Savoyard Vicar, M. de Luxembourg, and Lord Keith fit this description.[51] To these human virtues, the Romans, Spartans, and Genevans add robustness, martial valor, and dedication to public duty. While these characteristics distinguish the citizen from the real contemporary characters Rousseau admires, all these men certainly resemble one another more than any of them resembles the Parisian men who dedicate their lives to pleasing women (*D'Alembert,* 105).

But to what degree do Rousseau's ideal men and his ideal women resemble one another? The subject of coquettishness raises a difficulty with the argument here. I initially characterized Rousseau's ideal type as lacking vanity and as willing to defend truth and justice rather than compromise his integrity, even at the risk of offending others. But Rousseau's women are compelled to concern themselves with their reputations and constrained to submit to injustice without a murmur (*Émile,* 358, 361, 364, 381, 396). The contrast seems to belie the contention that there is a single ideal at work here.

Rousseau does identify distinctively female virtues. Modesty is foremost among them, and it is modesty that motivates the concern for good reputation. But, a concern to maintain a good reputation is not the same as a concern for reputation simply (i.e., a competitive concern for status or popularity). The two are as far from each other as modesty is from vanity. Female modesty functions to support female virtue in every polity in much the same way that male pride functions to support citizen virtue in

50. For a few of Rousseau's comments on Parisian men and women, see *Émile,* 141n, 350–51, 355, 389–90. For Rousseau's comparisons of Émile to corrupted young men, see *Émile,* 227–30, 243, 292–93, 433.

51. *Confessions,* 478 ff., 508–9, 550–53; *Émile,* 262–63. The Savoyard Vicar's closing advice is this: be "sincere and true without pride," do not be deceived by private interest, and do not be overly concerned with the opinion of others—just what is needed to maintain integrity as Rousseau understands it. *Émile,* 313.

the best polities, whereas vanity corrodes virtue in females and males alike.[52] A modest woman's concern to maintain a chaste reputation cannot lead her to vices that would compromise her integrity; quite the contrary. In this respect, integrity and a woman's concern for public opinion are not in conflict with each other, according to Rousseau.

Moreover, Rousseau argues that, if there should be a conflict between the particular female virtues and the moral requirements of humanity, the latter take precedence in every instance. Girls should only say pleasing things, but the first law is never to lie (*Émile,* 376, see 383), and the human rule of the "inner sentiment" takes precedence over the rule of public opinion even for women (*Émile,* 382). Rousseau asserts the priority of the "human" virtues over the "female" ones (although as a matter of the realities of psychological development, I doubt that the two can be as easily blended as he supposes).[53]

While there are specific female virtues, such as modesty, and specific citizen virtues, such as devotion to public service, a core set of qualities remains the same for all of Rousseau's exemplary types. In other words, though each of these types may behave differently given their circumstances, their admirable behavior is always admirable for the same reasons. They are honest and trustworthy people in whom benevolence and virtue are not sullied by personal interest and private passions. The essentials of good character are identical for men and for women, for citizens of the best polities as well as for members of modern society.

Above all, Rousseau's exemplary figures are concerned to preserve their own integrity. For example, the Savoyard Vicar would rather be poor than dependent (*Émile,* 262). Jean-Jacques at his best will not change even for a Prince (*Confessions,* 501). Émile declares that he will not change his beneficent habits or forget the rights of humanity even if it means losing his beloved Sophie

52. See chapter 5, note 28 and accompanying text.

53. Rousseau's understanding of men and women, of their relations, and of the political importance of them is extremely complex, and there is an extensive literature on the subject. Interesting treatments of the issues raised here can be found in Lynda Lange, "Rousseau and Modern Feminism," in *Feminist Interpretations and Political Theory,* ed. Mary Lyndon Shanley and Carole Pateman (University Park: Pennsylvania State University Press, 1991), 95–111, and Joel Schwartz, *The Sexual Politics of Jean-Jacques Rousseau* (Chicago: University of Chicago Press, 1984), 143–44, 149–53.

(*Émile*, 441).[54] In fact, it is Émile's insistence on this that prompts Sophie finally to agree to become his wife. What these two love in each other is the reflection of their own virtue, another indication of their essential similarity. Many of Rousseau's characters, female as well as male, are intemperate, impulsive, and lacking in judgment (*Émile*, 266, 395 ff.; *Confessions*, 483). The Savoyard Vicar, like Mme de Warens, is described as a lover of truth with a simple heart whose mistakes are errors of judgment rather than crimes (*Émile*, 266). Rousseau consistently portrays Jean-Jacques's "mistakes" in similar terms in the *Confessions*. Rousseauian integrity does not require moderation and good judgment; it requires only simplicity, purity, and unaffected goodness.

Through all of his various examples, Rousseau is teaching his readers to recognize integrity when they see it. But to see all of Rousseau's examples as similar, we must learn to judge people more by the heart than by the head, more by their sentiments and character than by their principles and actions. This is why the chaste and modest Sophie and the rather loose Mme de Warens can both be models. For the same reason, exemplary characters can be found among all social strata and regardless of religion or nationality despite Rousseau's strenuous arguments that certain social and political conditions are much more conducive to virtue and happiness than others. It is a good heart and good character that really count, and these are available in principle to everyone whatever their social situation, religion, or politics.[55] Proud, without vanity or vindictiveness, truthful and disinterested, and for these reasons, possessing an incorruptible integrity; these are the qualities Rousseau would have us admire wherever we find them.

People who possess these qualities necessarily possess the unity of self that also characterizes Rousseau's ideal. It is not possible to be good in the way that the person with integrity is good, and, at the same time, to be divided against oneself. Like unity, autonomy and authenticity are also elements of Rousseau's ideal, but only because these qualities are inseparable from the moral

54. Sophie simply gives him new reasons to be himself (*Émile*, 433).

55. In fact, it seems to be some part of a good character to be able to remain unchanged despite the vicissitudes of one's social circumstances. Like Rousseau himself, the pupil in *Émile* must be someone who will be able to survive changes in his fortunes (*Émile*, 41–42, 52).

components of integrity as Rousseau understands them. For example, Rousseau's exemplary characters are authentic because they lack vanity. They have no desire to be anyone else, and thus they are themselves, genuine and unified. Lacking vanity, Émile will not be led into conflict with himself by exposure to history's heroes for example (*Émile*, 243). Moreover, lacking vanity, Rousseau's characters also lack vengeance. Vengeance and vindictiveness arise only when insult can be added to injury (*Second*, 149; compare *Émile*, 65–66). The man who is vain, spiteful, and driven by vengeance acts in response to others. He is less than fully autonomous insofar as autonomy implies authoring one's own actions.[56]

Truthfulness and disinterestedness are also both moral qualities and elements of the unity of the self. The opposite of truthfulness is duplicity: a liar is two-faced and divided; insincerity divides a man between what he is for himself and what he is for others. Self-interestedness too is a source of internal conflict, while disinterestedness is a protection against it. For example, the Spartan mother in Rousseau's account is not even conflicted about sending her sons to battle; she is wholly governed by patriotic duty (*Émile*, 38–41).[57] Duty for the citizen is sweet because the inclinations have been trained to accord with its demands. The citizen is denatured to prevent conflicts between private interests and public duties. Émile is the opposite case. He is unconflicted because he never develops any personal interests or desires that are not natural inclinations, and therefore his inclinations do not lead to conflict so long as he remains outside of society.[58] The natural man is an absolute unity; the civil man is a part of a unity by which he defines himself. Neither suffers conflict.

If, for man or citizen, psychic unity is maintained, a person will experience peace and happiness. There is nothing new in the observation that psychic unity is an essential condition for happiness in Rousseau's view.[59] But this conception of psychic

56. "Authentic" derives from the Greek *authentikos,* adjective of *authentes,* one who acts on his own authority, a chief.

57. See note 44.

58. In this, he is directly contrasted with the bourgeois. *Émile*, 38–41, 443–49.

59. See Christopher Kelly, *Rousseau's Exemplary Life: The "Confessions" as Political Philosophy* (Ithaca, N.Y.: Cornell University Press, 1987), 147–60, 203–4; Melzer, *Natural Goodness,* 20–23, 42 ff., 104; Jean Starobinski, *Jean-Jacques Rousseau: Transpar-*

unity is sometimes treated as if it were morally neutral—as if it
might be possible to be a happy, unconflicted, and bad human
being. What I wish to stress is that psychic unity is not merely
a formal quality of the self; it has substantive moral content in
Rousseau's view. Psychic unity cannot be maintained without
goodness, and both are produced by the same qualities, the qualities that have been identified as the elements of the Rousseauian
ideal of integrity (*Émile*, 38–40). In contrast, the conception of
authenticity as the highest ideal allows for the possibility that to
be true to yourself and to maintain your psychic unity might
require abandoning the constraints of morality.[60] Such a diremption between unity and goodness is simply inconceivable in
Rousseauian terms.

Wholeness is preserved only by particular moral characteristics, and the converse is also true: it is precisely the transformation
of these particular characteristics that produces alienation and inauthenticity and constitutes corruption. In his *Second Discourse*,
Rousseau describes how, with the development of civilization,
disinterestedness gives way to conflicts of interest, duplicity replaces truthfulness, and vanity and vengeance are born (*Second*,
148–50).

In Rousseau's account, dividedness and moral decay arise very
early in human history and are as closely linked as unity and integrity. With the development of social inequality,

> for one's own advantage, it became necessary to appear to be other
> than what one in fact was. To be and to seem to be became two
> altogether different things; and from this distinction came conspicuous
> ostentation, deceptive cunning, and all the vices that follow from
> them. (*Second*, 155–56)

---

ency and Obstruction, trans. Arthur Goldhammer (Chicago: University of Chicago Press,
1988), 47–58.

   60. Rousseau is capable of admiring certain qualities in men who are not good.
In the "Discours sur la vertu du héros," he praises the hero's strength of soul, though
heroes are not virtuous in every respect, *O.C.*, II, 1262–74. See also "Observations
de Jean-Jacques Rousseau de Genève sur la réponse qui a été faite à son discours,"
where Rousseau writes, "There are lofty characters who bring even to crime an unde-
finable quality of pride and generosity." Such criminals, in contrast to hypocritical
ones whom Rousseau does not admire, can sometimes be reformed. But when "great
scoundrels" reform, in Rousseau's words, they "return to themselves [*rentrer en eux-
mêmes*]" (*O.C.*, III, 51–52). It is not at all clear that heroes or lofty criminals, however
admirable, possess either psychic unity or happiness.

The internal conflict, the alienation, the hypocrisy can be found everywhere in society; in the decaying aristocracy and in their fawning servants, but preeminently in the bourgeoisie.

The bourgeois type stands as the opposite of the Rousseauian ideal. Either a natural man or a denatured citizen may possess integrity; but the bourgeois cannot.

> He who in the civil order wants to preserve the primacy of the senti-
> ments of nature does not know what he wants. Always in contradic-
> tion with himself, always floating between his inclinations and his du-
> ties, he will never be either man or citizen. He will be good neither
> for himself nor for others. He will be one of these men of our days:
> a Frenchman, an Englishman, a bourgeois. He will be nothing.
>
> *To be something, to be oneself and always one, a man must act as he*
> *speaks;* he must always be decisive in making his choice, make it in
> a lofty style, and always stick to it. I am waiting to be shown this
> marvel so as to know whether he is a man or a citizen, or how he
> goes about being both at the same time. (*Émile,* 40, emphasis added)

The bourgeois is characterized particularly by internal conflict and by hypocrisy in the simple sense of saying one thing and doing another.

That this hypocrisy may be unselfconscious is crucial for the critique of the bourgeois. The bourgeois is the sincere but inauthentic man who is unaware of his own inauthenticity, who suffers from false consciousness, who is a phony without even knowing it. His sincerity itself becomes suspect, a sign of his naiveté. According to Rousseau's general account, men become corrupted by a process that is not self-conscious to become self-deceived role players made dependent by their vanity.[61] The model of the hypocrite has become, since Rousseau, this oblivious role player, epitomized by the bourgeois, rather than the con man, on the one hand, or the self-righteous type, on the other. Rousseau leads us to see what look like ordinary, decent moderate people as embodying a particularly destructive sort of corruption, one that trivializes and blurs the distinction between good and evil. This is a more serious problem than the presence of evil among those who recognize it as such. Rousseau prefers the open wickedness of the criminal, Cartouche, for example, to the hy-

61. See *Second,* 148–49, 155–56.

pocrisy of a Cromwell. But he writes of the Philinte type that "[t]here is no greater enemy of man."[62] In rejecting Philinte, and in rejecting the bourgeois, Rousseau rejects the politic moderate as well. He offers instead his own version of Alceste. Is his case for the improved Alceste sound? And what are its political implications? In making this choice, is Rousseau rejecting political efficacy as a standard?

Evaluating the Alternatives: Moralist or Moderate?

The discussion thus far has produced four portraits in response to the question, What are the moral limits of political compromise? This is because there is a genuine version and a degenerate version of those who advocate a strict adherence to principle and a genuine and a degenerate version of those who advocate moral flexibility. A good deal may be said about the relationships among all four of these types, and so the evaluation of Rousseau's position will be made in the context of a more general evaluation of the alternatives.

The alternatives can be formulated as follows: (1) Molière's Alceste (or Orgon), the righteous hypocritical antihypocrite; (2) an improved Alceste, the true moralist, whom Rousseau describes in the *Letter to D'Alembert;* (3) Rousseau's Philinte, the complacent hypocrite, and (4) an improved Philinte, equivalent to Cléante, the decent moderate.[63] The first two alternatives represent the moralistic types while the last two represent the moderate types. This formulation reveals possibilities that are obscured

---

62. *D'Alembert,* 38. On the dangers of a Cromwell, see *S.C.,* IV, viii, 129. On Cartouche and Cromwell, see "Observations de Jean-Jacques Rousseau de Genève sur la réponse qui a été faite à son discours" (*O.C.,* III, 49–51). Here and in his "Lettre à Grimm," Rousseau attacks the notion that hypocrisy, especially as politeness, can have the positive effect of masking vice (*O.C.,* III, 60). Contrast "Préface de *Narcisse,*" where he praises the public simulacrum of virtue in corrupted times, though he does not call it hypocritical (*O.C.,* II, 971 ff.).

63. Again, the alternatives can be expressed diagrammatically. Compare note 16.

	Moderation	Moralism
Integrity	Cléante	Rousseau's Alceste
Hypocrisy	Rousseau's Philinte	Molière's Alceste

by the "Aristotelean" sort of continuum that identifies only one virtuous type. First and most important, it makes visible the true political alternatives: the choice is between the best type of Alceste and the best type of Philinte, or the best type of moralist and the best type of moderate. Second, it allows us to compare the best and the worst of each type. Thus we can specify general criteria with which to distinguish true moralism from hypocritical self-righteousness and true moderation from rationalization in defense of the status quo.

We begin the comparison with the moralists. Rousseau's picture of the righteous man of integrity must be compared to Molière's portrait of the righteous hypocrite. Is Rousseau's modified Alceste a distinct alternative to and a significant improvement over Molière's original? Molière's Alceste was originally characterized as severe, rigid, indiscriminate in his judgments, blind to his own faults, highly critical of others', indignant, and hypocritical. Of these characteristics, Rousseau's alternative shares only the indignation and, in a certain sense, the rigidity. He is indignant and uncompromising; he is a moralizer. But he has been purged of sanctimoniousness. His moralizing is neither smug nor tyrannical; his principles are not used to enhance his private interests or his own sense of superiority; he is not a hypocrite. Moreover, his indignation never becomes vengeance or spite. His anger at the sight of injustice is a natural impersonal response, unmixed with vanity.

In contrast, the two moderate types are cool-headed, tolerant, and forgiving peacemakers. But the complacent moderate, Rousseau's Philinte, is concerned to maintain the peace even if it is not a just peace. His true concerns are his own comfort, position, and reputation; and he cannot be trusted to do the right thing if that would involve personal risk. His moral position is in fact an unselfconscious rationalization for his self-interest.[64] This is what characterizes both of the negative types, the hypocritical moderate and the hypocritical moralist: they appear to be defenders of a sound moral position, and they believe that they are, but they are actually self-serving and vain. The moderate with these char-

---

64. It should be noted that Rousseau's characterization of Philinte is not quite fair to Molière's portrait of him. For example, consider his behavior toward Eliante (4.1).

acteristics is no statesman; the moralist with these characteristics has certainly abandoned the high ground.

The two positive types also share key characteristics, and this is why they are both attractive. The politic moderate and the uncompromising moralist are neither fooled by appearances nor governed by concern for their own appearance or reputation. For this reason, they are able to act autonomously, doing what they believe is right without undue anxiety about the consequences for their own position. Neither is vindictive, though both are genuinely concerned with justice. They are disinterested and forgiving. In short, neither is a hypocrite; both are men of integrity.

These are true alternative possibilities; there is neither a synthesis of them nor a mean between them that can provide the definitive answer to the question of what our stance ought to be toward principled political action. Instead, there seem to be two attractive but mutually exclusive possibilities: passionate moralistic commitment or cool and considered flexibility. It makes a great deal of difference for politics which of these types we admire, and, without a fair contest between them, we will not know which of them we ought to admire.

Why do we so rarely see a clear comparison between them? Too often, in making the case for one type, the argument is set up so as to compare the best version of the favored type with the worst version of the alternative type. And of course, this makes the argument very easy to win. Rousseau, for example, would have had greater difficulty comparing his improved version of Alceste to Cléante than he has showing his superiority to Philinte. With Molière the situation is reversed. In *Tartuffe,* Molière gives Cléante a speech detailing the characteristics that distinguish true religion from false piety (1.5). Religious charlatans are described as spiteful, self-serving, vain, and censorious, while the true religion is moderate, humane, and merciful. The moderate type looks very attractive when its only alternative appears to be false religious zeal.

There is a tendency to collapse the distinction between the best and the worst in each category in theory because that distinction tends to collapse in practice. Rousseau, for example, might blur the distinction between the best and the worst of the moderates because even the best pursues a path that leads down a "slippery slope."[65] A legitimate compromise will lead to many illegitimate ones; a lack of passion will become complacent indifference. Cléante in practice will become indistinguishable from Philinte. Some critics of Rousseau take the same approach in criticizing the Rousseauian ideal, arguing that Rousseau himself cannot escape the charge of hypocrisy. They argue that, while claiming to teach sincerity, he provides only a "cult of sincerity" that feeds the vanity of its adherents.[66] Rousseau, the author of the *Confessions,* evades his moral responsibilities in the same way that Molière's Alceste does, blaming the world for his weaknesses while priding himself on his honest admission of his faults. Jean-Jacques, the character in the *Confessions,* does the same, particularly early on. He always seems to manage to excuse himself immediately after an abject confession of guilt (e.g., *Confessions,* 88–89). Moreover, his unwillingness to compromise, his preoccupation with maintaining the purity of his behavior, leads to ridiculous extremes of exactly the sort of vain posturing he claims to oppose. For example, he will not alter his mode of dress in order to appear appropriately attired at a royal performance of his work and becomes totally preoccupied with the likely effects of his nonconformist behavior (*Confessions,* 352–55, see also 343, 502). In this he seems to resemble nothing so much as Molière's version of Alceste.

But Rousseau deserves the benefit of the doubt. That Jean-Jacques does not consistently display all the virtues of the ideal type is certainly not surprising. Rousseau never claimed that Jean-Jacques was without weaknesses—he even admits that his ideal type has distinct characteristic weaknesses (*D'Alembert,* 40). What the criticisms amount to is the charge that the truly righteous man can be easily corrupted to become hypocritical, that is, that the distinction between the two often collapses in practice.

Granting that this is the case, the theoretical distinction remains intact and important. The best type of uncompromising moralist must be compared to the best type of politic moderate.

65. Recall the statement quoted above: "For if one permits oneself . . . the first alteration of the truth, where is the sufficient reason for stopping before one becomes false as a courtier?" (*D'Alembert,* 43).

66. See, for example, Peter Gay, *The Party of Humanity* (New York: W. W. Norton, 1971), 143–44.

Is Rousseau's modified Alceste a significant improvement over
Molière's Cléante or not? The Cléante type was originally described as a good judge of character, measured, tolerant, forgiving, dispassionate, and for these reasons, politically effective.
Rousseau's Alceste is neither tolerant nor dispassionate; he remains uncompromising and indignant, "hard and unbending"
(*D'Alembert,* 40), and for these reasons he is not politically effective. In fact, he cares less for political efficacy than for preserving
his integrity. Recall that he would rather lose in a just cause than
act badly (*D'Alembert,* 43–44). Cléante, Elmire, and Dorine, on
the other hand, would rather achieve justice even if that requires
lying or withholding the whole truth, for example. Which is superior: cool and effective worldliness or ineffective indignant purity?

Rousseau's case against the politic moderate is a critique of the
dispassionate spirit of compromise and tolerance that approaches
every conflict as if it were negotiable. It is the spirit of the *homme
du monde.* That Rousseau rejects worldliness, the *homme du monde,*
cannot be doubted. What "worldly" means for Rousseau is col-
ored by the fact that its opposite is no longer "otherworldly," as
it is in the Christian context of Molière's *Tartuffe.* In *Tartuffe,*
Molière depicts the true Christian as a worldly gentleman superior to the otherworldly impostor. In his view, true Christian
morality does not require the sacrifice of human involvements,
withdrawal from society, nor the denial of the pleasures of this
world. But in Rousseau's analysis, a spiritual commitment to
Christian principles cannot defend a man against the corrupting
effects of involvement with society. The "Christian gentleman"
is no longer available as a solution. For Rousseau, the opposite
of "worldly" is "natural," and, since the natural condition of man
is a condition of goodness, all human evil and corruption can be
ascribed to man's social condition. The worldly man is too
attached to the advantages and standards of the social, conventional world for his moral integrity to remain secure.

In contrast, for Molière, the *honnête homme,* the good man,
and the *homme du monde,* the gentleman, are one and the same.
And if Molière's plays have a moral purpose, it is often said to
be the promotion of this type.[67] This is certainly the intention that

---

67. For the place of this interpretation in the history of Molière criticism, see
Laurence Romero, "Molière's *Morale:* Debates in Criticism," in *Molière and the Com-*

Rousseau ascribes to Molière's theater. Molière was not alone in developing the ideal of the *honnête homme* in the seventeenth century. Pascal, La Bruyère, Méré, and La Rochefoucauld are among those whose work is associated with the ideal of *honnêteté*, an ideal shared by the generation of the French elite who comprised Molière's audiences.[68]

What is this *honnêteté* that Rousseau attacks in attacking Molière?

> [T]he *honnête homme* was essentially a product of polite society outside the Court . . . [*Honnêteté*] implied modesty, discretion, and the refusal to assert oneself. In social intercourse, the *honnête homme* was a good listener . . . the cultured amateur, never the professional. . . .[69]

La Rochefoucauld wrote that "Le vrai honnête homme est celui qui ne se pique de rien."[70] And the definition in the 1694 *Dictionnaire de l'Académie* identifies *honnêteté* with *les manières du monde*, and *homme de bonne conversation, de bonne compagnie*. The *honnête homme* is always identified with *de raison, de bon sens*. He is a moderate and sensible gentleman who gets along easily in high society. A sense of balance and good judgment, which require a realistic assessment of limitations, are his preeminent characteristics.[71] Alongside this elite conception, there was also a bourgeois usage of the term associated with the moral quality of the adjective, *honnête*.[72] Rousseau's usage drives a wedge between the two connotations joined in the term, those of social status and of morality. For Rousseau, the *honnête homme* and the *homme du monde* are opposing alternatives, and this is a radical change. Rousseau

---

monwealth of Letters: Patrimony and Posterity, ed. Roger Johnson, Jr., Edita S. Neumann, and Guy T. Trail (Jackson: University Press of Mississippi, 1975), 706–27. For contemporary interpretations along these lines, see Lionel Gossman, *Men and Masks* (Baltimore: Johns Hopkins University Press, 1963), and J. Morel, "Molière ou la dramaturgie de l'honnêteté," *L'Information Littéraire* 15 (Nov.–Dec. 1963).

68. Morel, "Molière ou la dramaturgie de l'honnêteté," 187. For an excellent brief discussion of the ideal of *honnêteté*, see Jean Starobinski, *Blessings in Disguise; or, the Morality of Evil*, trans. Arthur Goldhammer (Cambridge: Harvard University Press, 1993), 36–43.

69. Howarth, *Molière: A Playwright and His Audience*, 57.

70. Maxim no. 203. Variously interpreted: *se vanter, se fâcher, rien ne blesse l'amour-propre* (a man whose vanity is not easily bruised, who is not insulted by anything).

71. Morel, "Molière ou la dramaturgie de l'honnêteté," 189–90.

72. Howarth, *Molière: A Playwright and His Audience*, 57–63.

means to distinguish clearly between goodness and respectability. The change is reflected in his frequent use of the term *homme de bien* as an equivalent for *honnête homme,* with *homme du monde* in opposition to them both.[73] Rousseau's critique of the moral impact of Molière's theater centers on Molière's confusion of the good man with the man who is honored in society. In Rousseau's view, it is precisely the man of the world who is most likely to be corrupted. His lauded good judgment is, in reality, contemptible complacency. Moreover, he is likely to be not only morally suspect but lacking in grandeur. His moderate sense of balance, like his good judgment, is more properly a target of criticism than praise. At the height of Parisian society there is no true honor, nobility, or heroism. The salons are frequented by little men.[74] The moderate man "avec de raison et de bon sens" lacks imagination and he lacks passion.

The man of the world particularly lacks indignation, a passion Alceste possesses in abundance. Recall that Rousseau condemns Philinte for the cool and phlegmatic attitude that produces complacency in the face of injustice. If Molière had to choose between the excess and deficiency of indignation, in all likelihood he would choose the deficiency. Damis, for example, like his father Orgon, is a dangerously volatile character even though his rage is directed against true injustice. If Rousseau had to choose between an excess or deficiency of indignation, he would choose the excess.

> [F]anaticism, though sanguinary and cruel, is nevertheless a grand and strong passion which elevates the heart of man, makes him despise death, and gives him a prodigious energy that need only be better directed to produce the most sublime virtues. On the other hand, irreligion—and the reasoning and philosophic spirit in general—causes attachment to life, makes souls effeminate and degraded, concentrates all the passions in the baseness of private interest, in the abjectness of the human *I,* and thus quietly saps the true foundations of every society. . . . If atheism does not cause the spilling of men's blood,

---

73. Note Rousseau's usage of *homme de bien, honnête homme, homme du monde,* and *honnête homme du grand monde* in his discussion of *The Misanthrope. Lettre à M. D'Alembert sur son article Genève, O.C.,* V, 33–43. See also Morel, "Molière ou la dramaturgie de l'honnêteté," 191.

74. This is the thrust of Alceste's complaint throughout *The Misanthrope.*

it is less from love of peace than from indifference to the good. Whatever may be going on is of little importance for the allegedly wise
man, provided that he can remain at rest in his study. . . . Philosophic
indifference resembles the tranquillity of the state under despotism.
It is the tranquillity of death. It is more destructive than war itself.
(*Émile,* 312)

Unlike the fanatic, whose passion elevates the heart and makes
him despise death, the modern bourgeois has philosophers, doc-
tors, and priests who "debase his heart" and "make him unlearn
how to die" (*Émile,* 55). Rousseau's critique of both worldliness
and dispassionateness, the two qualities that clearly distinguish
Cléante from his Alceste, is that they are the dominant characteristics of a base and petty life and that they are ultimately incompatible with devotion to justice.

In the quotation above, Rousseau refers to dispassionateness
as "indifference to the good" and to worldliness as "attachment
to life." His own alternative prescription for a passionate devotion
to justice is, paradoxically, coupled with what can only be called
disengagement from life. All the various models Rousseau presents are either outsiders by choice or socially marginal outcasts,
with the exception of the Spartan or Genevan citizen.[75] And their
form of citizenship is possible only in rare circumstances. Rousseau's uncompromising moralist appears apolitical, if not antipolitical.[76] At the least, he will choose marginality over engagement if that is what is required to preserve his integrity.

Rousseau's model is of a free individual with the courage of
his convictions who is consistently principled and who cannot
be deflected from his commitments to justice and truth by any
personal interests. The true moralist is a man who insists on maintaining the highest ethical standards along with the highest expectations for man's moral possibilities. His integrity can be characterized in terms of moral unity, moral simplicity, or moral purity.
And this particular conception of integrity derives from Rous-

75. See Bronislaw Baczko, "Rousseau and Social Marginality," *Daedalus* (summer
1978): 27–40. M. de Luxembourg and Lord Keith might be considered exceptions.
See *Confessions,* 478 ff., 508–9, 550–53.

76. The extent of Émile's involvement is to set an example and act as a benefactor
for the locals. He will concern himself with brawls in the marketplace, but that is all.
See *Émile,* 435–36, 474–75; *Second,* 132. Note that Molière has his Alceste withdraw
from society as well.

seau's fundamental premise of the natural goodness of man. Human goodness is not achieved in the first place by suppressing natural passions that lead to evil, nor is it a goodness complicated by original sin. People are not naturally divided and morally torn. Instead, their goodness is the ground of their unity, their wholeness. This is man's natural state, one that may be experienced to the extent that a person can escape the conflicting pressures generated by social life. Because Rousseau conceives of man as naturally good, he conceives of integrity as purity and incorruptibility. And that conception of integrity, in turn, is the ground for his defense of the uncompromising moralist. Integrity so conceived could find its expression in moral outrage and its protection in withdrawal from the conflicting pressures generated by social life.

By way of contrast, the model of the *honnête homme* suggests a very different conception of integrity. Integrity can mean purity, but it also can mean completeness, that is, a wholeness composed of a balance of competing elements.[77] This is the integrity of the politic moderate. To defend the politic moderate and criticize Rousseau's position is to argue from a very different conception of integrity than Rousseau's. Here the model is of an individual who is able to integrate a variety of conflicting demands, including conflicting ethical demands. From the perspective of this alternative model, even the improved version of Alceste seems adolescent. It is not accidental that a certain kind of moralism is called "adolescent idealism." Unlike the adolescent, the mature adult is able to compromise without compromising himself. He is not defined by a complete commitment to a single overriding set of principles. The model for maturity is of complexity, rather than consistency; of tolerance of the tragic and the seamy side of life, rather than of moral purity.

This moral attitude presumes that conflict is the natural human condition.[78] Men are both good and bad, and, while it is necessary

77. Rousseau uses *probité* most often where we might use "integrity." But *probité* has only the former sense—honesty, uprightness.

78. For a very suggestive contemporary discussion, see Erik Erikson, *Identity, Youth and Crisis* (New York: W. W. Norton, 1968), 74–90. Erikson differentiates wholeness from totalism. Wholeness as an ideal is connected in this case to the Freudian premise of man's natural psychic and moral complexity. See also Sigmund Freud,

to recognize the importance of the difference between the two, it is also necessary to accommodate in some way the inevitable presence of evil within the self. A man of integrity must recognize both human weakness and the validity of competing ethical pressures; for example, justice and loyalty to loved ones. Even Philinte, despite his casual attitude toward social vices, can be defended both as truly caring, because his love is directed toward particular human beings rather than humankind in the abstract, and as realistic, because he knows the limits of what can be expected of men in public life. Orgon, on the other hand, despite his efforts to achieve moral purity, must be condemned as inhumane.[79] Integrity, when conceived as a balanced integration of competing elements, finds its expression in moderation, tolerance, and forgiveness and is not threatened by active involvement in worldly affairs.

George Orwell, in criticizing a certain sort of idealism, exemplifies a critique that might be leveled at Rousseau. He wrote:

> The essence of being human is that one does not seek perfection, that one *is* sometimes willing to commit sins for the sake of loyalty, . . . that one is prepared in the end to be defeated and broken up by life, which is the inevitable price of fastening one's love upon other human individuals. No doubt alcohol, tobacco, and so forth, are things that a saint must avoid, but sainthood is also a thing that human beings must avoid.[80]

From this perspective, moral purity is not a fulfillment of one's humanity; it is a betrayal of it.

The critique of the moral implications of Rousseau's ideal is as sharp as the Rousseauian critique of the *honnête homme*. At the same time, both the uncompromising moralist and the politic moderate share characteristics that entitle them to be classified as men of integrity. But integrity does not mean the same thing in each case. A conception of purity grounds the moral claims of

---

Civilization and Its Discontents, trans. James Strachey (New York: W. W. Norton, 1961).

79. For a similar argument, see Susan Wolf, "Moral Saints," *The Journal of Philosophy* 79, no. 8 (Aug. 1982): 419–38.

80. George Orwell, "Reflections on Gandhi," in *A Collection of Essays* (Garden City, N.Y.: Doubleday and Co., 1954), 182

Rousseau's ideal while a conception of balance grounds the moral claims of the alternative to it.

Conclusions

How should one choose between the two positive types? The choice can be made on the basis of a philosophic consideration of the validity of the premise of man's natural goodness and unity. To accept that premise implies acceptance of Rousseau's ideal; to reject it in favor of the premise of man's natural moral complexity is to take a more tragic view that inclines toward political moderation. Or, it might be argued that there is no real necessity to choose; "it takes all kinds" in political life. Politic moderates need uncompromising moralists to set the goals and to keep them honest, while the latter need the former to see their goals realized in practice. There is certainly some truth in this, but it does not relieve individuals from the need to make a choice.[81]

The choice can also be made on the basis of a judgment as to which alternative carries with it the greatest political dangers. The danger of those who would be principled moderates is that they may become complacent hypocrites instead. Rousseau seeks to avoid this danger by rejecting the kind of prudence and engagement represented by the *honnête homme*. If, in so doing, he rejects prudence and engagement altogether, the case can be made that his own ideal is at least as dangerous.

Two kinds of political dangers accompany the Rousseauian ideal: one associated with unleashed indignation and the other with resignation or withdrawal. The first and most obvious of these is the danger of rejecting Rousseau's preference for political disengagement while accepting his model of integrity as purity. As Blum has convincingly demonstrated, this is the model that inspired Robespierre and Saint-Just.[82] Fanaticism was the product of adopting moral purity as the exclusive guide for political action. According to Blum, the quest for a virtuous republic was

---

81. To the extent that these are character types, people may not be psychologically free to make such a choice as to their own behavior, though they are always free to make a judgment.

82. See also Hannah Arendt, *On Revolution* (New York: Viking, 1965), 91–102; Lionel Trilling, *Sincerity and Authenticity* (Cambridge: Harvard University Press, 1971), 67–72.

inseparable from the use of terror against its enemies, and both were the realization of a reading of Rousseau faithful to the core of his teachings.[83]

There is an alternative view of Rousseauian politics that, when carried to extremes, produces its own quite different political dangers. According to this view, "the founding that Rousseau himself hoped to accomplish was only an indirectly political one. He hoped to change the way people saw themselves and to cause a dissatisfaction with the prevailing forms of social life that would lead them to value private life, domestic life, and participation in small communities."[84] Rousseau seems to confirm that his political goals were modest: "If his doctrine could be of any use to others, it was by changing the objects of their esteem and thus perhaps delaying their decadence."[85] Rousseau aimed only at a revolution in judgment:

> Rousseau's preference for peace, stability, and resignation is incompatible with any sort of social activism or programmatic politics. And in fact, Rousseau was intent on only one thing: judgment. To reveal the failures of actuality and to condemn the unpardonable was enough. It was an exercise in indignation.[86]

What are the potential dangers of this sort of revolution? At the least, to encourage the virtuous to abandon public life cedes the field to the vicious. Rousseau acknowledges that the virtuous will not necessarily have a salutary effect on the others simply by the example of their private virtue. He understands that it is a naive illusion to believe that hatred and evil in some people will be overcome by gentle, honest, and truthful behavior in others (*Confessions*, 438). Rousseau also makes his argument easier by failing to confront the most difficult sorts of conflicts for his position. For example, in praising the true Alceste for his integrity in preferring to lose his suit than to corrupt a judge, he does not consider the case where Alceste might be confronted with the question of whether to intercede with a judge on behalf of some-

---

83. Carol Blum, *Rousseau and the Republic of Virtue: The Language of Politics in the French Revolution* (Ithaca, N.Y.: Cornell University Press, 1986), 277.

84. Kelly, "Reading Lives," 29.

85. Jean-Jacques Rousseau, *Rousseau, Juge de Jean-Jacques: Dialogues, O.C.,* I, 935.

86. Judith N. Shklar, *Men and Citizens: A Study of Rousseau's Social Theory* (Cambridge: Cambridge University Press, 1969), 30.

one else who is the victim of injustice. This is the difficult case. Good men often are tempted more easily to compromise certain of their principles on behalf of the good of others than they would be on their own behalf.[87] It is hard to fault Philinte entirely for wishing to do what he can to secure justice for his friend, even if that involves moral compromise. In the most general terms, it is Rousseau's position that can be faulted as ultimately incompatible with justice if moral purity is purchased at the price of the just result.

Disengagement from public life, however, is not the most serious source of the danger. Rather, the greater danger lies in the judgment that this disengagement is necessary because a life of integrity is impossible in this corrupted world. When integrity is viewed as purity, anything less may be condemned as unpardonable. And if this standard is in fact too high, we may be led to condemn behavior that is not only tolerable but necessary. The result is not only ceding the field to the vicious but weakening the good ones who remain in the fray. Crucial moral distinctions are obliterated when all who are engaged in the world are condemned as equally corrupt. The danger lies in undermining the moral legitimacy of what may be the only practically viable moral stance, and this is a very great danger indeed.

The fundamental question is whether Rousseau's conception of moral purity can form the basis for a practical ethics, one that neither plunges headlong into fanatical revolutionary politics nor stops short of providing a useful guide for action, producing instead only an indignant rejection of the modern world. Despite the historical testimony to these twin dangers of the Rousseauian ideal, there is reason to suspect that they flow from a distorting oversimplification of it. In both cases, the source of the danger is a certain rigidity thought to be necessary in order to sustain purity. Blum claims that Rousseau "rejected compromise and mixed solutions to human dilemmas as impure."[88] Similarly, the rigidity of the misanthropic posture flows from the fear that any involvement in a corrupted world will bring contamination (the typical concern where authenticity, rather than integrity, is iden-

---

87. Rousseau defends lying on behalf of others but condemns lying on one's own behalf. His position is discussed and contrasted with Immanuel Kant's position in chapter 4.

88. Blum, *Republic of Virtue,* 131–32.

tified as the ideal). Alceste cannot even allow himself to be polite, for example. No subtle moral distinctions and no flexibility can be found here. But neither the revolutionary posture nor the misanthropic one does justice to the prudential aspects of Rousseau's thought.

As I noted above, at many points in Rousseau's work he endorses compromise, political flexibility, and exceptions to his general moral critique. And by characterizing his ideal as "uncompromising moralism," I have accentuated thus far one aspect of his thought while obscuring another. The crucial problem is to identify the criteria that distinguish the compromises that he found acceptable from the ones he considered to be corrupting. It is possible that Rousseau's ideal does not preclude sufficient flexibility to provide a useful ethical standard. In other words, it may be that Rousseau provides a genuine alternative to the ethics of integrity understood as balance; that he offers a "mature idealism" in contrast to the adolescent variety; and finally, that he delineates a kind of prudential moderation that could not be condemned as complacency quite so readily. Perhaps then the high aspirations represented by Rousseau's ideal would not need to be condemned in turn as dangerously unrealistic.

To pursue this further, we need to know more precisely what the possibilities are for flexibility and compromise within the boundary set by the uncompromising character of the man of integrity. Is there a politics of integrity to be found in Rousseau, or does he offer only his odd combination of resignation and indignation?

4

Rousseau's Political Ethics
Integrity, Prudence, and Deception

INTRODUCTION

In chapter 3 I described Rousseau's ideal type as an uncompromising moralist. It is time to reevaluate that characterization. Throughout Rousseau's works there are examples of compromises he considers tolerable, lies he considers acceptable, and political manipulations he considers beneficial. He presents his readers with many cases where judgments must be made between competing values and in difficult circumstances. There is a Rousseauian prudence that requires examination. Where does Rousseau the moralist actually draw the line in making personal and political judgments? On the one hand, the problem is to determine whether he distinguishes between a legitimate compromise and a "sell-out" by any consistent criteria. On the other hand, the problem is to determine whether he maintains a principled stance that can be consistently distinguished from fanaticism. And in every case, we must wonder whether his prudential judgments are consistent with the ideal of integrity that he himself establishes as the new standard for moral-political judgment.

The prudential aspects of Rousseau's thought have not been given the sustained attention they deserve.[1] For understandable reasons, the tendency has been to read Rousseau in the light of Robespierre, i.e., to answer the question of the political implications of Rousseau's thought historically rather than analytically. As a result, some interpreters have looked in Rousseau's texts for

---

1. Roger Masters has consistently brought this problem to our attention. See his introduction in *S.C.*, 21, and his *The Political Philosophy of Rousseau* (Princeton: Princeton University Press, 1968), chap. 8.

the seeds of a new kind of modern political fanaticism.[2] They have found those seeds, paradoxically, both in Rousseau's moral rigidity and in his infinite moral flexibility. On the one hand, Rousseau is portrayed as a moral absolutist who has no room for pragmatic flexibility in his politics. On the other hand, Rousseau's moralism is seen as collapsing into subjectivism so that, finally, no moral rules bind the individual and anything that the individual's conscience can approve is permissible.

In what follows, I begin by analyzing instances in Rousseau's directly political works in which he seems to deviate from his principles or make exceptions to his own rules. These cases represent political compromises that bow to the necessities of the circumstances. In Rousseau's view, acting on the basis of prudential calculations of political consequences does not in itself compromise personal integrity. Next I focus on truthfulness and lying to explore Rousseau's treatment of personal ethics. As part of a complex argument on this issue, Rousseau defends lies that benefit others but condemns lying on one's own behalf. This ethical distinction, between action on behalf of others and for one's own sake, partially accounts for the perplexing mix of moralism and flexibility in Rousseau's writing. While Rousseau is strict with regard to action on his own behalf, he allows considerable latitude when acting in pursuit of justice for others. He even allows deceiving people for their own good. This is evident in the Legislator's relation to the citizens and in the tutor's relation to Émile. I turn to these cases to explore Rousseau's treatment of deception in ruling. That Rousseau justifies the deception of the ruled calls into question his commitment to personal autonomy and political freedom. At the very least, it requires that we reexamine the meaning of autonomy and freedom in his work. Rousseau countenances a certain sort of paternalism as well as certain sorts of prudential compromises, and in both cases, he grounds his case in necessity. Even the "uncompromising" moralist bends to necessity.

2. For examples, see Hannah Arendt, *On Revolution* (New York: Viking, 1965); Carol Blum, *Rousseau and the Republic of Virtue: The Language of Politics in the French Revolution* (Ithaca, N.Y.: Cornell University Press, 1986); Lester G. Crocker, *Rousseau's "Social Contract": An Interpretive Essay* (Cleveland, Ohio: Case Western Reserve University Press, 1968); and J. Talmon, *Origins of Totalitarian Democracy* (London: Secker and Warburg, 1952).

Rousseau's Political Prudence:
Tolerable Compromises

Rousseau made policy recommendations and advised his contemporaries on the reformation of their political institutions in
several of his works: the *Letter to D'Alembert, Project for a Constitution for Corsica, Government of Poland,* and *Letters Written from the
Mountain.* In addition, much of *The Social Contract* treats the art
of legislation, as distinguished from the principles of political
right. Even if Rousseau did not expect that his recommendations
would be implemented, these writings reveal how Rousseau
thought about practical political decisions and, by implication,
how he believed we ought to think practically about politics.[3]
For the purposes of this inquiry, the types of arguments he used
to justify departures from his political principles in their pure theoretical form are more important than the recommendations
themselves. And in every case, Rousseau's prudential writings
exhibit similar argumentation and a similar set of criteria for making political judgments.

Central among these is the view that policies and institutions
ought to be judged by their consequences. Since in every actual
case the consequences will be both good and bad, political judgment must be a process of balancing advantages and disadvantages. Moreover, no policy ought to be rejected unless it is found
wanting when weighed against the available alternatives. In politics, one must not seek perfection, only the best that is possible.
From this it follows that whether a policy is good or bad will
vary with the particular circumstances of a nation and its people.
Where a people retains some of its health and vigor and is not
yet completely corrupted, the prudent course is to act gradually
and to change as little as possible.[4]

It is important to recognize that this sober, cautious approach
is neither moderate nor conservative. That a calculating prudence
differs from moderation can be made clear by a moment's reflec-

3. Contrast Judith Shklar, who argues that Rousseau is a thoroughly utopian
writer. See Judith N. Shklar, *Men and Citizens: A Study of Rousseau's Social Theory*
(Cambridge: Cambridge University Press, 1969), 14–16.

4. Evidence to support this characterization of Rousseau's views can be found
throughout the works cited above, but some particular references follow: *D'Alembert,*
66, 107–10; *Mountain,* letter 6, p. 811, and letter 9, p. 873; *Poland,* 17–18.

tion on Machiavelli's counsel to princes to pick "the least bad as good" (*Pr.,* chap. 21, p. 91). Rousseau's approach is essentially the same: he weighs the relative advantages and disadvantages of competing policies. Yet in weighing alternatives, one might find that the least bad is a policy of exemplary executions or equally extreme measures. Rousseau's own extreme rhetoric, for example, can be justified on prudential grounds. Given a situation where the greatest danger is complacency, rousing rhetoric can be defended despite its inherent risks. Where the consequences of extreme political measures are better than the consequences of moderate ones, extremism is prudent.

Similarly, while Rousseau often counsels minimal, gradual change, his apparent conservatism is altogether conditional. Though Rousseau often sounds like Edmund Burke, unlike Burke his conservatism is not grounded in fundamental philosophic convictions concerning the inherent moral limitations of human beings, the dependence of every society on its heritage, and so forth. Precisely because Rousseau approaches a political situation prudentially, everything depends on the circumstances of the case. Conservative policies are appropriate only in situations where there is something left that is worth preserving or where change is certain to bring only further decline.

The question now becomes whether Rousseau's prudential approach is guided by any fundamental principles at all. Are there limits to the political flexibility found in his practical political works? Of these works, the *Government of Poland* is most interesting in confronting this question because it contains recommendations that seem to directly contradict the egalitarian political principles of *The Social Contract.* Rousseau here recommends against the immediate enfranchisement of the Polish serfs. And whereas in *The Social Contract* Rousseau writes, "the instant a people chooses representatives, it is no longer free; it no longer exists," the same Rousseau recommends a representative system for Poland that he claims to deduce from the principles of *The Social Contract.*[5] How does he justify these recommendations?

Rousseau's positions on representation and on serfdom in Poland illustrate the prudential approach already described in general terms. Poland is too large to do without some representative

5. *S.C.,* III, xv, 103; *Poland,* 38.

system. Rousseau's goal is to devise a system that approximates the democratic ideal as closely as possible given these circumstances. He stresses the advantages of federalism and proposes mechanisms, such as mandates and frequent rotation in office, to tie representatives closely to their constituents. Rousseau also suggests various means of protecting against the most likely abuses of representative systems (*Poland,* chap. 7). Frequent rotation of representatives, for example, guards against their corruption. If you must make do with a defective institution, the least you can do is to identify its characteristic deficiencies and attempt to mitigate their worst consequences.[6]

In the case of serfdom, the goal is to approach the ideal in a different sense, gradually over time. Despite the obvious injustice of serfdom, Rousseau recommends against immediate enfranchisement of the serfs, arguing that their enslavement has produced vices that leave them ill-prepared for true liberty. Given their condition, the consequences of a course of action dictated solely by the principles of justice would be license, rather than liberty, and political disaster for all. As one expedient, Rousseau recommends gradually rewarding with enfranchisement those serfs who have proved themselves worthy of it—a policy with the paternalistic implication that liberty must be earned rather than claimed as a right (*Poland,* 29, 43, 82, 94–97).

But Rousseau also insists on a clear statement of principle. Immediate emancipation may be impractical, but serfdom is wrong. The right to consent to the laws is "sacred and imprescriptible." In characteristic style he proclaims,

> Nobles of Poland, be more than nobles, be men; only when you are men will you be happy and free. But do not flatter yourselves that you are either so long as you keep your own brothers in bondage. (*Poland,* 29)

The style here is worthy of comment. Rousseau appeals to the pride of the nobles and pricks their vanity by implying that, as masters, they are not the men they think they are. And, of course, as a matter of justice, they ought to free the serfs even if it makes them miserable, rather than truly happy and free. The appeal here

---

6. See *Poland,* 17–18, for a similar approach to the evils of luxury.

is not to compassion or any similar sentiment. Still, Rousseau does not shrink from declaring moral truths to those unlikely to find them agreeable.

Neither does he expect this sort of rhetoric alone to persuade them. Rousseau is "politic" not only in his advice but also in his manner of dealing with the opponents of his reforms. Knowing that men are motivated by their interests as they perceive them, Rousseau takes every opportunity to point out the advantages to the nobles of eliminating serfdom; he recommends a policy that produces benefits, rather than burdens, for the master of a freed serf; and he counsels gradual reform. When changes are slow, men who had a stake in the status quo can come to see and feel the benefits of the reform. Moreover, by proceeding gradually, you can leave most current officeholders in their positions. These are the sorts of concessions that can be made to the political necessity to secure support for reform measures. Rousseau does not condone the attempt by reformers to secure support under false pretenses by concealing their intentions. Rather, reformers should reveal their plans in detail but implement them gradually (*Poland*, 114–15).

Rousseau's stance with respect to Polish serfdom adds up to this: state clearly that it is a moral evil; tolerate it for now, but put it on a course of ultimate extinction; and arrange incentives as far as possible for the masters to favor its elimination. Rousseau's position on serfdom bears a striking resemblance to Abraham Lincoln's on slavery. This must come as a surprise to readers of Rousseau who have formed an impression of him as a rigid moralist through reading his more polemical works alone. Lincoln, after all, portrayed himself as an opponent of both the moralistic abolitionism of men like Henry David Thoreau and the politic compromising of men like Stephen Douglas. Those who see only Rousseau the moralist would expect Thoreau, not Lincoln, to show a much stronger resemblance to him. Locating Rousseau's position on serfdom with respect to Thoreau's and Douglas's positions on slavery illustrates why a certain sort of political prudence and flexibility is compatible with his ideal of integrity, as well as where the limits to that flexibility lie.

Rousseau's notion of moral purity differs from Thoreau's. For Thoreau, association with a system that promotes evil supports the evil and stains one's personal integrity.[7] Rousseau does not express this notion that involvement in a corrupt society is contaminating in and of itself. By the same token, he does not describe dissociation from society as a public moral act of bearing witness to social injustice. Moreover, I believe that Rousseau would have criticized an abolitionism advocating dissociation from the South because it would not have freed a single slave. He criticized Christianity for leading citizens to care so much for the salvation of their souls that they become indifferent to the political consequences of their actions (*S.C.,* IV, viii, 129).

At the root of Rousseau's differences with Thoreau is a disagreement as to what constitutes a morally compromising act. In Rousseau's view, personal integrity is not threatened by accepting necessary limits, even when this means tolerating injustice. To "compromise" with reality, to bow to necessity, cannot be equated with compromising one's principles. Personal integrity is only corrupted when private desire, whether for gain, satisfaction of vanity or vengeance, or security of social status, is permitted to dictate a course of action contrary to the principles of justice. The conscience remains clear and natural purity is sustained so long as these degenerate desires have not been aroused. It is morally permissible to allow for the temporary continuation of slavery or serfdom so long as this position results from a truthful and disinterested attempt to secure justice as far as possible given the circumstances.

On the other hand, regardless of Stephen Douglas's personal intentions, it was not morally permissible to argue as he did in defending popular sovereignty in the territories. By allowing legislative majorities to vote on the slavery question, Douglas both permitted the expansion of the evil and obscured the moral issue, as if slavery need not arouse our indignation where it has been sanctioned by a democratic process. His position blurred the distinction between good and evil, allowing people to rationalize their wrongdoing.[8] Douglas wished to sustain the status quo com-

---

7. Henry David Thoreau, "On the Duty of Civil Disobedience," in *"Walden" and "Civil Disobedience"* (New York: New American Library, 1960), 222–40.

8. Douglas also suggested political subterfuge by arguing that authoritative court decisions could be undermined by "unfriendly legislation." See Robert W. Johannsen, ed., *The Lincoln-Douglas Debates of 1858* (New York: Oxford University Press, 1965).

promise at the price of truth and justice. Rousseau was prepared to proceed gradually out of deference to the strength of the opposition, but Douglas was willing to make common cause with them. This is "Philintism": a posture of moderation that encourages complacency toward evil, flatters the vicious, and protects the advantages of the status quo for the "moderates."[9]

This brief comparison suggests the outlines of Rousseau's "politics of integrity" by distinguishing it both from Thoreau's notion of political purity and from Douglas's notion of political moderation.[10] In Rousseau's eyes, a compromise is legitimate where it is dictated by the necessities of the circumstances even if it requires accepting considerable injustice. Rousseau distinguishes between association with a pre-existing evil and actually personally committing an evil act. To do what can be done for the good, and only what can be done, can never stain the conscience. In making a political judgment, the question to be asked is, What good will it do? and not, Will it implicate me in evil? Rousseau cannot be charged with the kind of political extremism or fanatical politics that can develop where the practical consequences of political action are deemed irrelevant so long as an abstract moral standard of personal purity is upheld. Similarly, Rousseau's notion of integrity as purity must be distinguished from purity understood as strict adherence to prescribed codes of conduct, as for example in certain forms of religious orthodoxy.[11] Where morality is equated with obedience to authoritative rules, consideration of consequences again has no place. By contrast, in Rousseau's politics no rigid set of prescriptions guides a fanatical political program. Rousseau's conception of integrity permits considerably greater flexibility than does the con-

See especially the Second Joint Debate, Freeport, 27 August 1858, p. 88, and the Fifth Joint Debate, Galesburg, 7 October 1858, p. 217.

9. See chapter 3, text accompanying notes 37 and 38.

10. In terms of the ideal types defined in chapter 4, the comparison is equivalent to comparing the improved Alceste (Rousseau—the moralist with integrity) with Molière's Alceste (Thoreau—the self-righteous hypocrite) and Philinte (Douglas—the complacent hypocrite).

11. Rousseau emphasizes intention more than conduct in religious matters. His argument for religious toleration depends on this emphasis to a certain extent. See *Mountain,* letter 1, p. 692.

ception of purity understood either in the Judaic sense, as legal orthodoxy, or in the Christian sense that underlies Thoreau's position.

Nonetheless, Rousseau's flexibility is political, not moral flexibility. The principles themselves cannot be compromised. Douglas's position represents an illegitimate compromise because it promotes and extends evil while lying about what evil is. This is compromise at the level of principle. Moreover, despite Rousseau's political flexibility, he nowhere recommends doing evil, even when the situation seems to require it.[12] In this respect, Rousseau's prudential politics also differs from Machiavelli's. His flexibility neither extends as far as Machiavelli's, nor does it rest on the same foundation. Machiavelli argues that the distinctive character of political life requires the ability and willingness to violate the usual moral constraints when necessary. In effect, the moral rules themselves differ among friends, enemies, and political allies. While Rousseau acknowledges that politics may be a dirty game, in his view, the rules for personal conduct remain the same within and outside of the political arena.

In making political judgments, Rousseau offers a more complex mix of considerations of pragmatism and principle, of consequence and intention, than is usually thought. The result is a prudential politics grounded in moral principle yet clearly distinguishable from fanaticism. But another aspect of the problem remains to be examined. The charge of fanaticism leveled against Rousseau arises as much from the apparent subjectivity of Rousseau's moral judgments as from the apparent rigidity of his political ones. If it were Rousseau's view that a clear conscience is the only true test of moral rectitude, he would provide an entirely subjective and thus infinitely flexible ethic. And this is but another route to fanatical politics. Robespierre's speeches confirm that the most extreme measures can be justified where sincerity or inner purity of intention has become the highest value.[13] What place do purity of intention, sincerity, and truthfulness hold in Rousseau's moral universe?

12. Recall that Rousseau's Alceste is a man who would rather lose a just cause than act badly (*D'Alembert*, 44).

13. Arendt, *On Revolution,* 69–75, 85–89; Blum, *Republic of Virtue,* 153–80; Trilling, *Sincerity and Authenticity,* 68–72.

ROUSSEAU'S PERSONAL ETHICS:
ACCEPTABLE LIES

Having established that Rousseau's ideal of integrity is compatible with flexible political judgments, I must establish now that it does not produce infinitely flexible moral ones. Blum makes this charge against Rousseau and illustrates it with Rousseau's treatment of his children. She argues that abandoning them did not trouble his conscience; he felt that his intentions were pure, and so he did not condemn his action as immoral.[14] There is no action, however horrible, that could not be justified in this way. Blum's charge is a serious one, particularly in the light of my claim that integrity, as opposed to authenticity or unity, is an ideal with some moral substance. But Blum's objection holds only if intention is the sole standard for morality and only if each is the sole judge of the purity of his own intentions. Neither of these is a fair statement of Rousseau's views.

The relation between intention and action is too complex to encapsulate with the claim that Rousseau's is an ethic of intention. An example from Rousseau's *Confessions* should clarify the issue. At the end of Book II, Rousseau confesses to a crime: while working as a house servant he stole a ribbon, which was soon discovered. When asked how he acquired it, he falsely stated that it had been given to him by a servant girl whose character was beyond reproach. Rousseau describes this as a wicked crime and portrays himself as stricken with remorse for the lasting harm he undoubtedly did to this girl by ruining her reputation. It is impossible to depict Rousseau's behavior as an act of goodness or as a well-intentioned error. But, immediately after stressing his wickedness, Rousseau begins to explain why his action was at least pardonable. He states that he had no intention to harm the girl and that he acted simply out of weakness, afraid of disgracing himself. While he describes himself as weak, rather than wicked, on the basis of an analysis of his intentions, he continues to describe what he did as a crime and a wicked lie on account of its evil consequences.[15]

14. Blum, *Republic of Virtue*, 78 ff.
15. It is noteworthy that he does not actually confess stealing the ribbon, only blaming someone else for having done so. See also *Julie*, 690, on the distinction between weakness and wickedness.

Intentions can be good (to help others), bad (to harm others), or, in a sense, indifferent (to benefit oneself without regard to the consequences for others). By and large, those with good intentions will act well, though certainly good people sometimes do bad things. They may misjudge, for example, whether their actions will be helpful or harmful. Nonetheless, for many actions there can be no mistake in this regard. There are some things a man of integrity will not do. These actions could never proceed from good intentions; they are simply corrupt (e.g., accepting a bribe). Those with bad intentions may do many good things along with a few bad ones, but this does not excuse them. Finally, there are those who are simply self-concerned. This is the category that I suspect includes the bulk of humankind in Rousseau's view. They are liable to do evil out of weakness or corruption. Rousseau suggests that such people, when they do wicked things, may be deserving of forgiveness or pardon, but this certainly does not imply that their actions are any the less wicked or that they are good people. The absence of bad intentions is not sufficient to support a claim of goodness.[16]

The situation is complicated further because it can be extremely difficult to discern people's intentions, including one's own. People are often deceived by an unselfconscious process of rationalization so that they do not avow their true motivations even to themselves. Self-deception is particularly common where self-interest is involved (see, for example, *Confessions*, 61–62). Rousseau was well aware of this possibility; in fact, it is essential for his critique of the morality of the Philinte types. They are precisely smug and self-satisfied people whose very corruption consists in their inability to recognize their hypocritical complacency for what it is. Rousseau's ideal of integrity is meant to allow his readers to make that identification. He does not rely on the subjective testimony of the individual as to the purity of his intentions as the standard for judging ethical action.

Certainly, Rousseau's intentions in the case of his children are suspect. It would be easier to credit his claim that he truly intended their benefit had he troubled himself to learn (or allowed

16. Compare Blum, *Republic of Virtue*, 84. "[Rousseau insists] that goodness is equivalent to the absence of any inner wish to do harm and that actions are therefore irrelevant to morality."

himself to acknowledge) the conditions in the Foundling Hospital. Knowing that the fate of his children was likely to be a tragic one, we are entitled to say that Rousseau's justifications were rationalizations of a wicked deed.[17] And such a judgment would be consonant with Rousseau's own mode of moral argument. His emphasis on intentions does not necessarily collapse into limitless subjectivity or lead directly to fanatical revolutionary excess.

In the case of the stolen ribbon, Rousseau considers his lie unjustified despite his lack of malicious intentions. He makes this judgment on the basis of some external standard. Yet an absolute requirement of truthfulness is not that standard. Even though truthfulness is one of the prime components of integrity, Rousseau does see some lies as justified. In the Fourth Walk of the *Reveries of the Solitary Walker,* Rousseau reflects again on the incident of the stolen ribbon and embarks on a detailed discussion of lying and truthfulness. This is the one place in Rousseau's writings where he discusses at length the grounds for making exceptions to his moral maxims, and consequently it is very important for this investigation.

Rousseau's general theoretical discussion of lying in the Fourth Walk is prompted by his consciousness of his own hypocrisy with respect to telling the truth. At the same time that he is proud of his dedication to the truth, that he is sacrificing his own interests to tell the truth, that he has adopted the motto *vitam impendere vero,* he nonetheless finds that he has often presented his own fabrications as true and that he has done so without remorse. In matters of some consequence where the truth has cost him dearly, he has maintained his integrity and been truthful nonetheless. Yet in small matters where it would be easy to speak truthfully, he finds that he often lies. This is the puzzle he seeks to explain: not so much why he has behaved in this way, but why his conscience has allowed him this behavior without pangs of guilt.

Rousseau writes here, as elsewhere, of the reliability of the moral sense and particularly of the need to trust the voice of conscience as a more reliable guide to ethical conduct than reason

17. See *Confessions,* 320–22, 332–35, and *Reveries,* 138–41, for Rousseau's explanations for what he did. See also Maurice Cranston, *The Noble Savage: Jean-Jacques Rousseau, 1754–1762* (Chicago: University of Chicago Press, 1991), 285–88, for evidence that he showed some remorse later in life.

or philosophy. But his reflections would lose their purpose entirely if he considered the conscience infallible. Rousseau's premise here is that he may have misjudged his conduct. The " 'Know thyself' of the temple at Delphi was not such an easy precept to observe as I had thought in my *Confessions*" (*Reveries,* 63), he remarks at the outset of his reflections, and he closes with a new, and considerably more critical, judgment of his past conduct than the one with which he began.

Between his initial and his final personal reflections on this subject, Rousseau conducts a theoretical inquiry that begins with the following definition: "to lie is to conceal a truth one ought to make known" (*Reveries,* 65).[18] This definition has two unusual features. First, it presumes that there are truths that one is not always obliged to make known. Rousseau accepts this premise. He then proceeds to consider truth as if it were a tangible possession and argues in the language of property rights to reach the conclusion that we owe one another only those truths that are potentially useful. Thus one who conceals trivial, indifferent, or useless knowledge is not lying. The problem, of course, is to ascertain what is useful, a problem that Rousseau concedes is significant.

The second unusual feature of the original definition is that it speaks only of withholding truth and not of uttering falsehood. According to Rousseau, falsehoods concerning trivial and indifferent matters are no more culpable than silence on such matters. For a falsehood to be a moral offense, both a deliberate intent to deceive and the possibility of a harmful effect from the deception must be present. Again, Rousseau considers both intentions and consequences in making moral judgments. And for the person wondering whether to proceed with a particular deception, the consideration of the consequences is the essential thing.

But to determine what may be harmful is no easier than to determine what may be useful. Since we can rarely be certain that the effects of our actions will be harmless, very few intentional deceptions are innocent. Those that are innocent are called "fic-

---

18. Victor Gourevitch identifies Fontenelle as the source of this definition and notes that Helvetius quotes it in a passage commented on by Rousseau, "Notes sur 'De l'Esprit' de Helvetius," *O.C.,* IV, 1126. My discussion of the Fourth Walk owes much to Gourevitch's, "Rousseau on Lying: A Provisional Reading of the Fourth *Rêverie*," *Berkeshire Review* 15 (1980): 93–107.

tions" rather than "lies." The distinction between fictions and lies is the distinction Rousseau's conscience rightfully made in warning him away from certain untruths and allowing him others.

There is an important category of fictions whose purpose is to present useful truths in a pleasing form: moral fables or parables. They make use of fabrications in order to allow people to benefit from truths they might not otherwise recognize. These, then, are not precisely innocent deceptions but are more accurately considered as good ones. Yet it turns out that this statement must be qualified. Only good fables are fictions; some fables are immoral and are therefore lies. They deceive people about the moral status of the imaginary people and events they present. These are intentional deceptions with harmful effects, and their authors are liars. "[E]ven if he is not lying about facts, he is betraying moral truth, which is infinitely superior to factual truth" (*Reveries*, 71).[19]

The distinction between moral and factual truth governs the distinction between lies and fictions, which in turn replaced the attempt to distinguish lies from truthtelling in the ordinary sense. Thus to lie means to betray the moral truth whether one adheres to the actual facts or invents them. Conversely, one can tell the truth while deliberately falsifying the facts, in Rousseau's view. The only falsehoods that deserve to be called lies are those that deceive us about moral judgments. They are the ones that lead us to make incorrect judgments about the moral significance of events and the real worth of human beings.[20]

To give someone more or less than their due is to act unjustly, and so Rousseau's definition of lying comes to this:

> To give an advantage to someone who does not deserve it is to pervert the order of justice; falsely to attribute to oneself or to another an act

19. "If *The Temple of Gnidus* is a useful work, the story of the Greek manuscript is no more than an innocent fiction; but it is a reprehensible lie if the work is dangerous" (*Reveries*, 73).

The distinction between moral and factual truth corresponds to the distinction between general, abstract truth and particular individual truth with which Rousseau begins this analysis (*Reveries*, 66).

20. Rousseau's position here helps to explain his judgments of Machiavelli as author of *The Prince* and of Frederick as author of *Anti-Machiavel*; see discussion in chapter 1.

> which can be praised or blamed, declared innocent or guilty, is to act
> unjustly; and everything which by being opposed to truth offends jus-
> tice in any way is a lie. That is the line which must not be crossed
> [*Voilà la limite exacte*], but everything which although opposed to truth
> does not offend justice in any way is no more than a fiction, and I
> confess that anyone who holds a mere fiction against himself as a lie
> has a more tender conscience than I have. (*Reveries,* 70–71)

Justice is the standard by which truthtelling and deception are to
be judged. And if falsehoods that do not offend justice are innocent, presumably *caeterus paribus* the same can be said for falsehoods that actually serve justice.

Rousseau does not mention this possibility in this passage, but
this is the possibility suggested by the consideration of moral fables. Moreover, the same line of argument that justifies moral
fables justifies the Legislator's deception of the people.[21] In both
cases, useful truths are clothed in deceptions that are justified by
the moral benefits they produce. In the *Reveries,* Rousseau rhe-
torically equates speaking truthfully with speaking justly so that
lies like this cannot even be called by that name. But if what this
actually means is that the truth may be abandoned for the sake
of justice, Rousseau's commitment to "truthfulness" may permit
quite a variety of fabrications. In order to determine the scope
of permissible deceit involved in Rousseau's identification of
speaking truthfully with speaking justly, we must examine further
what he means by justice in this context.

Speaking justly involves both being just to others and being
just to oneself. The former is a relatively straightforward matter.
Being just to others requires giving each his due and doing no
harm by what one says. Rousseau's lie about the ribbon violated
both requirements: "This lie, which was a great crime in itself,
was doubtless still more evil in its effects" (*Reveries,* 64). To falsely
attribute blame to Marion was itself a crime; it gave her less than
she deserved of moral estimation. But in disclosing the ribbon
lie in the *Confessions,* Rousseau did not do justice to himself.
Throughout that work, he was careful to expose all his weaknesses while omitting tales that would have brought him credit.

---

21. Kelly argues that, for Rousseau, politics is the proper arena for moral fables.
Christopher Kelly, *Rousseau's Exemplary Life: The "Confessions" as Political Philosophy*
(Ithaca, N.Y.: Cornell University Press, 1987), 19.

These omissions were permissible though they misrepresented the facts. To give oneself less than one deserves is not a serious injustice in Rousseau's view. False self-aggrandizement is the far greater vice.

Nonetheless, in the *Reveries* Rousseau counterbalances the ribbon tale with two stories of his deceptions that lead us to see him in a favorable light. Twice as a youth, Rousseau protected other children who hurt him quite severely, through lies or silence as to the true cause of his injuries. Rousseau's merciful falsehoods allowed the other children to escape just punishment. Apparently, these falsehoods are justified because the requirement that what we say accord with justice may be tempered by considerations of mercy. And in addition, the stories themselves may be fictions invented to communicate the moral truth that Rousseau is motivated more by pity than by revenge and so deserves our admiration. In either case, this sort of falsehood is permissible in Rousseau's view.

But by his own account, most of Rousseau's lies are prompted not by considerations of justice or mercy but by the fear of embarrassment. He invents trivial fabrications to fill the silences in conversation; he answers "no" and blushes when asked if he has any children; the ribbon lie itself he attributes to embarrassment. Lies of this kind are the ill effects of dependence and vanity. They are told in order to win the approval of others or to hide one's weaknesses and are therefore demeaning. For this reason, though they do no injustice to others, they are a kind of injustice to oneself.[22] One owes it to oneself to be true. Justice toward oneself in this sense might more properly be called integrity or honor.[23] Telling the truth is an aspect of dignified and autonomous behavior. "Truth is an homage that the good man [*l'honnête homme*]

22. These lies are bad because their intention is to impress others or to avoid their contempt, which is a venal motive. Consideration of consequences does not come into play here.

23. Compare Immanuel Kant, "On a Supposed Right to Lie from Altruistic Motives," in *Critique of Practical Reason and Other Writings in Moral Philosophy,* ed. and trans. Lewis White Beck (Chicago: University of Chicago Press, 1949). In a note commenting on his principle that truthfulness is the duty of each to everyone, Kant writes: "I should not like to sharpen this principle to the point of saying, 'Untruthfulness is a violation of duty to one's self.' This principle belongs to ethics, but we are here concerned with a legal duty. [Ethics as a] theory of virtue sees in this transgression only worthlessness, which is the reproach the liar draws upon himself" (347).

pays to his own dignity" (*Reveries,* 80). Truthfulness is a requirement of integrity and its demands are stricter than the demands
of justice toward others.

This is why Rousseau passes a double judgment on himself at
the end of the Fourth Walk. On the one hand, he defends himself
in these terms:

> I have often made up stories, but very rarely told lies. . . . I have
> injured no one and have not laid claim to more than was owing to
> me. In my opinion, this is the only sort of truth that may be called
> a virtue. (*Reveries,* 79)

On the other hand, he concludes that he is indeed at fault. He did
not pay enough attention to what he owed himself. And having
adopted *vitam impendere vero* as his motto, he ought to have been
able to overcome his weakness and embarrassment and spoken
and written the truth without fictional embellishment (*Reveries,*
80). With respect to truthtelling, Rousseau met the standards of
justice and his conscience was clear. But while he did nothing
impermissible, he did not meet the stricter demands of personal
integrity. He is not culpable, but neither does he deserve unqualified praise.

Rousseau reserves unqualified praise for his ideal type and
compares him favorably to society's ideal type in a passage remi-
niscent of the comparison between Alceste and Philinte in the
Letter to D'Alembert. The man who is called truthful by society
("dans le monde," *O.C.,* I, 1031) is scrupulous about factual details but allows others to be misled into forming impressions favorable to himself and his interests. Rousseau's truthful man behaves in the opposite way, caring little for the facts in matters of
indifference but insisting on honesty in matters affecting people's
opinions of each other's worth. The former is truthful only when
it costs him nothing; the latter is never more faithful to the
truth than when he has to sacrifice himself for its sake (*Reveries,*
71–72).

There is, of course, a third possibility: a truthteller who simply
tells the truth. This is the Kantian truthteller whose actions are
governed by duty and not by any calculation of consequences to
himself or to others. The extent to which Kantian morality is

indebted to Rousseau has been a matter of considerable controversy.[24]

On the question of truthfulness, the differences between Kant and Rousseau are stark, and not only with respect to whether a judgment of the likely consequences of one's action is a necessary element of moral judgment. Kant considers two different cases where a person might be tempted to lie: (1) the case of making a false promise to extricate oneself from a difficult situation,[25] and (2) the case of lying to extricate someone else from a difficult situation.[26] Kant makes no distinction between the two. A person has a duty to make truthful statements "whether they harm himself or others."[27] To distinguish the two situations would be to deny to oneself the very action that one might demand of another. It would be to say that I cannot lie on my own behalf, but I can expect others to lie to my advantage. In Kant's words, this creates a claim "opposed to all lawfulness."[28]

For Rousseau the distinction between lying for oneself and lying for the benefit of others is critical. He would concur with Kant in the first case and condemn a lie for one's own benefit, for to sacrifice oneself for the truth is a noble thing. To sacrifice others, however, is an entirely different matter. We have already seen that Rousseau justified lying to save his childhood companions from punishment. In an even more dramatic example, Rousseau describes in the *Confessions* his decision to flee France rather than allow himself to be arrested. He claims that he was prepared to face his accusers and to say "nothing but the truth" even at great personal cost. But that course of action would have compromised Mme de Luxembourg, and so he decided "to do for

24. See Ernst Cassirer, *The Question of Jean-Jacques Rousseau,* trans. Peter Gay (New York: Columbia University Press, 1954), 70–71; Melzer, *Natural Goodness,* 61–63; Patrick Riley, "Why Rousseau Is Not Kant: The Theory of Moral Sentiments in the *Lettres Morales*" (paper delivered at American Political Science Association annual meeting, Chicago, 1990); Bernard Yack, *The Longing for Total Revolution: Philosophic Sources of Social Discontent from Rousseau to Marx and Nietzsche* (Princeton: Princeton University Press, 1986), chap. 3.

25. Immanuel Kant, *Fundamental Principles of the Metaphysic of Morals,* trans. Thomas K. Abbott (New York: Bobbs-Merrill, 1949), 20–21.

26. Kant, "On a Supposed Right to Lie," 346–50.

27. Ibid., 349.

28. Ibid.

her on this occasion what nothing would have made me do for myself.''[29]

A kind of double standard characterizes Rousseau's ethics, and it accounts for no small part of the paradox in his writings that prompted this discussion. Alongside rigid and righteous professions of the noblest moral purity are prudential calculations producing flexible moral judgments. The former generally apply when Rousseau considers action on his own behalf; the latter when action on behalf of others is at issue. This characteristic duality already appeared in the observation that integrity, honor, or "being true to yourself" required a more stringent truthfulness than did justice toward others.

Rousseau's ethical double standard is the result of his concern to ensure disinterestedness, and there is some plausibility to it. For example, we can admire the way that Rousseau lied to protect his childhood friends, but, had he lied to protect himself from punishment, we would at least suspect his motives. We can only be certain that an action is disinterested if it requires some sacrifice. It is characteristic of Rousseau's approach that he describes his ideal truthteller as "never more faithful to the truth than when he must sacrifice himself for its sake" (*Reveries,* 71–72).

Nonetheless, situations will arise where what is to one's own advantage is also required by justice. Rousseau's ethical approach and his concern to ensure disinterestedness do not allow him to take sufficient account of this possibility. Disinterestedness was identified as a major component of Rousseau's ideal of integrity. In the initial discussion of this element of his ideal, the man of integrity was described as enraged by injustice against others, and calm in the face of injustice toward himself.[30] Why? Why not the reaction of righteous anger in both cases? Is there any reason to deny myself a remedy that I would willingly provide for others? In maintaining a distinction between acting in one's own behalf and acting on behalf of others, an odd situation is created where one may be forbidden to do for oneself precisely what one

---

29. *Confessions,* 536. See Maurice Cranston, *The Noble Savage: Jean-Jacques Rousseau, 1754–1762* (Chicago: University of Chicago Press, 1991), 356–58. While it would have been quite painful to be arrested, Rousseau also portrays fleeing as a sacrifice, a sacrifice of his reputation or honor, which he wanted Mme de Luxembourg to appreciate.

30. See the section in chapter 3 entitled, "Rousseau's Ideal of Integrity."

is obliged to do for others in a situation similar to one's own. And of course those others are under precisely the same set of moral obligations so that each may help the other in ways that neither may help himself.

By emphasizing disinterestedness in the way that he does, Rousseau seems to foreclose any self-regarding action even when it might be justified by the logic of his ethical arguments. To allow self-regarding action is to create an opening wedge for personal corruption; this is what Rousseau seeks to avoid above all. Rousseau's extreme concern on this matter produces a moral tone or a psychological posture of both righteousness and passivity along with a glorification of self-sacrifice as a testimony to one's righteousness. This is the result of drawing the line in moral matters between selfishness and altruism, self-interestedness and disinterestedness.

It would be more consistent to draw the moral line between behavior that serves particular interests (one's own or others') and behavior that serves the cause of justice (in one's own case or others'). Kant recognizes the possibility that justice and personal interests may coincide and insists only that the individual's actions be grounded in the obligations of justice and not in personal desires. An equally consistent utilitarian or consequentialist position would require consideration of the effects of one's actions whether acting on one's own behalf or on behalf of others. Speaking loosely and anachronistically, Rousseau seems to lean in a Kantian direction in acting on his own behalf and in a consequentialist direction in acting on behalf of others. The result is a more rigid morality when one's own interests are at stake and greater flexibility for the sake of others.

To return to Rousseau's truthteller: this person will never speak falsely to his own advantage, out of vengeance against his enemies, or even out of personal vanity or embarrassment in minor matters. He will always consider whether a falsehood might have harmful consequences before he speaks, and, in the vast majority of cases, he will have to conclude that it might and hold his tongue. Justice requires truthfulness in serious matters and honor requires it in trivial matters. Rousseau upholds a very high standard of truthfulness.

But with all this said, Rousseau's truthteller may sometimes speak falsely. He may falsify the facts with disinterested motives in an effort to be helpful to others. And if he abandons the facts for the sake of the moral truth, according to Rousseau, he does not lie; he merely becomes the author of a moral fable. In *Julie, ou La Nouvelle Héloïse,* Rousseau puts a similar argument into Julie's mouth as she urges St. Preux to abandon his vow never to marry.

> [I]t is a second crime to hold to a criminal vow. If yours were not so before, it is become so now; and that is sufficient to annul it. The promise which no man ought to break is that of being always an honorable man [*honnête homme*] and always firm in his duty; to change when that is changed, is not levity, but constancy. . . . Act at all times as virtue requires you to do and you will never break your word.[31]

Apparently, to keep your word is not itself a part of virtue independent of the content of the promise. And in characteristically exaggerated Rousseauian rhetorical style, a broken promise in the name of virtue cannot really be called a broken promise, just as a lie in the name of justice cannot really be called a lie.

Rousseau's definition of truthfulness includes selfless lies. Does this mean that any and every falsehood may be justified in the end with the claim that it serves justice, virtue, or the moral truth? This is a politically important matter central to the problem of hypocrisy in politics. It is not a matter of deceit and trickery for self-interested gain, but of lies sanctified by moral purpose whose authors remain convinced of their own righteousness. I have already suggested the analogy between the author of a moral fable and the Legislator.[32] If Rousseau's claims regarding moral fables are problematic, so too may be his claims regarding deceitfulness in politics.

Consider Rousseau as the author of the *Confessions*. This work is certainly a moral fable in the terms of the Fourth Walk.[33]

31. *Julie,* 690–91. Compare *Pr.,* chap. 18.

32. The suggestion is supported by the particular example of a moral fable Rousseau chooses for his discussion in the *Reveries. The Temple of Gnidus* is a modern work that pretends to be the translation of an ancient text in an effort to lend authority to its message. Similarly, the Legislator deceives the people as to the divine source of the laws in order to increase their authority. *S.C.,* II, vi.

33. See Ann Hartle, *The Modern Self in Rousseau's "Confessions": A Reply to St. Augustine* (Notre Dame, Ind.: University of Notre Dame Press, 1983), 9–24; Kelly, *Exemplary Life,* 13–19.

According to Jean Starobinski, Rousseau's self-portrait in the *Confessions* cannot but be "true." However Rousseau portrays himself, it will be an authentic portrait, revealing of his own self-conception. The author's creative freedom is unlimited because authenticity is the governing conception behind Rousseau's notion of truthfulness. "The law of authenticity prohibits nothing."[34]

But here again the substitution of authenticity for integrity distorts Rousseau's position. His position does not endorse unlimited subjectivity, creativity, and moral boundlessness. If it did, it would be impossible to make sense of his condemnation of certain fictions as lies. He condemns Molière's portrait of Alceste, for example, as a misrepresentation of the misanthropic type. "The character of the misanthrope is not at the poet's disposal."[35] And by his own account, Rousseau is under a moral obligation to portray himself in the *Confessions* as no better than he is in fact. There is an objective truth about himself against which his self-portrait can be measured. Moreover, in presenting himself to his readers for judgment, he is obliged to present us with all the facts about his virtues and vices, strengths and weaknesses, and even crimes. To distort these things in his own favor would be a despicable lie, though to falsify the particulars of his experiences is not.

Nonetheless, this position is tenable only if we can accept the notion of a recognizable class of trivial facts concerning which what we believe to be true is a matter of complete indifference. In relying on the distinction between moral truth and factual truth, Rousseau seems to sever the connection between the two. Yet certainly "the facts of the case" have some bearing on our moral judgments, and rightfully so. How can we distinguish between knowledge of moral truth and dogmatic prejudice unless there are some facts against which we can test our moral knowledge? At the end of the *Reveries,* Rousseau seems to acknowledge that the line between moral truth and even trivial factual truths cannot be so starkly drawn. He writes, "when the pleasure of writing led me to embellish reality with ornaments of my own invention,

---

34. Starobinski, *Jean-Jacques Rousseau: Transparency and Obstruction,* 196–200, especially 198.

35. *D'Alembert,* 39. See Victor Gourevitch, "Rousseau on Lying: A Provisional Reading of the Fourth *Rêverie,*" *Berkshire Review* 15 (1980): 94.

I acted even more wrongly, because to decorate truth with fables is in fact to disfigure it" (*Reveries,* 80).

The thrust of the argument of the Fourth Walk is precisely to justify disfiguring the truth in the name of justice. Beneficial fictions and moral fables may be easier to accept in the realm of literature, where the facts of the situation are clearly invented and meant to be merely illustrative, but if the general argument is applied to politics and if the distinction between trivial and nontrivial facts cannot be sustained, the dangerous tendencies of the argument become obvious. The political realities, the "facts of the matter," may be willfully distorted to gain adherents to a righteous cause. The argument justifies the characteristic behavior of the demagogue: propagandizing, ideological indoctrination, or any political practice whose object is moral suasion rather than rational persuasion.[36]

Moreover, its underlying premise is that there are those who cannot benefit from, and may even be harmed by, the unadorned truth. The author of a moral fable or the political leader who falsifies the facts for the sake of the general good stands apart from his audience and above it; his relation to them is paternalistic. He is able not only to appreciate the naked truth but to see that the others do not share this capacity. To the extent that Rousseau justifies deceitfulness of this sort, he undermines his own case for democratic government and personal autonomy.

The issues raised by the consideration of acceptable lies are preeminently political ones, and are the same issues raised in considering the figure of the Legislator, Émile's tutor, and the characters in *Julie.* In all these cases, Rousseau justifies deceit and manipulation in relations of governance. In analyzing them, the central questions to consider are (1) what is it about relationships of rule that requires deceit in Rousseau's view? (2) does his defense of deceitfulness accord with his ethical ideal of integrity? and (3) is Rousseau himself hypocritical in advocating manipulation of the ruled while professing principles of egalitarianism and liberty?

36. George Kateb stresses the dangers of dogmatism and intolerance of inquiry in Rousseau's thought, though he denies that Rousseau defends well-intentioned lies. "Comments on Gourevitch," *Berkeshire Review* 15 (1980): 122–28.

Rousseau's Political Ethics:
Beneficial Manipulation

Rousseau's condemnation of the manipulative dimensions of so-cial and political relationships in existing societies, particularly powerfully expressed in the *Second Discourse*, is well known. This makes it all the more surprising to find elements of manipulation and deceit in the relationships he lauds as models. In fact, these elements are essential to the success of the political, familial, and social relationships Rousseau describes. In every case, the "ruler" can only truly benefit the "ruled" by disguising his own author-ity. As a result, the independence of the "ruled" is always partially illusory.

The Legislator is the clearest political example of this pattern (*S.C.,* II, vii, 67–70). He is the founder of a people, creating laws that transform a collection of individuals into citizens. But in one crucial respect, the Legislator depends on the people for the success of his project: they must accept the laws as their own. On the one hand, the Legislator cannot force them to do this because the laws can only become authoritative on the basis of consent. Rousseau explicitly reminds the reader of the principle of consent in discussing the Legislator's task (*S.C.,* II, vii, 69). To impose the laws on the people would negate their authority rather than establish it. On the other hand, the Legislator cannot convince the people to consent to the laws by any sort of rational explanation of their benefits or justice. For the people to willingly consent to accept the moral discipline imposed by these laws, they would already have to have the moral character of citizens, which is the very thing the laws are meant to create. Thus, with neither force nor reason at his disposal, the Legislator turns to deception to secure the consent of the people.

The example of the Legislator conforms to Machiavelli's un-derstanding that hypocrisy and deception will arise in relation-ships of mutual dependence between those with conflicting inter-ests. Force can be used with enemies, reason with friends, but only deceit works in politics. The Legislator depends on the con-sent of the people, but the people are not capable of understand-ing their interests as the Legislator understands them. The Legisla-tor persuades the people that the laws are divine in origin and authority. He tricks them into wanting what is good for them and believing that they have done only what they wanted.

This is a statement that could apply to the exemplary relationships of governance throughout Rousseau's writings: in every case the subjects are led to want what is good for them and to believe that they have freely chosen the yoke of virtue. The parallels to the tutor's relationship to Émile are most obvious. Émile's experiences are carefully designed so that any opposition to his will appears to be the spontaneous consequence of necessity or accident. He never experiences the interposition of his tutor's will.[37] Instead, the tutor is the hidden architect of Émile's world, often engaging the cooperation of other people to arrange the precise experience that will teach Émile a particular moral lesson.[38] The tutor's guiding hand, like the Legislator's, is hidden from view, and, just as the citizens are "subjected to the laws of the State as to those of nature" (*S.C.,* II, vii, 69) because they have been led to believe that the author of both is one and the same, Émile is subjected to the guidance of his tutor as if he were subjected only to natural necessities (*Émile,* 85–86).

In both cases, the reasons for this deception are also the same. Were Émile's tutor to forcefully impose his will, he would defeat his own purpose, which is to preserve Émile's natural freedom and to prevent his moral corruption (*Émile,* 137, 178, 207). Were he to rely on reason alone, he certainly would fail as well. Émile is a child, after all, who needs a guide for the moral and intellectual development he must undergo before he will be susceptible to rational argument. In the case of the child as in the case of a people, the development of both freedom and virtue depend on a ruse that disguises the fact that they are being led, guided, indeed ruled.

Other commentators on Rousseau's work have recognized these characteristics of his ideal modes of governance throughout his writings. Arthur Melzer argues that Rousseau's vision of "in-

37. There is a period in adolescence during which Émile's relation to his tutor changes and he submits himself to the tutor's guidance voluntarily, and there is one moment when the tutor relies on the promise of obedience made at that time, but this is the exception. See *Émile,* 325, 449; Judith N. Shklar, *Men and Citizens: A Study of Rousseau's Social Theory* (Cambridge University Press: Cambridge, 1969), 149.

38. The episodes between Émile and the gardener and Émile and the magician are prime examples of this technique of education. *Émile,* 98–99, 173–75.

direct rule" operates not only in the Legislator at the moment of founding but perpetually in the governing executive, too.[39] Lester Crocker describes *la main cachée* throughout the relationships of *Julie* and in all of Rousseau's major works.[40] Judith Shklar compares Wolmar to the Legislator in his rule at Clarens and in relation to St.-Preux.[41] Even the ideal marriage, according to Rousseau, involves manipulation where the true relationships of rule are disguised. The husband, the ostensible ruler of the household, can be led to want what his wife wants him to want because of his dependence on her. Like the people and like Émile, he is insufficiently cognizant of his dependence, unaware of his subjection, and therefore experiences himself as entirely autonomous.[42]

To be sure, there are differences between domestic and political rule, and these examples are not alike in every respect.[43] Émile is a child; the people are not. Wolmar's rule is more paternalistic than directly deceitful. He tells no lies comparable to the Legislator's whopper concerning the divine origin of the laws. Various distinctions of this kind could doubtless be multiplied, but the essential similarity remains. Unbeknownst to the "ruled," the "ruler" directs their wills toward morality while encouraging their belief that they are self-directed. It is the relationship of rule itself that is disguised. Crocker has suggested that the appropriate metaphor for Rousseau's vision of governance is the garden in *Julie,* where the impression of the free growth of nature has been made possible only by the consummate skill and constant care of

39. Melzer draws evidence from the *Political Economy* as well as from *The Social Contract.* See Melzer, *Natural Goodness,* 232–52, for his discussion of indirect rule as Rousseau's solution in all his writings to the problem of combining consent and wisdom in governance.

40. Lester Crocker, "Julie, ou La Nouvelle Duplicité," *Annales de la Société Jean-Jacques Rousseau* 36 (1963–65): 105–52.

41. Shklar, *Men and Citizens,* 127–63.

42. See Melzer, *Natural Goodness,* 248; Joel Schwartz, *The Sexual Politics of Jean-Jacques Rousseau* (Chicago: University of Chicago Press, 1984), 92–95. In *Émile,* Sophie is said to take over the role of tutor (*Émile,* 479).

43. Shklar notes that Wolmar does not have political power at his disposal at Clarens and that therefore he must gain authority over the wills of the workers there. Shklar, *Men and Citizens,* 150. I have already indicated why I think that the Legislator and Wolmar are actually alike in this respect. The use of political power, or force, for the Legislator would be self-defeating, and he must also seek to gain authority over the wills of the people.

the gardener. The gardener works to produce a garden that appears to have had no gardener.[44]

The metaphor is apt up to a point, but it deflects attention from the element of consciousness in the human material of the ruler that is absent from the vegetable material of the gardener. It is this element that gives Rousseau's account its disturbing mix of paternalism and egalitarianism. The marriage of Sophie and Émile illustrates my meaning. This is essentially an arranged marriage. The two have been chosen for each other and even raised for each other since infancy. But Sophie and Émile believe that they meet by accident, fall in love, and decide to marry of their own free will, asking only the blessing of their elders. The truth is that they could hardly have chosen otherwise, and they are never made aware of the role that their elders have played in ensuring that they would choose as they do (*Émile*, 407, 476–77). An old-fashioned arranged marriage is paternalistic once. This arrangement is paternalistic twice: once in the old-fashioned way and once in fostering an illusion of autonomy. The deception compounds the paternalism while it threatens to undermine Rousseau's stated commitments to freedom and equality. At the same time, it is presented as the only means to secure whatever freedom and equality is compatible with virtue.

There is considerable consensus that what I have described here as "beneficial manipulation," what Melzer calls "indirect rule," and what Crocker refers to as *la main cachée,* accurately characterizes Rousseau's vision of good governance. However, there is only disagreement as to how this vision ought to be evaluated. Judgments range from the claim that it represents a liberating vision of authority (Shklar) to the claim that it is central to Rousseau's totalitarian tendency (Crocker). How ought Rousseau's position to be judged and how does Rousseau himself justify it?

Three distinct standards are involved in evaluating Rousseau's position: truth, justice or morality, and freedom. "Beneficial manipulation" seems to violate the first and the third in the name of promoting the second. It sacrifices truth and freedom to promote justice or virtue. While the case of freedom turns out to be con-

---

44. Crocker, "La Nouvelle Duplicité," 123. Rousseau uses a gardening metaphor at the beginning of *Émile* (*Émile*, 37–38).

siderably more complicated than this statement suggests, it is accurate with respect to the standard of truth. We have already seen Rousseau's general argument justifying falsehood for the sake of moral education and deceit in the name of justice more generally.

George Kateb takes issue with this characterization of Rousseau's position, arguing that to lie *is* to act unjustly and maintaining that Rousseau does not endorse beneficent fictions. He explains that the civil religion of the Legislator is, in fact, true in Rousseau's view. Rousseau was not an atheist, but a "troubled Deist." The doctrines of the civil religion described in *The Social Contract* are the same as the doctrines of the natural religion Rousseau promotes through the Savoyard Vicar's profession of faith. Moreover, to the extent that the Legislator is merely a conduit of divine wisdom and benevolence, the true source of the authority of the laws is divine in a very important sense. Kateb goes on to cite Rousseau's criticism of pagan religion in *The Social Contract:* "it is bad in that, being founded on lies and error, it deceives men, makes them credulous and superstitious, and drowns the true cult of the Divinity in empty ceremonial" (*S.C.,* IV, viii).[45]

But this statement immediately follows a paragraph which begins by praising pagan religion as "good in that it combines the divine cult and love of the laws." The question at issue is whether, in weighing the good against the bad, Rousseau doesn't conclude that the political benefits of a false religion may outweigh the falsehood. Moreover, even if Kateb is correct that Rousseau considers the doctrinal content of the civil religion true and the Divinity as the ultimate source of the laws authored by the Legislator, the people are still deceived. They do not understand the respective roles of the Deity and the Legislator in this way. They may believe, for example, that Moses actually received stone tablets from God on Mount Sinai (see *S.C.,* II, vii, 70). In a sense, Kateb's argument recapitulates Rousseau's claims in the Fourth Walk: so long as the moral truth is maintained (or so long as the essential religious teaching is true), it is unimportant if the particular facts are distorted or abandoned. This is precisely the position that justifies beneficent lies.

The question then arises, if lies are justifiable only when they serve justice or morality, how do we know when they do indeed

---

45. Kateb, "Comments on Gourevitch," 126.

serve this purpose? May those with power and influence deceive others who depend on them so long as the deception is beneficial to all? Such a notion is clearly open to serious abuse. While there are never any guarantees against abuses, it does help to know that there are some criteria for distinguishing beneficial manipulations from harmful ones. The moral wisdom and, even more important, the disinterestedness of the "rulers" is the chief security here, and there are some outward signs by which that disinterestedness can be known. Neither the Legislator nor the tutor, for example, stands to benefit personally from his position.[46] The task of each is a task of founding. If they do it well, they make themselves obsolete. There would be good reason to distrust a Legislator who did not follow the example of Lycurgus and begin by abdicating the throne. The Legislator's task "has nothing in common with human dominion." If he were to exercise authority over men, "his laws, ministers of his passions, would often only perpetuate his injustices, and he could never avoid having private views alter the sanctity of his work" (*S.C.,* II, vii, 68).

Wolmar's case differs from the Legislator's and the tutor's in that his function is not temporary. Shklar nonetheless emphasizes his disinterestedness. "The end of Wolmar's managerial cares is not his property so much as the peasants and servants who work for him. They must be kept on the land and away from Paris."[47] Wolmar works to preserve them from corruption. Crocker, on the other hand, depicts Wolmar as personally benefiting from his manipulative rule, forming the peasants, not as ends in themselves, but to serve his own ends.[48] The two interpreters concur only in identifying the dominance of private interest as the element that would taint this sort of governance and disinterestedness as the quality of character that might redeem it.

Interestingly, Rousseau seems to trust that the people will be able to judge the character of the "ruler" well. Precisely because neither force nor reason is at his disposal, the person who would lead must be a person who inspires respect and admiration.[49] He must establish his authority by the force of his personality and

---

46. "The first quality I would exact of [the tutor], and this one alone presupposes many others, is that he not be a man for sale" (*Émile,* 49).

47. Shklar, *Men and Citizens,* 150.

48. Crocker, "La Nouvelle Duplicité," 123; see ibid., 118–23.

49. See Shklar, *Men and Citizens,* 150–58; *Julie,* 468–69, 611; see also *Émile,* 246.

the greatness of his soul. Both Wolmar and the Legislator have the extraordinary capacity to reach people and to influence them in this way. But they are able to establish their influence only because ordinary people are moved by genuine greatness. In speaking of the Legislator, Rousseau concedes that although the people may be occasionally and temporarily misled by a charlatan or an impostor,

> it is not every man who can make the Gods speak or be believed when he declares himself their interpreter. *The legislator's great soul is the true miracle that should prove his mission.* Any man can engrave stone tablets, buy an oracle, pretend to have a secret relationship with some divinity, train a bird to talk in his ear, or find other crude ways to impress the people. One who knows only that much might even assemble, by chance, a crowd of madmen, but he will never found an empire, and his extravagant work will soon die along with him. (*S.C.,* II, vii, 70, emphasis added)

Of course, the final test of whether the "rulers'" manipulations are beneficial is not only the longevity of their projects but the moral character and happiness of the "ruled"; whether of the citizens, of Émile, or of the workers at Clarens.

The most difficult problem is to determine whether we can say, with Rousseau, that their virtue and happiness is also combined with freedom. At first glance, it seems that this cannot possibly be the case. The paternalistic manipulation Rousseau describes puts people in a position of unselfconscious subjection. Freedom, like truth, is sacrificed to produce morality and justice.[50] But Rousseau would deny this. In fact, he does not even seem to recognize that the two are put in tension with each other in his discussion. "For some reason, Rousseau is willing to claim that so long as the people actually consent to the laws, even though they have been tricked into doing so, they remain free and sovereign."[51] Our question is, for what reason is Rousseau willing to make this claim?

It is important to begin with a clear understanding of precisely

50. See, for example, Crocker, "La Nouvelle Duplicité," 64–5.

51. Melzer, *Natural Goodness,* 236. See also Gourevitch, "Rousseau on Lying," 96: "Rousseau is sometimes charged with justifying paternalism. He takes the charge seriously, but he simply does not think it necessarily demeaning to provide or to conform to wise guidance."

what claim is made. Rousseau does not argue that freedom is maintained *in spite* of manipulative and deceitful practices. He claims instead that freedom is maintained *because of* those very practices.

> [The fathers of nations] attribute their own wisdom to the Gods; *so that* the peoples, subjected to the laws of the State as to those of nature, and recognizing the same power in the formation of man and of the City, *might obey with freedom* and bear with docility the yoke of public felicity. (*S.C.*, II, vii, 69, emphasis added)

Similarly, in the case of Émile, it is because the tutor disguises his authority and because Émile is unaware of the true causes of much of his experience that he retains his natural freedom and his sense of himself as autonomous. Deception is necessary, not only for the sake of moral improvement but also for the sake of freedom itself.

How does Rousseau justify this claim? And what could he mean by freedom if these relationships qualify as examples of it? Arthur Melzer suggests in a lengthy note to his discussion of "indirect rule" that freedom for Rousseau is nothing more than a "salutary illusion." Human freedom in fact is only "extreme malleability," which is to say that men are mere creatures of their environment and, hence, unfree.[52] While I think that he overstates the case (as will become clear below), Melzer is certainly correct to question what Rousseau might mean by freedom considering that he grounds it in deceit. Rousseau's position with respect to political and personal manipulation cannot be understood without recognizing that his understanding of freedom differs markedly from a liberal, Enlightenment, or Kantian understanding. The intimate link between freedom and reason in these dominant conceptions of freedom is considerably attenuated in Rousseau's thought. Rousseau's distinctive understanding of freedom accounts for his defense of beneficial manipulation, and that defense is an important part of his general critique of the Enlightenment attempt to rationalize political life.

The primary meaning of freedom in Rousseau's thought is the absence of personal dependence, that is, the absence of subjection to the private will of another individual. This is why the ruses

52. Melzer, *Natural Goodness*, 249 n. 29.

that disguise personal authority can be understood as necessary conditions for political freedom and personal autonomy. On account of the deception, the people subject themselves to neutral general laws, and Émile feels only the impersonal pressures of necessity. Looked at in this way, Rousseau's models of good governance appear to be positively liberating. This is the position that Judith Shklar elaborates. She depicts Wolmar, for example, as St.-Preux's liberator. Wolmar forces St.-Preux to face reality and frees him from his obsession by employing all the familiar techniques of manipulation: carefully arranging situations for him, deceiving him, acting against his will in his own best interest.[53] In Shklar's view, this is an example of a genuine authority that promotes, rather than stifles, freedom. "Authentic authority liberates. It gives liberty to those who are incapable of creating it for themselves. Better a will dominated by a tutor than no will at all."[54]

As this last statement indicates, the defense of Rousseau's position depends on the view that the practical alternatives to it are severely limited. The premise of the entire discussion is that men need masters; children need tutors; some form of authority is necessary. Absolute freedom is not a real possibility. The people do depend on the Legislator, as Émile depends on his tutor, for their moral transformation. The very fact that such a transformation is necessary is sufficient to conclude that it cannot be done autonomously. The difficulty is to find a form of authority that can accomplish the moral task while preserving the capacity for autonomous action.

I have already indicated that deception is necessary to this task because, in Rousseau's view, reason does not provide a viable option. This leaves force as the only practical alternative form of rule, which makes Rousseau's defense of deception and manipulation considerably more persuasive. This is the thrust of Christopher Kelly's excellent discussion of the Legislator.[55] What I have called "deception and manipulation," Kelly describes much more favorably as "symbolic politics and nonrational forms of persuasion." The Legislator speaks a musical language that reaches the

53. Shklar, *Men and Citizens,* 141–43.
54. Ibid., 162.
55. Christopher Kelly, " 'To Persuade without Convincing': The Language of Rousseau's Legislator," *American Journal of Political Science* 31 (May 1987): 321–35.

affections of the people.[56] His appeal to their feelings provides "a middle road between coercion and rational argument. It is the abandonment of this middle road that Rousseau regards as a decisive mark of the defects of modern politics."[57] Because we have forgotten the need for nonrational appeals in politics, our politics is governed by self-interest and force alone. Symbolic politics or beneficial manipulation, even with all its dangers, is the only alternative to coercion.[58] Beneficial manipulation thus appears to be perfectly defensible, since without it freedom of any kind is doomed.

Recall the example of Émile and Sophie's marriage discussed above. If the only alternatives are traditional arranged marriage and the hidden arrangement of this marriage, perhaps the latter is preferable. Despite the deception involved and despite its double paternalism, Sophie and Émile are free in principle to choose differently than they do (*Émile*, 407). Similarly, the people are free to change their laws for the worse. Rousseauian freedom is something more than a salutary illusion. The will is free to choose, and the question is what will govern the choice. The answer, however, is not individual autonomous reason but sentiment and character. And these are shaped in turn by external forces, and particularly by dependencies on other people. Given that this influence is inescapable, it is best that it be exercised in a manner that encourages the greatest possible autonomy and in a manner that allows for the psychological experience of autonomy.[59] If this requires deception, it also justifies it as the necessary condition of the only sort of freedom that is available to us.

This is the most positive statement of Rousseau's claim, but it is not unassailable. Rousseau's position is open to criticism both on its own terms and from the perspective of an alternative conception of freedom. Rousseau's own claim is that beneficial manipulation promotes freedom in that it provides an escape from personal dependence, or at least from the experience of personal dependence. But the element of personal admiration and emulation in the relations between the people and the Legislator, Émile

---

56. See also Shklar, *Men and Citizens*, 156–57. This depiction makes the Legislator look very much like the author of a moral fable.

57. Kelly, "To Persuade without Convincing," 331.

58. Ibid., 323.

59. This is the problem of moral education for a free people.

and his tutor, and the inhabitants of Clarens and Wolmar cast some doubt on this claim. Moreover, the people, in accepting the laws as divine commands, presumably understand themselves as subjects of divine authority rather than as autonomous agents exercising the legitimating power of consent. The Rousseauian deception may not succeed in achieving its intended psychological effect in this case either. In every case, the subjects of manipulation may continue to experience themselves as childlike dependents.

This situation would be less problematic if we were sure that the paternalism of Rousseau's vision of good governance was meant to be a temporary condition. Temporary paternalism is a fairly standard way of resolving the inevitable tension in child rearing, for example, between the need for moral habituation and the desire to produce an autonomous adult. This is, of course, the very same dilemma Rousseau is attempting to resolve. He seeks a form of authority that will secure both moral virtue and freedom. The difficulty is that it is not quite clear that either Émile, St.-Preux, or the citizens of *The Social Contract* ever really "grow up." At the end of the *Émile,* when Émile expects to become a father, he says to his tutor,

> God forbid that I let you also raise the son after having raised the father. God forbid that so holy and so sweet a duty should ever be fulfilled by anyone but myself. . . . But remain the master of the young masters. Advise us and govern us. We shall be docile. . . . I need you more than ever now that my functions as a man begin. You have fulfilled yours. Guide me so that I can imitate you. And take your rest. It is time. (*Émile,* 480)

The passage is somewhat ambiguous in tone. On the one hand, it is a declaration of Émile's willingness to assume an adult role in life. On the other hand, the language of mastery, docility, and need leave the impression that even the adult Émile will never be entirely self-governing.

This impression will be particularly strong for those who have a certain understanding of what it means to be "grown up," self-governing, or autonomous—an understanding that Rousseau does not share. If to be fully autonomous requires critical self-consciousness, or in this case the ability to stand outside of one's moral education and evaluate it critically, then Rousseauian autonomy falls short of the ideal. The same point can be made in considering Rousseau's vision of the free citizen.[60] The Rousseauian citizen is free as a subject of the general will and not primarily as an individual governed by his own reason. Consequently, Rousseau's citizens seem passive and docile when compared, for example, to Alexis de Tocqueville's portrait of an ideal democratic citizenry. Tocqueville's ideal citizen has a sense of his own efficacy; he is a "problem solver," active and proud.[61] A similar comparison could be made between Rousseau and John Locke. For Locke, a truly free human being not only adopts a position in accordance with reason, he adopts it through his own reason and not by uncritically accepting authoritative opinion.[62] While this view does operate in the education of Émile, Rousseau's citizens are certainly not noteworthy for their independence of mind. Rather, they are decisively governed by mores or authoritative opinions.[63] If freedom is understood to require full self-consciousness and to depend on the individual's capacity to govern himself according to reason, then Rousseau's ideal modes of governance do indeed sacrifice freedom to moral virtue.

But Rousseau is operating from a very different conception of freedom. Nothing illustrates this better than Rousseau's treatment of consent as the grounds for free government. Generally, for consent to be a meaningful act, it must be both voluntary and rational. In Rousseau's view, the case where the people consent to the laws, having been deceived as to their divine origins, qualifies as a genuine example of consent. Consent is voluntary in this case in the sense that there is no coercion involved and the people could choose otherwise than they do. Moreover, consent in this case is rational to the extent that accepting the obligation of the laws is a reasonable means to a reasonable end. In this, it can be contrasted with the case of consenting to slavery which Rousseau

---

60. See Zev M. Trachtenberg, *Making Citizens: Rousseau's Political Theory of Culture* (New York: Routledge, 1993), chap. 6, pp. 230–43.

61. Tocqueville, *Democracy in America*, vol. 2, pt. 2, chaps. 4–5.

62. See especially John Locke, *Of the Conduct of the Understanding*, in *John Locke, "Some Thoughts Concerning Education" and "Of the Conduct of the Understanding,"* ed. Ruth W. Grant and Nathan Tarcov (Indianapolis: Hackett Publishing Co., 1996).

63. This is clear in *Government of Poland*, in *Project for a Constitution for Corsica*, and in Rousseau's descriptions of Geneva in *Letter to M. D'Alembert* and the "Letter to the Citizens of Geneva" preceding the *Second Discourse*.

describes as "illegitimate and null" because a person who would do such a thing could not be "in his right mind." Consent to slavery is "absurd" and "inconceivable" (*S.C.*, I, iv, 49) whereas consent to the laws devised by the Legislator is a reasonable thing to do.

Nonetheless, it is not a rational action if that means an action guided by reason, deliberate, self-conscious, and informed. In the first place, the people do not understand what they are doing. The Legislator's laws are deliberately misrepresented to them as having the same status as the divine laws of nature. In their minds, accepting them is tantamount to accepting the law of gravity. They do not understand themselves to be granting legitimacy or creating their own obligations through their act of consent. Secondly, their consent is obtained under false pretenses, which compromises both its voluntariness and its rationality. The false pretenses are necessary because of the insufficiencies of reason, and they take the form of nonrational, symbolic appeals. Furthermore, these pretenses are necessary precisely because, without them, the inclinations of the people would most likely lead them to make the opposite choice. Their choice is manipulated, which makes it difficult to accept as an unconstrained voluntary action. Rousseau does not accept agreement secured under the threat of force as a legitimate example of consent. The constrained choice violates the principle of voluntariness.[64] A similar logic might be applied where choice is constrained by fraud.

In fairness to Rousseau, however, it must be acknowledged that consent theorists often allowed for legitimate consent to be something less than deliberate, self-conscious and fully informed. If consent were to be the only grounds for legitimate government, it had to include tacit or implied consent to avoid the conclusion that almost every government throughout history was illegitimate. The difficulties involved in making a strong argument for consent but allowing weak forms of consent are apparent in John Locke's political writing and they have received a great deal of discussion in Locke scholarship.[65] Curiously, little attention has

---

64. Contrast Hobbes, *Leviathan,* ed. C. B. Macpherson (Harmondsworth, U.K.: Penguin, 1968), pt. II, chap. 21, pp. 268–69.

65. See Ruth W. Grant, *John Locke's Liberalism* (Chicago: University of Chicago Press, 1987), 124–28, and 123 n. 30, for the literature on this controversial issue in Locke studies. See also Ruth W. Grant, "Locke's Political Anthropology and Lockean Individualism," *Journal of Politics* (Feb. 1988): 52–54.

been paid to this issue in Rousseau studies, though surely Rousseau's argument confronts many of the same difficulties as Locke's.

Locke allows for the legitimacy of tacit and unselfconscious acts of consent in early patriarchal societies but demands more explicit and deliberate forms of consent at later stages of political development.[66] It is clear in his political writings that express, deliberate, and informed action is always to be preferred. For Rousseau, like Locke, a legitimate act of consent need not be self-conscious and deliberate; free government may be established by actions that are not rational in every respect. But for Rousseau, unlike Locke, the development of consciousness and rationality are not always seen as improvements. In fact, their development threatens freedom. Both the *First Discourse* and the *Second* recount how the development of consciousness and rationality brings about the slavishness of the human race. Freedom is severed from individual reason in Rousseau's account in very important respects. I began this discussion by asking, For what reason is Rousseau willing to claim that consent obtained through deception establishes the freedom of the people? The answer is that in Rousseau's view self-consciousness is simply not a necessary requirement for freedom.

Freedom means the absence of personal dependence. In the terms of the social contract, each one "obeys only himself" (*S.C.,* I, vi, 53). Personal dependence is not only enslaving, it is the primary source of moral degradation, according to Rousseau.[67] To experience oneself as subject to another person's will is corrupting. Thus the most important aspect of freedom is the subjective experience of personal autonomy. Given this conception of freedom, Rousseau's models of governance do not require the sacrifice of freedom for virtue despite the manipulation involved. Rather, through manipulation and deception, freedom and virtue together are purchased at the price of a highly developed rational self-consciousness.[68]

This particular combination of goods can only be obtained through deception. Once moral education is accepted as a legiti-

66. Grant, "Locke's Political Anthropology," 53.

67. This issue is discussed further in chapter 5.

68. Always in Rousseau's writings sophisticated people are portrayed as corrupted and enslaved in contrast to free and virtuous simple folk.

mate aim of governance, the problem becomes how to shape another's will and at the same time leave it an autonomous will; i.e., how to secure both virtue and freedom. The problem is solved by a ruse that disguises the fact that any shaping has been done by a human agent. In the final analysis, the necessity of the deceit is itself an admission of the necessity of personal dependence, of authority, and of governance. Like it or not, we do depend on one another and we are formed by those dependencies. Only by hiding that fact from ourselves can we attain the greatest possible measure of autonomy. Free government and personal autonomy are possible, but they remain partial illusions always.

POLITICS AND DECEIT

Ironically, Rousseau, the apostle of sincerity and honesty, the critic of modern society for the manipulation and hypocrisy it breeds, recognizes the necessity of deceit in even the best case. And paradoxically, while personal dependence is the source of the deceitfulness of modern life Rousseau condemns, deceit is required precisely in order to escape personal dependence. Slave or free, corrupted or pure, deceit is inescapable. Moreover, Rousseau is able to defend political duplicity because in his view freedom does not require full disclosure. While Rousseau's thought is an important source of the modern turn toward personal sincerity, it is not Rousseau who seeks political honesty. Rather, it is Enlightenment liberalism that both requires and thinks possible honesty in politics. In aiming for an honest, open, and rational politics, it aims too high, in Rousseau's view, and is bound to be disappointed. Rousseau is more realistic and hence more pessimistic.

Rousseau and Machiavelli share a skepticism concerning the possibilities for rational politics that arises from a common appreciation of the dependencies that are at the root of political relationships and the manipulation and deceit that always accompany relations of dependence. Their understanding of the nature of political life stands as a sharply contrasting alternative to the Enlightenment liberal view. Enlightenment liberals exaggerate the potential political efficacy of reason and minimize the power of force and will. And because they mistakenly believe that the impossible is possible, they are too quick to condemn what is in fact, according to Rousseau, our best possibility.

Because Rousseau accepts manipulation and deceit as inescapable, the serious question for him becomes how to distinguish beneficial manipulation and acceptable lies from the destructive and unacceptable kind. This discussion has brought to light some of the criteria according to which Rousseau makes these distinctions. A tolerable compromise, acceptable lie, or beneficial manipulation always remains faithful to the moral truth, promotes justice as far as possible given the particular circumstances, is prompted by disinterested motives, and does not require the compromise of personal integrity. The man of integrity may make prudential calculations and must consider the consequences of his actions when making ethical and political judgments. Prudence is not in itself a threat to integrity.[69]

While prudence sometimes requires deception, all deception is not alike. Rousseau makes a sharp distinction between deception that is self-aggrandizing and deception that is self-effacing. The former is a hypocritical form of deceit: one pretends to greater virtues than one possesses in fact. The latter is deception that is neither hypocritical nor self-serving but rather noble in character. The Legislator and the tutor are almost literally self-effacing in their attempts to render their own authority invisible. Self-effacing deception is compatible with integrity, while hypocrisy is a sure sign of corruption.

These are some of the distinctions Rousseau develops in considering what might be required for his principles of political right and personal morality to operate in practice. The evaluation of Rousseauian prudence challenged the claim that fanaticism is implied by Rousseau's political thought. Rousseau's conception of integrity allows for prudential judgment and thus does not require fanatical politics in the name of sustaining a pure inner state. Yet, Rousseau's prudential politics is depicted only with respect to extremely rare cases (viz., Geneva, Poland, and Corsica), ancient cases (Sparta, Rome, and the Hebrews), or in his fiction (*Émile* or *Julie*). These depictions establish in principle how we should think about politics and how we might act politically with integ-

---

69. But, still unlike the *honnête homme,* Rousseau's man of integrity is to be admired more for his disinterestedness than for his judgment.

rity. But whether Rousseau offers any practical guidance for political ethics in the modern world is still open to serious doubt. We are entitled to wonder why the positive possibilities are so rarely actualized in human history according to Rousseau. And we need to understand better why Rousseau is so skeptical of any claims that the development of human rationality will enhance those possibilities.

Thus we turn in the next chapter to the subject of corruption. Why is corruption inevitable in Rousseau's view? In investigating the sources of corruption as Rousseau portrays them in the *First* and *Second Discourses,* the role of the development of rational consciousness will become clear. The development of man's rational capacities is inseparable from the evolution of vanity, in Rousseau's account, and is thus a major threat to integrity as well as to freedom. Integrity is threatened not by prudence but by personal dependence and by intellectual sophistication, because both are psychologically bound to vanity. To maintain one's integrity, then, would seem to require a posture of detachment from modern society, defined as it is precisely by the continual growth of dependence and sophistication. The discussion that follows thus addresses an alternative opinion, outlined earlier, concerning the political implications of Rousseau's thought, viz., that it leads not to fanaticism but to withdrawal.

5

Rousseau's Political Ethics
Corruption, Dependence, and Vanity

INTRODUCTION

One of Rousseau's central political aims was to alter the standards of ethical judgment so that people would come to revile what they had hitherto admired and to admire what they had previously held in contempt. He was equally critical of the status quo and of the alternative standards of progressive social critics of his day. In opposition to both, Rousseau developed an ideal of integrity that has tremendous critical import. Once his readers apprehend his vision of natural purity, goodness, and simplicity, the sight of the modern world becomes repugnant; the greatest glories of civilization appear as nothing more than the telltale signs of degeneration, corruption, and decay. How does Rousseau bring about this great revolution in vision? How do we come to recognize corruption for what it is?

Rousseau's first step is to present his readers with attractive images of an earlier or original uncorrupted condition to serve as a standard. This is the initial task of the *First* and *Second Discourses*. But once he persuades us that men are naturally good and that integrity is our first condition, he must then explain why integrity is now so rare. How does corruption take place at all? Why is it ubiquitous and, apparently, inevitable? We need to know both the meaning of corruption and its sources if we wish to assess Rousseau's estimate of the power of corrupting forces and of the inevitability of degeneration.

Moreover, the process of corruption takes place on several different levels: in the soul of each individual human being, in the history of the species, and in the development of societies. These developments are not necessarily simultaneous, and the question arises whether there are resources for the individual to resist the forces of corruption even if he finds himself in a corrupted society in an historically degenerate period. It may be that, if Rousseau has taught us well to recognize corruption when we see it, our only option is to withdraw into solitude if we wish to preserve our personal integrity. But it is also possible that understanding the process of corruption and the precise threats to integrity will allow us to better guard against them.

There are three distinct but interrelated sources of corruption: intellectual progress, the development of *amour-propre,* and personal dependence. Each is a threat to personal integrity to the extent to which it stimulates vanity. We learn from Rousseau to recognize as corrupt anything that either produces or is produced by vanity. Intellectual progress does both. At a minimum, it produces comparative ideas like "better" and "worse" without which vanity would be simply impossible. *Amour-propre,* which can be characterized as the desire to be preferred, awakens with the first need of other human beings. Once that need takes the form of personal dependence, *amour-propre* manifests itself primarily as vanity.[1] Because vanity and dependence are inevitably accompanied by hypocrisy (as people wish to appear to have those qualities that please those on whom they depend), hypocrisy emerges as the most significant indicator of corruption in Rousseau's view. Like Machiavelli, Rousseau sees dependency relations among those with conflicting interests as the source of hypocritical behavior. But Rousseau adds that the psychological companion of hypocritical behavior is vanity with all its corrosive effects. In Rousseau's view, vanity is the intractable problem at the root of social, political, and economic corruption. It is only

---

1. *Amour-propre* is the kind of self-love that depends on recognition and therefore on social relationships. In this it differs from *amour de soi,* which is self-concern of a sort that can occur in isolation, like a concern for self-preservation. *Amour-propre* can be manifested positively, as pride or self-esteem, or negatively, as vanity. See *Projet de constitution pour la Corse, O.C.,* III, 937–8. See also *Émile,* 213–5; *Rousseau, Juge de Jean-Jacques,* First Dialogue, *O.C.,* I, 668–69: "[A]mour-de-soi, which is a good and absolute feeling, becomes *amour-propre,* which is to say a relative feeling by which one compares; which demands preferences, whose enjoyment is purely negative, and which no longer seeks satisfaction in our own benefit but solely in the harm of another."

because Rousseau can imagine social relationships that are not afflicted by the corrosive effects of this passion that he can provide some guidance for maintaining integrity in a corrupted world.

THE MEANING AND SOURCES OF CORRUPTION

Rousseau identifies a wide variety of phenomena as corrupt: the decline of martial valor produced by luxury; physical illness and weakness; flattery of those on whom you depend; and actions against duty for the sake of gain. All of these are corrupt.[2] The variety indicates both the core meaning of the concept and the difficulty with its usage. Whether applied to physical, moral, or political phenomena, corruption means change for the worse by a process of decay. A corrupted thing has deteriorated from its natural, healthy, innocent, or virtuous condition (each a legitimate antonym for "corrupt").

But of course this formal definition is useless as a guide for recognizing when something is corrupt, since it does not specify what it means to change "for the worse." For example, in the *First Discourse,* Rousseau identifies as corrupting precisely those developments identified by Enlightenment thinkers as the greatest achievements of a progressive human history.[3] He makes his case by recurring to particular criteria for judging the health of a political society (for instance, the ability to conquer rather than be conquered). What constitutes corruption and what constitutes progress can be determined only with reference to some such independent criteria. But to establish those criteria and to identify something as corrupt requires knowledge of the pristine condition of the thing in question.

Rousseau illustrates the difficulty in an ironic and amusing fashion with a citation from Aristotle on the title page of the *Second Discourse.* "Not in corrupted things, but in those that are well placed according to nature, should one consider that which

2. These examples are taken from the *First Discourse.* Yves Lévy suggests some interesting comparisons with Machiavelli's understanding of corruption in the *Discourses.* Lévy, "Machiavel et Rousseau," 169–74.

3. Rousseau added "or corrupt" to his statement of the question posed by the Academy. Their question was, "Has the restoration of the sciences and arts tended to purify morals?"

is natural."[4] Aristotle makes this remark in defense of his argument for the naturalness of slavery. Rousseau uses it to preface his case for the naturalness of equality and freedom. Clearly, Aristotle and Rousseau do not share an understanding of what is according to nature. Rousseau's task in the *Second Discourse* is to lead his readers to recognize inequality as a corrupted condition of corrupted men by creating a new vision of the original, natural state. It is a vision of independence, health, happiness, peace, and plenty. Rousseau's very use of the language of "corruption," where he might have spoken simply of change, development, or history, has the effect of reinforcing his theoretical defense of this vision. He is arguing that men are not originally or naturally evil or contentious. If the species begins in a good and healthy condition, then the process of change must be a process of decay.[5]

Yet it is not a simple linear decline. It is critically important to see how human progress and corruption are inextricably intertwined, for it is that vision which grounds Rousseau's rejection of any hope for humanity arising from the further development of our rational faculties or of civilization altogether. Progress cannot be a purifying force; it cannot even be a bulwark against corruption. On the contrary, human perfectibility, while it is a unique capacity, is nonetheless inseparable from corruption and highly problematic for human beings.

Rousseau's account of human history begins with the natural condition of vigor, innocence, and peace. Consequently he immediately must confront a problem that does not arise for someone like Hobbes, for example. It is not difficult to explain why men might wish to change their original condition if that condition is a state of war.[6] But if the natural condition of man is one

---

4. See *Politics*, 1.5.1254a. Rousseau uses the Latin: "Non in depravitis, sed in his quae bene secundum naturam se habent, considerandum est quid sit naturale." The Greek is, "dei de skopein en tois kata phusein exousi mallon to phusei, kai ma en tois diephtharmenois."

5. Rousseau can be contrasted both with Aristotle, for whom the original is not the standard for the natural, and with Freud, for whom the natural is not the standard for the good. Corruption for either Aristotle or Freud might mean precisely a return to the original condition.

6. It is difficult, of course, to explain how the change can be brought about on Hobbesian assumptions. Hobbes has recourse to religion to solve the problem. "[B]efore the time of Civill Society, or in the interruption thereof by Warre, there is nothing

of happiness and harmony, one must account for the changes that have produced the misery we see everywhere around us. "Man is born free, and everywhere he is in chains." This famous statement from *The Social Contract* (I, i) suggests the very question that occupies much of the discussion of the *Second Discourse:* what causes human corruption?

This question can be taken in two ways. It asks what the specific sources of corruption are, but it also raises the prior question as to how it is possible for a species to become corrupt at all. Corruption, in whatever form, is a process that takes place over time. Cumulative degeneration is possible only for a species that is capable of a history. Surprisingly enough, in Rousseau's view, the possibility of corruption is thus a mark of *the* distinguishing characteristic of humanity, its historicality. And again, surprisingly, Rousseau calls this unique human capacity "the faculty of self-perfection." In other words, perfectibility is the cause of corruption in that it makes corruption possible. Certainly this requires explanation.

Human beings are uniquely capable of making permanent changes in their constitution both as individuals and as a species.

> [T]he faculty of self-perfection [is] a faculty which, with the aid of circumstances, successively develops all the others, and resides among us as much in the species as in the individual. By contrast an animal is at the end of a few months what it will be all its life; and its species is at the end of a thousand years what it was the first year of that thousand. (*Second,* 114–15)

Perfectibility is the preeminent distinguishing feature of human beings.

But perfectibility is impossible without man's other distinguishing characteristic, freedom.[7] Freedom is understood here as the capacity to acquiesce in or to resist the promptings of me-

---

can strengthen a Covenant of Peace agreed on . . . but the feare of that Invisible Power, which they every one Worship as God." *Leviathan,* pt. I, chap. 14, p. 200. There is an interesting comparison here to Rousseau's recourse to religion at the founding of civil society.

7. And as between perfectibility and freedom, perfectibility has a certain preeminence. Whereas there is "some room for dispute" as to the status of freedom, "there can be no dispute" about perfectibility as a distinctly human characteristic (*Second,* 114). Moreover, in a lengthy note concerning the status of orangutans, Rousseau refers

chanical nature. Man is not simply governed by instinct. He can choose where nature is silent or resist its commands. Freedom thus understood is possible without perfectibility. Choices might simply have no cumulative effects. But the contrary is not the case. If man's actions were simply governed by instinct or by any natural mechanical process, there could be no development over time, no possibility for the individual to acquire a "second nature" or for the species to acquire civilization. What makes human freedom particularly meaningful is that it can produce history: the choices people make have lasting consequences. Thus perfectibility, because it is the faculty that accounts for development, is itself the source of human corruption in the sense that it makes degeneration possible as well.

But if this is what Rousseau means by "the faculty of self-perfection," why does he use this term instead of, for example, "the capacity for development," or even "corruptibility"? His choice of language here seems oddly Aristotelean. The individual is depicted as a composite of potentialities that are actualizable by virtue of a particular faculty of self-perfection. The implication is that the individual's original condition is defective or, at the very least, incomplete. By actualizing these potentialities, a man can become what he is by nature. Rousseau, of course, does not reach this last Aristotelean conclusion. In Rousseau's account, the perfection of man's faculties is not equivalent to the perfection of man or to the fulfillment of his natural end. Instead, the progressive development of human capabilities destroys man's natural happiness forever.

Nonetheless, Rousseau refers to this development as "self-perfection" because natural man is indeed deficient and incomplete. Rousseau depicts natural man as human before he is capable of rational operations more sophisticated than those of other animals; reason is not considered among the defining characteristics of the human species (Second, 114). Memory, foresight, judgment, even the ability to make simple comparisons, are all acquired characteristics (Second, 135, 137, 143, 145). Pride, love, indeed all the passions save pity are also the products of development. The savage is, after all, a stupid and unfeeling brute. Rous-

---

to "the faculty of perfecting itself" as "the specific characteristic of the human species" without mentioning freedom at all (Second, 208).

seau nowhere recommends a return to the savage state. A human being who loses his historical acquisitions becomes lower than the beasts.

> Why is man alone subject to becoming imbecile? Is it not that he thereby returns to his primitive state; and . . . losing again . . . all that his *perfectibility* had made him acquire, thus falls back lower than the beast itself? (*Second*, 115)

Moreover, only after man emerges from his natural condition of complete independence does he reach "the happiest and most durable epoch" (*Second*, 151). The development of social institutions cannot be simply condemned as corrupting. Rousseau even concedes that the perfection of the individual is possible only within a highly developed civilization, although individual progress may take place at the expense of the species (*First*, 35–36; see also *Second*, 148–50, 156).

Thus Rousseau's account of man's origins and development is not a simple story of an idyllic beginning followed by gradual degeneration along a continuous downward slope. Instead, it is an account of progress and corruption proceeding hand in hand in a complex process in which incremental changes in one direction spur further developments in the other. Development brings enlightenment and virtues as well as error and vices, and the fact that these develop in tandem is by no means accidental. As a particularly important example, the intellectual ability to make comparisons is a prerequisite for the development of vanity, while vanity in turn motivates the development of the intellect.[8] Paradoxically, the perfection of man is itself the source of his corruption, *and* vice versa.[9] In Rousseau's account, the best and the worst for the species often flow from the same source.[10]

8. See *First*, 48, and *Second*, 175; compare *Second*, 179. Generally, "human understanding owes much to the passions, which by common agreement also owe much to it." *Second*, 115–16.

9. It might seem as though Rousseau is simply saying that intellectual progress is accompanied by a corruption of the passions, particularly when considering the *First Discourse*. But Rousseau's position is more complicated than that. Progress and decay proceed simultaneously even when considering the development of the sentiments alone. For example, love results from a progressive development of the passions but is always associated with jealousy. *Second*, 148–49.

10. For example, see Rousseau's use of the Prometheus myth in the *First Discourse*, 47–48.

The *First Discourse* illustrates the point. In this work, Rousseau attempts to establish the links between the perfection of human intellectual capacities and the corruption of morals and politics. On the one hand, the development of the arts and sciences necessarily creates new needs that prepare men for servitude. Enlightenment leads to urbanity and a culture where hypocrisy is the dominant mode of social interaction. Increasingly dependent and needy, and able to conceal themselves from one another, people become increasingly vicious. The development of the arts and sciences corrupts by replacing our original freedom, goodness, and simplicity with servitude, vice, and hypocrisy. On the other hand, "the sciences and the arts owe their birth to our vices" (*First,* 48, 50). And it is vanity that spurs their continued development. There is a symbiotic spiral of cause and effect between the perfection of human faculties and human degradation. Each is the cause of the other.

For this reason, Rousseau argues, it is utter foolishness to look to the development of the human rational faculties and their products in the arts and sciences for resources for resisting corruption, maintaining integrity, sustaining progress, or overturning tyrants. He thoroughly rejects the project of Enlightenment rationalists. Sophistication cannot save us from corruption; the two go hand in hand. Rousseau's attempt to demonstrate that sophistication and corruption are inseparable resonates with the implications of the language itself. In English, "to sophisticate" is synonymous with "to adulterate" or "to corrupt." The same can be said in French.[11] On account of our distinctive human capacity for development, the "faculty of self-perfection," we are doomed to continual progress, progress which will always be a mixed blessing at best.

In the *First Discourse,* Rousseau asserts that the development of the arts and sciences is linked with slavery, vice, and hypocrisy, but he fails to provide a complete argument explaining the dynamics of the connections between them. In a general sense, the development of the arts and sciences is one source of corruption. But in the *Second Discourse* Rousseau provides a more complete

---

11. *Grand Larousse,* 6:5598. For examples of usage from Voltaire, Montesquieu, and others, see Émile Littré, *Dictionnaire de la langue française,* tome 7 (Paris: Gallimard and Hachette, 1958), 281–82.

analysis of the process of corruption, one that goes beyond considerations of the effects of intellectual development alone. We turn to the *Second Discourse* for Rousseau's understanding of the specific sources of corruption and of the dynamics of the process that brings it about.

Having initially tried to persuade readers of the *Second Discourse* of the proposition that people are naturally good, Rousseau must demonstrate the corollary; that human evil is the product of an historical process.[12] According to Rousseau, that process is set in motion by the introduction of social, economic, and, eventually, political inequalities. But these developments have their sources in turn. Once people have been brought into continual contact with one another, two revolutions in human affairs (one in sexuality and one in knowledge) introduce inequality with all its concomitant evils. But even this is not the whole story. It turns out on closer inspection that neither the developments in sexuality and knowledge nor the inequalities they produce are corrupting in and of themselves. All these things have their greatest negative effects only because the development of *amour-propre* is associated with them.

Consider the transformation in sexuality Rousseau describes. Natural sexuality, which is perfectly innocent among savage people, is transformed with the development of sexual preference. Sexual preference emerges only after people have begun to live in groups and only after they have developed the capacity to make comparisons. People begin to compare, and thus develop the idea of inequality, long before inequalities are instituted among them. The ability to compare is an intellectual development that has immediate moral consequences. The ideas of better and worse lead people to desire to be among the best and to be considered as such. *Amour-propre* is born and soon after takes the form of vanity. With vanity comes the possibility of insult, and vengeance appears on the scene. Vanity and vengeance are corrupt and cor-

---

12. Like the Biblical account of the Fall, Rousseau's account initially attributes the genesis of evil to knowledge and to sexuality. But unlike the Biblical account, in Rousseau's tale the loss of innocence does not result from a deliberate act of an individual human will. An evil act in the primal state of individual isolation that Rousseau describes is almost inconceivable. See also Starobinski, *Jean-Jacques Rousseau: Transparency and Obstruction,* 290.

rupting passions unknown to the savage. These passions arise in conjunction with sexual preference and produce their most terrible effects when joined with sexuality. Love, the gentlest and sweetest of human sentiments, produces violent jealousies, bloodshed, and cruelty. In this case again, the best and the worst of human possibilities are indissolubly linked (*Second*, 134–35, 146–50).

The second major source of corruption is an economic revolution sparked by advances in knowledge, viz., the arts of metallurgy and agriculture. These advances produce revolutionary changes because they forever destroy economic self-sufficiency. The new economic order introduces division of labor among men (in addition to the division of labor between men and women established earlier), division of property, and economic inequalities. But in what way does economic inequality cause moral corruption? Economic inequality certainly produces the relative economic misery of the poor, but it is not at all obvious that it will produce moral degradation. Rousseau, however, insists that it does, and this claim is central to his effort in the *Second Discourse*. Despite the title of the piece, he is as interested in persuading his readers of the devastating effects of inequality as he is in explaining its origins.

In Rousseau's view, universal corruption is born of inequality because inequality creates a system of personal dependence for masters as well as slaves, rich as well as poor. Similarly, sexual preference, and not sexuality simply, is corrupting because it too creates dependence. Even dependence on things can be a source of moral corruption. This is the thought that animates Rousseau's attacks on technology and on false "needs."[13] If there is something you cannot do without, you are subject to those who are able to provide it.

> [S]ince the bonds of servitude are formed only from the mutual dependence of men and the reciprocal needs that unite them, it is impossible to enslave a man without first putting him in the position of being unable to do without another. (*Second*, 140)

13. Dependence on things produces moral corruption when it implies further dependence on human beings. In and of itself, it produces only physical corruption (*Second*, 100–13). See also Schwartz, *Sexual Politics*, 14–15.

Dependence is corrupting in two respects. First, to depend on the will of another is in itself, and almost by definition, a corruption of your natural status as a free man. Second and more important, dependence produces vice as well as servility. It is a profoundly corrupting status in a moral sense.

Rousseau describes the moral impact of economic dependence in the following terms:

> [B]ehold man, due to a multitude of new needs, subjected so to speak to all of nature and especially to his fellowmen, whose slave he becomes in a sense even in becoming their master; rich, he needs their services; poor, he needs their help; and mediocrity cannot enable him to do without them. He must therefore incessantly seek to interest them in his fate, and to make them find their own profit, in fact or in appearance, in working for his. This makes him deceitful and sly with some, imperious and harsh with others, and makes it necessary for him to abuse all those whom he needs when he cannot make them fear him and does not find his interest in serving them usefully. Finally, consuming ambition, the fervor to raise one's relative fortune less out of true need than in order to place oneself above others, inspires in all men a base inclination to harm each other, a secret jealousy all the more dangerous because, in order to strike its blow in greater safety, it often assumes the mask of benevolence: in a word, competition and rivalry on one hand, opposition of interest on the other; and always the hidden desire to profit at the expense of others. All these evils are the first effect of property and the inseparable consequence of nascent inequality. (*Second,* 156)

The economic revolution adds ambition and hypocrisy to vanity and vengeance in the development of human psychology. The human heart becomes so corrupt that the natural sentiment of pity is replaced in all men by "a base inclination to harm each other."

As one would expect, in describing the process of corruption that proceeds from dependence, Rousseau explicitly details the destruction of each of the elements of integrity we identified in chapter 3. Dependence produces a man who is fragmented, vain, vengeful, slavish, deceitful, ambitious, self-interested, and corrupt in the particular sense that his virtues give way before the slightest temptation and are nothing but a "mask of benevolence" to cover his self-aggrandizement. Corrupted man is portrayed as the opposite of the man of integrity in every respect, and this confirms that the elements of integrity were identified correctly in the initial discussion of it.

We are now in a position to refine the sense in which dependence causes corruption. The root of the problem is the dependence on the opinion of others, which is to say, *amour-propre*. As we have seen, economic inequality is most destructive morally when tied to "the fervor to raise one's relative fortune less out of true need than in order to place oneself above others" (*Second,* 156). Similarly, the social revolution comes about when public esteem first becomes important: "Each one began to look at the others and to want to be looked at himself . . . and that was the first step toward inequality and, at the same time, toward vice" (*Second,* 149). Inequality itself arises in this case from the desire for preeminence and the aversion to being overlooked.

According to Rousseau, the concern for reputation is a predominantly destructive force whether as the fear of embarrassment or as the desire for distinction. The fear of embarrassment figures repeatedly in the *Confessions* as the cause of immoral behavior. The incident of the stolen ribbon is one of many such examples. And as for the desire for distinction, he wrote: "to this ardor to be talked about, to this furor to distinguish oneself, which nearly always keeps us outside of ourselves, we owe what is best and worst among men . . . that is to say, a multitude of bad things as against a small number of good ones" (*Second,* 175). Dependence on opinion emerges as the true source of corruption.

This is as true of political relations as it is of social and economic ones in Rousseau's account. Rousseau describes the historical stages of the degeneration of governments until they reach the extreme of their corruption in tyranny and arbitrary power. The source of this decay is said to be ambition. But Rousseau does not focus on the political ambitions of rulers or potential rulers, as one might expect. Instead, he stresses the pervasive ambition of citizens to rise in the social hierarchy once a system of civil and political inequalities has been instituted. Each wishes to achieve a position of superiority with respect to some others and will gladly yield his independence in order to achieve some small degree of honor, reputation, or dominance. Ambition is a weakness; only this desire to dominate allows one to be dominated.

It is also a need—a need for the obedience or deference of others (*Second,* 172–75). In Rousseau's view, it is not power that corrupts but the desire for preeminence, a desire that can be found in almost everyone. Moreover, the desire for preeminence is not only morally corrupting, it also creates a personal psychological dependence that destroys natural freedom. This is why political power cannot serve as an avenue by which to secure autonomy, as it does in Machiavelli's writings. The powerful in Rousseau's accounts are always at least as servile and corrupted as the powerless by the situation of inequality in which they find themselves. They are utterly dependent on those who serve and obey them.

In every case, whether in discussing politics, sexuality, intellectual development, or economics, whatever evils might be inherent in hierarchy are infinitely exacerbated by the passion for recognition, ambition, or vanity. And if moral corruption is the issue, *amour-propre* is always at its root. In concluding the *Second Discourse,* Rousseau describes the results of the historical transformation of the human soul that created social beings where once there were only savages. The "true cause" of all their differences, he writes, is this:

> [T]he savage lives within himself; the sociable man, always outside of himself, knows how to live only in the opinion of others; and it is, so to speak, from their judgment alone that he draws the sentiment of his own existence. (*Second,* 179)

The transformation of natural man, free and good, into social man, dependent and corrupt, is fundamentally a psychological transformation.

Rousseau attributes all the vices associated with corruption to the desire for esteem, rank, or status in a system of social hierarchy. This is a central Rousseauian concern and a critical one for the political implications of his thought. Charles Taylor has written of the contemporary "politics of recognition" as an inheritance from Rousseau. In his view, Rousseau is the source of the demand that political life must satisfy the desire for esteem. In searching for a positive way to meet this demand, Rousseau rejects both a hierarchical system of honor and a Stoical indifference to public esteem in favor of a politics where all virtuous citizens are equally honored. Today, various groups seek public recognition of their claims to equal dignity as much as they seek equality of rights. Whether or not this was Rousseau's intention, one of the effects of his influence, in Taylor's view, has been to accentuate the desire for recognition in modern politics.[14]

Another effect of his influence has been to strengthen the view that inauthenticity or hypocrisy is the preeminent vice.[15] After all, these are the most direct manifestations of an excessive concern for the opinion of others. For followers of Rousseau, inauthenticity becomes emblematic of all the evils of society; hypocrisy *is* corruption. But for Rousseau himself, it is not that inauthenticity is itself the greatest evil, but that this "living outside of oneself" is the psychological mechanism that gives rise to the vices. *Amour-propre* in conditions of inequality leads people to care more for appearance than for reality; it compromises their independence; it destroys the unity of the self; most important, it leads people to do evil.

Rousseau's understanding of *amour-propre* is clearly important for his politics. But does Rousseau sufficiently explain its genesis and power? The desire for esteem is the source of corruption and even initially of social inequality. But what is the source of that desire? And is it true that dependence is always accompanied by the more negative forms of this passion, vanity and ambition, with all their destructive effects? A variety of political possibilities are brought to light by a critical analysis of Rousseau's position with respect to these questions.

AMOUR-PROPRE

According to Rousseau, "living outside of oneself" arises as inequalities are first recognized and then instituted. These are distinct moments in human history and the distinction between them is important. First, people acquire the capacity to make comparisons, recognize inequality, and rank things as better or worse. This purely intellectual capacity is both the ground for the possibility of *amour-propre* and the initial source of the sentiment of *amour-propre*. As soon as some things are recognized as better than others, one can develop the desire to be better and

14. Charles Taylor, *Multiculturalism and "The Politics of Recognition"* (Princeton: Princeton University Press, 1992).

15. Compare Judith Shklar, *Ordinary Vices* (Cambridge, Mass.: Belknap Press, 1984), who argues that cruelty, and not hypocrisy, is the preeminent vice.

to be recognized as such. Rousseau describes pride and vanity arising out of the mere recognition of inequalities. People "acquire ideas of merit and beauty *which produce* sentiments of preference" (*Second,* 148, emphasis added). As soon as savage man can intellectually apprehend his superiority to the beasts, he feels a pride that prepares him to "claim first rank as an individual" (*Second,* 144). In early human societies, people begin to make comparisons and to develop preferences, and soon each wishes to be the most highly considered by the others (*Second,* 149).

The striking thing about Rousseau's account is that, while preeminence can serve as a means to secure the satisfaction of other desires, the genesis of the desire for preeminence, according to Rousseau, is not tied to self-interest. Instead, it arises as a necessary concomitant of particular intellectual developments, and it continues to have a life of its own. People desire preference for its own sake apart from the tangible benefits that may attach to it, and they simply cannot stand the contempt of their fellows. For a victim of a wrong, the contempt associated with it is "often more unbearable than the harm itself" (*Second,* 149).

Why should this be so? It really is not obvious that the new intellectual capacity to recognize better and worse alone should induce in the sentiments of the individual the desire to be the best. For example, the savage man who comes to recognize his superiority to the beasts might simply appreciate the usefulness of his superior survival skills rather than take pride in himself on account of them. Or, the person who comes to recognize that there are better and worse dancers might wish to dance well. But certainly that desire is independent of the desire to be applauded for it. Why is the applause of one's fellows a satisfying thing in and of itself? And to take one further step, how do we come to want that applause even when we know that we cannot dance well?

Rousseau does not answer these questions fully in the *Second Discourse.* He does not classify vanity and pride as natural sentiments; if he did, he would have to abandon the major premise of his argument, viz., that men are naturally good.[16] Instead, he describes the first appearance of *amour-propre* as an automatic, even "natural," consequence of the earliest intellectual develop-

---

16. See Melzer, *Natural Goodness,* introduction.

ment. In so doing, he seems to make the same sort of error that he attributes to his predecessors, such as Hobbes, who tried to describe what people must have been like in the state of nature: he assumes that uncorrupted men will react as modern corrupted ones do (*Second,* 120, 129–30). He assumes that, if there is a hierarchy of better and worse, even men in the state of nature will need to be considered among the best.

A more complete explanation can be found in *Émile* and in the *Dialogues.*[17] *Amour-propre* begins with the ability to compare, which implies judgment. It is natural to prefer whatever we judge to be better than something else. But the desire to be preferred by others arises only with the development of society, with the need of others, and especially with the preference for a particular sexual partner. We want to be chosen by the one we have chosen. And once a person has experienced the pleasures of these loving sentiments, he will seek those pleasures more broadly and will pursue the positive regard of friends and others. From our desire to be preferred by others arises our tendency to assess our own worth on the basis of comparisons with others. *Amour-propre* thus emerges from an interaction of judgment and desire that is only possible in the context of established social relations.[18]

Amour-propre gradually develops and intensifies as social inequality increases and becomes institutionalized. It might even seem as if this passion is simply a byproduct of social inequality. And it is tempting to interpret Rousseau in this way—as if *amour-propre* were simply a useful attribute for people who find themselves in positions of dependence within a hierarchical social system. *Amour-propre* could then be understood as the handmaiden of self-interest in modern conditions of inequality. This interpre-

17. See *Émile,* 213–15, and *Rousseau, Juge de Jean-Jacques,* First Dialogue, *O.C.,* I, 668–72; Second Dialogue, *O.C.,* I, 804–7. I am indebted to Christopher Kelly on this point.

18. In fact, in such a context the development of *amour-propre* is not only possible, it is inevitable: "This species of passion, not having its germ in children's hearts, cannot be born in them of itself; it is we alone who put it there. . . . But this is no longer the case with the young man's heart. Whatever we may do, these passions will be born in spite of us" (*Émile,* 215).

It could be argued that the desire to be preferred arises much earlier than adolescence in the child's relationship with its mother. If that were the case, Rousseau's arguments both for natural asociality and for the unnaturalness of *amour-propre* would be weakened considerably.

tation is tempting because it would mean that the continued degradation of human life is not inevitable, since a change in social and economic institutions might radically alter man's moral psychology. Furthermore, it would mean that intellectual progress need not be accompanied by moral corruption. Vanity would find its roots in self-interest, rather than in the intellectual ability to compare and the increased occasions for comparison that sophistication brings, and the arts and sciences might be freed from the opprobrium heaped on them by Rousseau. And indeed, the argument that vanity has its source in self-interest has a certain plausibility. Within a hierarchical system of mutual dependence, it is foolish at the least and often seriously self-destructive to ignore the opinions and judgments of those on whom you depend. Obviously, it is often necessary both for workers to flatter the boss and for the boss to worry about his reputation. Manipulative and abusive behavior are necessities of the system in these circumstances, and, as we saw, this is precisely what Rousseau describes as the major moral effect of the revolution in metallurgy and agriculture.

But even after this second revolution, when concern for one's reputation could be understood to be useful, Rousseau describes it as a destructive concern. There are certainly reasons why people become vain, jealous, ambitious, and vengeful under conditions of inequality, but these passions cannot be understood as serving their interests. Moreover, in Rousseau's account, *amour-propre* is an independent motivating force unrestricted by considerations of utility. Ambition always exceeds true need. People seek vengeance for insults as well as reparation for injuries. Vanity is not limited by self-interest. In fact, *amour-propre* often leads people to act against their interest; that is one of its distinguishing features. To illustrate the difference between *amour de soi* and *amour-propre,* Rousseau uses the jealous lover who becomes more concerned with destroying his rival than with securing the affections of his beloved.[19] Moreover, by tying *amour-propre* to the intellectual development that is the inevitable result of man's perfectibility, Rousseau gives it a foundation that is independent both of self-interest and of the institutions of inequality.[20] *Amour-*

---

19. *Rousseau, Juge de Jean-Jacques,* First Dialogue, *O.C.,* I, 668.
20. Ibid., Second Dialogue, 806.

propre first appears before inequality is institutionalized. It should be recalled that *amour-propre* is not only a product of institutionalized inequality but also one of its sources. *Amour-propre* might be transformed, but it could never be eradicated by restructuring social and economic institutions. The consequences of this position for the political implications of Rousseau's thought are profound.

In Rousseau's view, *amour-propre* is a powerful human passion that must find some satisfaction in public life. Were vanity understood exclusively as a consequence of self-interest, were the desire to please merely an instrument for securing gains from those on whom you depend, were the thirst for distinction only the common companion of greed and nothing more, their political importance would be considerably diminished. The pleasures of recognition would be one of a number of exchangeable benefits, and the desire for revenge might be pacified by the acquisition of other sorts of goods. Political problems then might be resolved simply by negotiating differences of interest. But this is not Rousseau's view. The rage provoked by injured vanity, for example, is a permanent political danger. And the feeling of *amour-propre* itself "no longer seeks satisfaction in our own benefit, but solely in the harm of another."[21] The family of political passions associated with *amour-propre* (e.g., vanity, envy, ambition, vengeance, pride) create political problems that are much more difficult to resolve than conflicts of interest, if they are resolvable at all.

In giving *amour-propre* an independent status and a central place in his thought, Rousseau again opposes rationalistic, utilitarian, and interest-based views of politics. His opposition includes an implicit criticism of the Enlightenment rationalists' overly optimistic estimations of the possibilities for politics. Rousseau, for example, is pessimistic about the project for perpetual peace designed by the Abbé de St.-Pierre. While he concedes that it would be in the true interests of the monarchs of Europe to adopt the proposal, he argues that their ambitions and those of their ministers would prevent them from ever adopting it.[22]

Again, Rousseau resembles Machiavelli in this. Machiavelli

---

21. Ibid., First Dialogue, 669.
22. Jean-Jacques Rousseau, "Judgment on Perpetual Peace," in *A Project of Perpetual Peace,* trans. Edith M. Nuttall (London: Richard Cobden-Sanderson, 1927), 101–13.

too treats the concern for the opinion of others, particularly in the political form of the desire for honor and glory, as an independent motivating force. One sure way to make a political mistake is to underestimate its power. The Samnites made this mistake with respect to the Romans (*D.,* II, 23, p. 351; III, 40–41; see also II, 14, III, 26). A prince must take care to secure the admiration of his subjects and to avoid their contempt. Admiration for greatness can go a long way toward compensating for the absence of goodness in a prince (*Pr.,* chap. 19, pp. 72, 77; chap. 21, p. 88). Moreover, Machiavelli recognizes that, for some, dishonor is worse than death. He does remark that, for most men, the death of their father is a less serious injury than the loss of their patrimony, which seems to imply that self-interest is all that counts. But he also contends that the rape of a man's wife is not so easily forgiven (*Pr.,* chap. 17, p. 67; chap. 19. p. 72). The man who can accept the murder of his father, but not the rape of his wife, can only be reacting to the contempt for his own person, the insult to his honor, attached to the latter crime.[23] Machiavelli, like Rousseau, appreciates that the favorable opinion of others, as well as one's own sense of honor, are goods that many people seek for their own sake—goods for which people will often make real sacrifices.

Their approach stands in stark relief by comparison to that of Thomas Hobbes. Hobbes defines a man's power as his means to obtain some future apparent good. Reputation is merely an instrumental power; glory a joy in imagining our own power. Reputation, glory, worth, honor are all subsumed within Hobbes' "economic" logic. The value of all these is understood only as it relates to a man's ability to acquire other things that he wants.[24] They have no independent value. In contrast, one could sum up Rousseau's depiction of the corrupted condition of mankind as the condition in which the satisfaction of vanity has come to have an independent value.

23. See Hanna Fenichel Pitkin, *Fortune Is a Woman* (Berkeley: University of California Press, 1984), on the importance of Machiavelli's understanding of manhood for his politics.

24. *Leviathan,* pt. I, chap. 10. Hobbes's treatment of pride is complex. One could argue that he appreciates the power of pride and its associated passions, and that he describes them in such a way as to subordinate them to interests precisely in order to tame them. See chapter 2, note 32.

Amour-propre is not a natural passion in Rousseau's account, and in that respect there are grounds for some optimism in his thought. But the optimistic strain is overwhelmed by the pessimistic implications of Rousseau's analysis of corruption. Corruption is inevitable and ubiquitous to the extent that vanity and ambition are inseparable from both sophistication and dependence, and sophistication and dependence are inseparable in turn from the historical development of the species made possible by man's perfectibility. Corruption would seem to be inseparable from social relationships per se.

To state this somewhat differently: if there is to be a political solution for Rousseau, it would have to provide dependencies that do not arouse *amour-propre,* satisfactions for vanity that are harmless, and honors that are not corrupting.[25] Rousseau does explore these possibilities, though the likelihood of their actualization is extremely slim to say the least. Nonetheless, his exploration of them is part of his effort to establish new standards by which we might judge the difference between a healthy and a corrupted life. And these standards can serve as a guide for the behavior of individuals within corrupted situations. Thus, in what follows, we consider the political implications of Rousseau's analysis of corruption.

POLITICAL IMPLICATIONS

If corruption means change from man's natural condition and man's natural condition is one of individual isolation, then participation in the artificial, conventional world of society is corrupt by definition. Integrity can be preserved only by the solitary. Moreover, if social engagement necessarily involves concern for the opinion of others and autonomy means purely individual self-direction, then autonomy can only be preserved by the solitary. There is a tendency to reach these conclusions if authenticity is taken to be the core of Rousseau's ideal. The sign of the authentic is that it is not conventional. Thus if there is to be a politics of authenticity at all, it can only be a politics of opposition from a

---

25. Rousseau implies that not all systems of honor are equally corrupting when he condemns honors awarded on the basis of wealth as the most corrupting. *Second,* 174–75.

position of marginality. By remaining authentic, or genuine, that is, untouched by the contaminating effects of involvement with society, people can maintain their integrity and autonomy as well. And the sign that they have done so would be their individuality, uniqueness, or nonconformity; sure indications of a refusal to succumb to the corrupting concern for reputation.

But an analysis of Rousseau that ends in individuality has certainly gone awry. For Rousseau, after all, the citizen is one embodiment of the ideal. The citizen of a free republic is understood as autonomous, which is to say that autonomy has nothing to do with self-expression of individual uniqueness or idiosyncrasies. Autonomy is also entirely compatible with what we now call socialization. The citizen of Sparta or Rousseau's idealized Geneva, Poland, or Corsica cares a great deal for public esteem or humiliation. And if we turn to Rousseau's model individual in the modern world, Émile, we find that he is not striking for his individuality, but for the ordinariness of his tastes and habits. There is nothing bohemian about Émile. To analyze Rousseau's thought in terms of authenticity produces an emphasis on individuality and nonconformity that distorts the political implications of his thought.

It is by departing from the now customary focus on authenticity that I hope to recover or uncover a neglected aspect of Rousseauian politics. The question is not whether authenticity can be preserved but whether integrity can be. Integrity, unlike authenticity, is not a concept that is definitionally in tension with convention and society. We can sensibly ask whether there are forms of social engagement that are compatible with integrity. Are there resources for preserving integrity against the pressures toward corruption? The life of solitary withdrawal may not be the only available consistent outcome of a Rousseauian perspective on morals and politics.

That it seems to be, however, is not surprising. Rousseau's extreme concern to avoid the corrupting effects of certain forms of dependence lends powerful support to this view. Rousseau seems hypersensitive to the possibility that a person will unconsciously begin to rationalize self-serving behavior once he has put himself in a position of dependence. It takes a great deal of personal strength, in this view, both to hear the dictates of the inner voice and to act in accordance with them when one stands to gain or to lose. Because disinterestedness is an important component of integrity, personal involvement in the outcome of a course of action always threatens to corrupt one's integrity, whether consciously or unconsciously. The only certain indication that one has maintained the disinterestedness requisite for integrity is the sacrifice of private interest. For example, Rousseau testifies to his own integrity with the claim, "I have almost always written against my own interest" (*D'Alembert*, 131–32). He was often uncomfortable with receiving benefits from friends;[26] he avoided the offer of a pension from the King (*Confessions*, 352–55); his male ideal types treasure their independence. Rousseau even counseled against allowing yourself to be named in a friend's will for fear of the corrupting effects of anticipating benefits upon his death (*Confessions*, 62)! He depicts human beings, despite their natural goodness, as highly vulnerable to corruption. It does look as if avoiding corruption may require avoiding any kind of social relationship that would put one in a "compromising" position.

But it is not at all obvious that Rousseau's observations concerning the corrupting effects of dependence are equally applicable to every dependency relationship: to the relation between parent and child, between God and man, or to the mutual dependence of lovers, for example. Under what conditions does dependence produce the moral corruption that Rousseau describes and under what conditions might there be dependencies either that do not produce excessive concern for the opinion of others or that produce this concern without negative consequences? Much of Rousseau's work, but particularly *The Social Contract* and *Émile*, could be seen as an attempt to answer this question.

Rousseau's explanation of moral degeneration is set in the context of his discussion of economic and political relationships in the *Second Discourse*. In these relationships, dependence is conscious, unjust, and personal, and the interests of the parties involved conflict. These are the characteristics that make dependence destructive of integrity. Dependency relationships that do

---

26. Though he certainly accepted many. See Maurice Cranston, *The Noble Savage: Jean-Jacques Rousseau, 1754–1762* (Chicago: University of Chicago Press, 1991), 16–19.

not share these characteristics do not have the same destructive consequences.[27] For example, a person who is not conscious of his dependent status cannot become manipulative as a result of his dependence. If he is unaware that someone else is the source of benefits or that he is in need of another's help, he will not be led to seek what he wants through efforts to influence these others. As we have seen, Rousseau explores this possibility through the relation between Émile and his tutor and, in a different way, in the relation between the citizens and the Legislator. The citizens are not conscious of their dependent status and are therefore not corrupted by it (*S.C.,* II, vii, 69–70). The tutor takes care that Émile feel his weakness but not his subordination (*Émile,* 48, 66–68, 85, 91).

Similarly, it is clear that dependence will not produce the vices Rousseau describes (resentment, deceitfulness, hypocrisy, etc.) unless that dependence is personal. There must be someone to please. Dependence on things is corrupting only if the multiplication of needs also involves a multiplication of the people necessary to supply those needs. The desire for luxuries produces moral decay because these false needs increase one's dependence on other human beings (see *Émile,* 190–92). In contrast, the inability to satisfy one's desires due to simple scarcity is unrelated to moral decadence. Poverty is not corrupting in and of itself. To be limited by necessity is altogether different in its moral consequences from being limited by the opposing will of another human being. Again, the *Émile* offers ample illustration of the point (see *Émile,* 68, 85, 195 ff., 262; see also *Confessions,* 501).

There are important political illustrations of this point as well. For citizens to be subjected to impersonal laws or to the General Will is radically different from subjection to the will of a particular magistrate or ruler. Even the citizens' dependence on the Legislator is disguised as a subjection to divine authority. In both *Émile* and *The Social Contract,* Rousseau attempts to avoid the destructive moral effects of dependence by arranging things so that it is both concealed from consciousness and impersonal.

Yet, political subjection to an impersonal system seems an ambiguous case. While the benefits of impartiality are obvious, the

---

27. Again, Rousseau assesses consequences, rather than rejecting all dependency "on principle."

dangers of impersonality have been made clear in the totalitarian politics of the twentieth century. The impersonal character of general rules alone is no protection against vicious politics and moral decay. Something more is required: the general rules must be kept distinct from the will of particular magistrates in practice and they must embody a true unity of interest.

In Rousseau's model political communities, the citizens are united in their interests. The General Will is general not only in that it is impersonal but also in that its aim is the common interest of all the members of society (*S.C.*, I, vi, 53; II, i, 59). In contrast, the inequalities produced by the development of metallurgy and agriculture introduce an "opposition of interest" that makes it necessary for each man, whatever his place in the hierarchy, to "incessantly seek to interest [others] in his fate, and to make them find their own profit, in fact or in appearance in working for his" (*Second*, 156). Perhaps if there is no conflict of interest between the parties, even personal dependence can escape the destructive consequences Rousseau describes. The mutual dependence of friends and the desire of each to serve the other can be ennobling, rather than corrupting, precisely because of the unity of interest between them.

Finally, the corrupting political and economic relationships Rousseau describes are unjust. These are relationships where inequalities are imposed on equals. At first glance it seems obvious that unjust dependence of this sort breeds resentment, envy, and the desire for revenge. But is it the injustice of the relationship or the consciousness of its injustice that is psychologically and morally corrosive? Where the parties believe that the hierarchy is legitimate, they may be able to maintain their dignity and integrity despite its actual injustice. This is a highly problematic possibility. To the extent that the moral phenomena of integrity and corruption that concern Rousseau are psychological phenomena, appearance, belief, and intention become more important than reality. From this perspective, the negative moral consequences of unjust hierarchies might be mitigated by legitimating prejudices.

Nonetheless, the major thrust of Rousseau's argument is to delegitimize traditional inequalities precisely by bringing their deleterious moral effects to consciousness. From this perspective, those who find their dignity in playing their appropriate role within an unjust system of domination are enjoying a false dignity based on a false consciousness. And they do not escape the threats to their integrity that hierarchy entails. The experience of personal dependence is corrupting whether or not the parties to it believe it to be just. A servant will be led to be manipulative by the consciousness of his dependence even if he believes it to be entirely legitimate. A master will taste the pleasures of domination and seek to enhance them, particularly if he believes his authority is justified. And, of course, his position entails the pressure to generate rationalizations in support of that belief. Deception that hides the injustice of subordination is different from deception that hides its personal character: the latter can function to support integrity, as we saw in the case of the Legislator, but the former cannot.

Consider also the cases where the dependence produced by inequality is, in fact, just. For example, a child is in many respects the inferior of its parents. The citizens are inferior to the extraordinary Legislator. Émile is justly governed by his tutor. There are two possibilities in these cases as well: either the justice of subordination mitigates the deleterious moral consequences of personal dependence or personal dependence per se is corrupting. Some evidence suggests that Rousseau would support the first alternative. In his own early life, his dependence on adults became destructive only when he was unjustly treated (*Confessions,* 28–30). On the other hand, Rousseau does conceal from Émile his dependence on his tutor. This can only be because personal dependence is corrupting whether justified or not. Even though dependence is justified in these cases (Émile does need the tutor; the citizens do need the Legislator), as personal dependence it would be corrupting nonetheless if it were known. In a purely formal sense, dependence of any kind is a corruption from man's original condition of freedom. But it is the psychological character of Rousseau's claims that truly underlies his position. The experience of dependence on another human being cripples and distorts the child's own exercise of his will (*Émile,* 66), and the effect is the same among adults.

If something similar could be said of every form of dependence, we would be led to conclude that social life, with its essential dependencies, is inseparable from corruption and that virtue and freedom belong only to the solitary. The search for political solutions in Rousseau's thought would be at an end. Instead, the brief survey of the particular elements comprising the destructive political and economic dependencies that Rousseau describes was meant to suggest that Rousseau was well aware of alternative possibilities. Dependence that is just and also either mutual, impersonal, or personal but hidden, can actually nurture integrity.

In place of clashing individual interests and hierarchical dependence, Rousseau seeks mutual dependence and a common subordination to the demands of virtue. For example, he portrays the mutual subordination of men and women (each to the other in different respects) as just and ennobling, rather than corrupting, in the best case. He describes the playwright's dependence on his audience as corrupting, but only because the modern audience has corrupted tastes. As a substitute for the theater, Rousseau suggests various public entertainments that also involve the desire to win public acclaim (D'Alembert, 125–34).

Rousseau makes a similar argument concerning the dependence of citizens on one another. For citizens, unlike for presocial human beings, the natural pursuit of self-interest constantly pulls against the requirements of morality. Thus the citizen must undergo a continual process of public moral education that subordinates self-interest to virtue or that leads the citizen to identify his interest with the good of the whole. To accomplish this goal, Rousseau's systems for Poland and for Corsica depend heavily on public honors and the desire for esteem. Vanity is corrupting but pride is not, and Rousseau hopes to use pride precisely in order to inculcate integrity. Where the public values rightly and where reputations are publicly judged, concern for reputation is not necessarily corrosive.[28] On the contrary, that concern can produce a people with the requisite disinterestedness to sustain their integrity.

To the extent that social engagement is possible without personal dependence, integrity can be preserved.[29] This is the condition that Rousseau's ideal societies are designed to meet. But it is no less true even in a corrupt society. For those concerned to

28. See *Projet de constitution pour la Corse, O.C.,* III, 937–38.

29. Rousseau distinguishes between social bonds formed by "mutual esteem and benevolence" and those formed by "personal interest." "Préface de *Narcisse*," *O.C.,* II, 968. See Starobinski's comments on this passage, *Jean-Jacques Rousseau: Transparency and Obstruction,* 23.

maintain their integrity under corrupt conditions, the lessons are
clear. There is no reason to fear dependence on the esteem of
others where that follows from a mutual subordination to the
demands of virtue. You must choose your friends carefully. Economic dependence does threaten integrity, so one must seek to
acquire economic self-sufficiency. Cultivating simple tastes is essential for this purpose, as is finding an appropriate livelihood.
This is one reason why Émile learns the trade of a carpenter: it
protects his morality by putting him in a position where he can
always afford to lose his job (*Emile,* 195 ff.). A political lesson
may be drawn from this view of economic dependence as well:
place greater trust in the middle class than either the poor or the
rich on account of its greater self-sufficiency (*Mountain,* letter 9,
pp. 889, 896). In sum, avoid any situation of dependence on the
personal will of others or a situation where others depend on you
in this way as far as possible.

In a corrupted world, "as far as possible" is unlikely to be very
far. Rousseau's analysis does seem to lead people to value "private
life, domestic life, and participation in small communities."[30] But
in taking this position, Rousseau certainly does not recommend
a life of solitary withdrawal and a posture of philosophic indifference. Rousseau sharply criticized the philosophic type who
spends his time alone in his study engaged in constructing mathe-
matically sound demonstrations of moral principles while remaining aloof from the human drama around him. His egoism
has drowned out the voice of his conscience, and his moralizing
is worse than useless.[31] On the small scale of the local community,
a great deal of good can be done without compromising one's
integrity. Émile and Sophie engage in a variety of humanitarian
projects to improve the lives of the peasants among whom they
live (*Émile,* 435–36, 474–75; see *Second,* 132). Rousseau advises
Sophie D'Houdetot to work among the poor.[32] Julie's work with
local peasants is directed precisely toward preventing the corruption of young people who are tempted by city life and bourgeois

30. Christopher Kelly, "Reading Lives: Rousseau on the Political Importance of
the Hero" (University of Maryland, 1990), 29, cited at chapter 3, note 84.

31. Second, 132. See Jean-Jacques Rousseau, "Lettres Morales," letter 2, *O.C.,*
IV, 1087–91.

32. "Lettres Morales," letter 6, *O.C., IV,* 1117–18.

manners.[33] Rousseau sees the opportunity to do good for others as one element of a happy life.[34] Moreover, where there is the power to act against wickedness, there is the moral duty to do so.[35]

Rousseauian morality does not require a blanket rejection of society per se as corrupt and corrupting. Instead, it requires a series of careful judgments of the possibilities for doing good in any particular situation as well as a vigilant attitude toward the relationships that might undermine one's integrity. It should be recalled that one of the elements of integrity is this very willingness and ability to resist the pressures toward corruption. Rousseau encourages moral fortitude in the face of the pressures and temptations of the world. And he does so because, though the possibilities for effective public action may be severely limited, personal integrity remains a possibility everywhere and always.

Rousseau develops his ideal character type out of an analysis whose core dichotomy is integrity/corruption. I have tried to show that his conception of integrity is the ground for Rousseau's apparently disparate moral judgments and the standard of judgment he wishes to instill in his readers. Moreover, recognizing the centrality of this conception in his work allows us to give his practical political writings their due. I do not claim here that Rousseau's alternative is without difficulties, but I do mean to argue that his ideal both includes a greater moral content and permits a greater political flexibility than is sometimes supposed. If the question of the political implications of Rousseau's work is, How would Rousseau's ideal type behave politically? the answer is different than we have been led to expect.

By looking at Rousseau's writings through the lens of the conception of integrity, a neglected political possibility comes to light. Knowing the difference between integrity and corruption and having the fortitude to maintain integrity is certainly politically important, and this is what Rousseau meant to encourage.

33. *Julie,* 534–37.
34. See *Reveries,* 94, and *Second,* 179.
35. Jean-Jacques Rousseau, *Political Economy,* in *S.C.,* 218. Cranston recounts how Rousseau declined to intercede on behalf of persecuted Protestants in France, saying he would have no influence, and Cranston agrees with that self-assessment. See Cranston, *The Noble Savage,* 299–300.

He alerts us to the dangers of societies composed of complacent men whose rationalizations weaken ethical resolve.

In more contemporary terms, his analysis illuminates the problem of resistance and collaboration. Rousseau's righteous moralism, which has been condemned as the source of revolutionary totalitarianism, can also be the source of a very laudable sort of rectitude—a rectitude of the very kind that supports resistance to totalitarianism. A person of integrity as Rousseau understands it is one who prefers "exact probity" to the "practice and principles of society" and is not attracted by the "mean between vice and virtue."[36] Such a person is not attracted by collaboration.

People of this sort may be found anywhere, but they are more likely to be found among simple people who have not obscured the voice of conscience with a fog of sophistication, philosophic speculation, and the false moral ideal of balanced moderation. A Rousseauian political science would predict, for example, that the French peasants would be more likely to hide persecuted Jews in their homes, while the Parisians would rationalize collaboration with the Nazis.

The fanatical revolutionary, the romantic solitary, and the quiet resistor are all contraries to the calculating and complacent *homme du monde,* and they are all Rousseau's progeny. But the first two are the bastards, and the last has been little noticed. He comes to light by identifying integrity as the primary characteristic of the Rousseauian ideal.

---

36. D'Alembert, 45; see chapter 3, text accompanying note 37.

6

Conclusion

Two models of integrity compete in the modern political imagination. I have called them the moralist and the moderate. Each represents a principled, and at the same time political, stance. It is important to recognize that, as much as they differ, each is a legitimate possibility. More than one ethical alternative is available to us; more than one type of person can be trusted to respond to injustice and to do the right thing without undue regard for the consequences for his own personal position. And yet, these two alternative ethical types look so different from each other that it is often difficult to recognize them both as legitimate. Particularly if we approach the question of the role of principle in politics by seeking the mean between cynicism and fanaticism, we limit our vision so as to recognize only one possibility for principled politics, the statesmanlike moderate. We also blind ourselves to the variety of forms of hypocrisy. We see only the cynical hypocrite—the hypocrite who is arguably the least interesting as well as the least significant for politics—and overlook the hypocrisy both of the complacent moderate and of the righteous antihypocrite. These are the corrupted forms of the moderate and the moralist respectively. By recognizing the full variety of ethical possibilities, we can evaluate the alternative types of integrity, at least in part, in light of the respective dangers of their degenerate forms.

In both the complacent moderate and the righteous antihypocrite, hypocrisy is unselfconscious, consisting of rationalizations in moral terms for private ambitions and interests. In the former, the ethic of moderation covers a cowardly concern for reputation and for the preservation of a comfortable status quo. In the latter, the sense of moral superiority becomes a rationalization for self-aggrandizement; and this is so in the dupes of demagogues no less than in the demagogues themselves. Precisely because these forms of hypocrisy are unselfconscious, they are more common, more dangerous, and more culpable than the conscious manipulations of the cynical political con man.

But the differences between the two types of integrity go beyond the tendency of each to slide toward its peculiar hypocritical excess. The differences are substantial even if they appear most vividly as differences in character or temperament. The moderate is cool and deliberate, relying on careful judgment. While actively engaged in attempts to rectify injustices, he is a forgiving peacemaker. The moralist, by contrast, is passionate and impulsive, moved by his hatred of vice and outspoken in his condemnation of it. He may be lacking in judgment, but he is pure in motivation. Each appears defective in the eyes of the other. The moderate, with his tolerance and his efforts to find the acceptable compromise, may consistently minimize what is at stake morally in political conflicts and ultimately compromise our ability to see critical moral distinctions clearly. The moralist may sacrifice a just result to his unwillingness to deviate from high moral standards as well as to his insistence on publicly proclaiming them.

Beneath the competing preferences for one type over the other lies a theoretical disagreement of some magnitude. The integrity of the moderate is directed toward maintaining perspective and balance. Balance is required because the human soul is complex and divided between tendencies toward good and toward evil. On the basis of this presupposition, the moderate is a bit suspicious of those who appear to be too good and somewhat tolerant of those who allow themselves to be a little bad. He is more likely to excuse mixed motivations if the outcome is good. The person of integrity, in this view, is well-integrated, incorporating the various competing aspects of the self into a unified whole. The integrity of the moralist, in contrast, is directed toward maintaining purity and rests on the assumption of a primary innocent goodness. The person who is able to maintain his integrity is whole in that he remains unconflicted. Goodness must be protected by resisting the corrupting forces which constantly threaten it. I have drawn on Rousseau's writings to explore the integrity of the moralist and the conception of purity which it presupposes. In Rousseau's account, that presupposition depends on the claim that vanity is a passion that is not original to the human soul, which depends in turn on the claim for the original asociality of human beings. Because both of these claims are questionable, doubts remain as to the conception of purity that underlies the Rousseauian ideal.

Additional problems with Rousseau's ideal of integrity arise from his pessimism concerning the likelihood of corruption and from his skepticism concerning the power of reason. The first generates an emphasis on disinterestedness that is both psychologically implausible and theoretically questionable. Rousseau imagines a human type who reacts with cool indifference when he is the victim of injustice but with passionate rage when confronted with injustice perpetrated against others. And, as appears in his treatment of lying, Rousseau applies a double standard in judging moral action: no deviation is permissible for the sake of avoiding one's own suffering, however undeserved, while principles may be transgressed for the sake of alleviating the suffering of others. Because disinterestedness is the only sure bulwark against corruption and corruption is the danger to be avoided at all costs, self-sacrifice becomes the only certain test of rectitude. There is no room for those cases where what is good simply and what is good for oneself coincide. Instead, there is a tremendous concern to avoid self-concern, one which itself can become self-absorbing. The theoretical problem here is that Rousseau provides no ground for sustaining a moral distinction between action on one's own behalf and action on behalf of others. After all, justice denied in one's own case is still justice denied. The practical danger is that Rousseau's ideal—his improved Alceste—can too easily come to resemble the Alceste of Molière's play: far too concerned with the preservation of his sense of his own integrity, too little concerned with the consequences of his actions, and ultimately unwilling to become fully engaged in the world.

Moreover, Rousseau's anxiety about corruption, when coupled with his distrust of reason, leads to a disturbing element of paternalism in his thought. Even in the best case, that is, in the case of Émile's education or the polity described in *The Social Contract,* the full self-consciousness of rational decision is attenu-

ated for the sake of the requirements of morality and a more
limited autonomy. At crucial moments, people cannot be trusted
to make their own decisions well. Governance is required to
shape their choices; a governance that is indirect and deceptive.
As with Machiavelli, governance occupies that space between
outright force and reasoned discourse where fraud too resides.
Whether Rousseau's conception of governance appears benign
or malignant depends in large measure on one's judgment of his
estimation of the possibilities for human autonomy. If Rousseau
offers the best that we can ever reasonably hope to achieve, there
are no grounds for complaint. But if Rousseau's antirationalism
is excessive, so too is his pessimism.

Rousseau tells us that our sense of ourselves as fully self-
conscious, autonomous, and rational beings is always necessarily
at least a partial illusion, though a salutary one. This claim, quite
apart from the question of its validity, is certainly an affront to
our vanity; we do not like to think that we are not capable in
actuality of the fullness of freedom and rationality that we are
able to imagine. Rousseau invites us to imagine ourselves instead
as steadfast in our goodness, simple, and freed from the anxieties
of the concern for the good opinion of others. And one might
justifiably take pride in possessing integrity of this sort.

Despite the difficulties with Rousseau's conception of integrity, much may be said in its favor. Rousseau issues a challenge
to open a path to the heart through the sophisticated and sophistic
moral wrangling of the modern age. And because the heart speaks
clearly and with a voice common to us all, his ideal does not
collapse into the pure subjectivism of authenticity. It has a genuine moral core. Rousseau does not extol authenticity per se; to
the extent that Rousseau urges us to be ourselves, he does so
because those selves are good. Rousseau seeks to recapture the
perspective of the innocent and to find the resources with which
to forestall corruption and resist evil. Among these resources in
the political realm is the public praise of goodness, selfless dedication, and trustworthiness. But the public defense of moral principle does not preclude prudential compromise. Rousseau's work
provides an example of a combination of moral purity and political pragmatism. The combination is possible because moral purity
is threatened first and foremost by dependence and the vanity it
spawns. There is nothing corrupting about a compromise based

on a clear judgment of the practical possibilities rather than on a desire for personal advancement or reputation. To the extent that Rousseau's is a viable combination, it offers an escape from a dilemma: the political choices are no longer reduced to a dangerous apolitical idealism or an equally dangerous unethical realism.

Consideration of the Rousseauian ideal also focuses attention on a critical problem, and in this respect it serves a positive function as well. Ethical political action requires a combination of principle, prudence, and character: knowledge of what is right, an assessment of how far it can be achieved, and the resolve to act in accordance with that assessment. But in Rousseau's view, character has become particularly problematic. He alerts us to the political dangers of societies composed of complacent men whose rationalizations weaken moral resolve. In the modern world, reason has become the enemy of goodness. Rousseau's pessimism about our susceptibility to corruption further heightens our awareness of the dangers of complacency and rationalization. Before we congratulate ourselves on our political moderation, we must be very certain of the sort of moderate we are. It is all too easy to deceive oneself in this regard. As a critic of the genteel moderate, Rousseau criticizes at the same time the overestimation of reason as a moral touchstone and the underestimation of the irrational and the nonrational elements of political life.

The reflections on Rousseau's alternative to the moderate type that were developed in this book arose in response to the question, What are the ethical possibilities given the necessity of hypocrisy in politics? A particular understanding of the character of political relationships is the ground for the presupposition of that necessity. From Machiavelli we learn that political relations exist between parties who need one another's cooperation, resources, or support but cannot either coerce it or expect to receive it as a generous and sympathetic gift. Political relations are neither enmities nor friendships but friendly relations sustained among nonfriends. And in order to sustain them, one must cultivate one's reputation and care for the opinion of others. Vanity and pride inevitably are constituents of these relationships. Moreover, it becomes very useful to appear to be other than what you are and to appeal to whatever moral or religious norms constitute the commonly accepted vocabulary of justification for political action. Hypocrisy is generated by the particular sort of dependence that defines political relations. This is an insight that Rousseau shares with Machiavelli. Dependence, vanity, moral discourse, and hypocrisy are interwoven threads of the political and social fabric. For Machiavelli, this is a political reality that can be understood and manipulated. For Rousseau, these are immensely corrosive psychological realities. To overcome vanity, to achieve psychological independence, to create a political community without destructive dependencies are Herculean tasks, and even they require deception and manipulation.

Machiavelli's and Rousseau's shared understanding of political relations contrasts sharply with alternative visions, particularly of liberal democratic politics, according to which honesty is a crucial political virtue. The liberal democrat argues that political deliberation must be conducted in the open, for the people cannot judge if they cannot see. Hypocrisy is the characteristic vice of monarchies and aristocracies, and one that should disappear along with hierarchical dependency in an egalitarian regime. But in fact, as I have tried to show, the problem of hypocrisy is pressing in democratic politics because of the new kinds of dependencies that it produces. Where all are equal, no one can go it alone; no one is in a position to rely on his "own arms," to use Machiavelli's term. Democratic politicians are even more enmeshed than Machiavellian princes in a web of dependency relations. While most in need of honesty as a political virtue, liberal democratic regimes are most likely to produce the conditions that undermine that virtue. Oddly enough, in light of these reflections on the thoughts of Machiavelli and Rousseau, liberalism can be criticized, not for being hypocritical, but for refusing to acknowledge the necessity of hypocrisy.

At the outset, we noted the peculiar susceptibility of liberal democracies to charges of hypocrisy. This is a function of both aspects of what I have called the "paradox of democracy"; liberal democratic regimes make particularly strong claims to be able to provide open and honest political processes at the same time that those processes are structured so as to increase the dependencies conducive to hypocritical political behavior. Supposing that it is indeed the case that liberal politics will always include a good deal of hypocrisy, what ought to be our judgment of this situation? It is not obvious that a characteristic tendency to produce hypocrisy is cause for the condemnation of liberalism.

Throughout this book, I have written as if the appreciation of the necessity for political hypocrisy and the perspective of the liberal rationalist were simply at odds with each other. The former, represented by Machiavelli and Rousseau, stands as a critique of the political expectations of the latter, represented by Hobbes, Locke, and Smith. This observation led me to suggest in introducing this work that the analysis presented here does not fit neatly with the major competing accounts of the place of these authors in the history of political thought.[1]

Instead, this analysis involves a reconceptualization of the common ground between Machiavelli and Rousseau as well as a reconceptualization of the grounds of their distance from Hobbes, Locke, and Smith. The examination of the problem of political hypocrisy in the works of Machiavelli and Rousseau, along with the recognition that an investigation of that problem in the works of Hobbes, Locke, or Smith would be considerably less fruitful, leads to the following conclusion: liberal theory does not take sufficient account of the distinctive character of political relations, of political passions, and of moral discourse and so underestimates the place of hypocrisy in politics. This is a real and often unrecognized weakness of liberal theory. But what of the practice of liberal politics, as opposed to its theoretical self-understanding? What emerges from the exploration of the nature of political hypocrisy in the works of Machiavelli and Rousseau is the recognition that liberal political practice might actually be improved by the sort of political hypocrisy it generates.

Why do we not always speak the whole truth aloud in public, and especially political, settings? Public speech in liberal democracies is a matter of defending one's opinion and engaging in mutual attempts at persuasion in an effort to reach a collective decision. This much is generally taken for granted, so that we do not often acknowledge the constitutive components of the political system that generate this process. Public speech is conducted as it is, first, because the process of decision-making requires the consent of a number of different parties to the decision, and, second, because

---

1. See chapter 1, notes 18–28 and accompanying text.

there is a governing norm that decisions are to be made for some articulable reason and not on the basis of whim, or inspiration, for example. Under such circumstances, one's position must be defended on grounds that are at least potentially persuasive to others. Of course, the arguments are often hypocritical rationalizations; that is, they have been developed after the fact to justify positions that people actually support for self-interested reasons or on the basis of irrational preferences. Nonetheless, in a political forum, people are compelled to give plausible reasons for the course of action that they advocate. Similarly, government actions must be at least minimally defensible, whatever the real motivations of the actors. For example, while you may support a particular course of action because it will benefit you and those like you, to say so is not sufficient. And while often one group might truly say, "We don't have to listen to you because there are more of us than there are of you," this is not often said in practice. The whole truth can be both singularly ineffective and corrosive to the political process.

Moreover, the ethical offense involved in excessive truthfulness is part of the reason for its corrosive effect. Within the ethical framework of liberal politics, to be told that you are acting exclusively in your own interest is rightly understood as an insult. To act without reason or to advocate a position for which you cannot provide a rationale is an embarrassment. And to abandon any pretense of an attempt to persuade those whom it is in your power to simply overcome is divisive and polarizing. Liberal politics is sustained by an ethic of rationalism; it depends on the notion that the political process will seek the public good in a reasonable fashion and on reasonable grounds. The frank exposure of self-interested motivations is often a threat to that process. In this sense, honesty and openness can be destructive, not only of the political community, but also of rational discourse itself. Liberal politics needs a certain kind of hypocritical speech. Because the theorists are right that people are often self-interested, they are wrong that politics can be conducted through the rational adjudication of interests without hypocrisy. Because people are often self-interested, political hypocrisy of the kind I have just described is important and useful precisely to sustain the rational adjudication of interests.

For these reasons, I suggested that the practice of liberal politics is improved by a certain sort of hypocrisy, even though liberalism understands itself as an alternative to hypocritical politics. Liberal political theory might learn something about liberal political practice by attending to the criticisms inherent in Machiavelli's and Rousseau's perspective on political relations. Adam Smith's insight that an appeal to the self-interest of the butcher can replace a hypocritical appeal is not correct when applied to politics.[2] Self-interest, hypocrisy, and also honesty and virtue coexist in politics in ways that the usual competing liberal visions do not capture.

There are alternatives within liberalism that have often been conceptualized as competing models, not only of how liberal politics does work, but of how it ought to work at its best to provide political liberty and serve the public good. The models identify differently what is really at the foundation of liberal politics: legislative deliberation or pluralist bargaining; virtue and principle or interest; a dialogical or an adversarial process.[3] On the one hand, those who look to deliberation, principle, and dialogue are open to the charge that they are simply naive. The dialogue is merely rhetoric that obscures what is "really" going on, viz., the competition of particular interests. On the other hand, those who look to competitive bargaining among interests are open to the charge that they are reductionist. Their descriptions of the phenomenon will be flat, ignoring the real impact of ideas, norms, and opinions in politics. Moreover, their cynicism may itself have the deleterious moral effect of creating a world more like their own description of it. People will behave in frankly self-interested fashion if they come to believe that there is no real alternative or that to behave otherwise is contemptibly naive. Neither of these models gives hypocrisy its due: the first tends to minimize its presence, while the second recognizes hypocrisy but dismisses it as epiphenomenal.

Alternatively, let us recognize that people with interests to protect and advance, with opinions as to how best to do so, and

2. See chapter 2, note 28 and accompanying text.

3. The variety of existing interpretations of Madison's *Federalist,* no. 10 is suggestive here. Compare, for example, Robert Dahl, *A Preface to Democratic Theory* (Chicago: University of Chicago Press, 1956), chap. 1, with Garry Wills, *Explaining America: The Federalist* (Garden City, N.Y.: Doubleday and Co., 1981), pt. 4. These authors reach opposing conclusions by selectively stressing certain aspects of Madison's essay. Madison apparently did not think it necessary to choose between the "models."

with ideas about what is justifiable, come together and express those interests, opinions, and ideas in a deliberative process sometimes, but not always, hypocritically. There are, of course, plenty of honest discussions and disagreements as well as genuine aspirations to act in accordance with deeply held principled commitments. But there are also times when people act and speak hypocritically, and when they do, it is not always such a bad thing. Some sorts of hypocrisy do not compromise integrity. On the contrary, some of them sustain the public conditions for political integrity. Every act of hypocrisy involves a pretense of virtue, which necessarily includes public acknowledgment of moral standards for political action, and sometimes, that public statement is the best that can be done. Moreover, even the pretense can serve as a genuine constraint.[4] If the pretense is to rationalism, people are constrained to give evidence and to defend their position in the light of generally agreed-upon criteria. There is a limit to what can be proposed; in order to be defensible, a proposal must often actually be in the other's interest at least to some extent. In this way, the necessity of hypocrisy can have a moderating effect. Moreover, people who initially adopt a pretense of rationalism in order to advance their own interest are sometimes led to appreciate the ways in which the ethic of rationalism, which the necessity of the pretense presupposes, functions for the general good. At best, they may be led to a genuine openness to reasonable persuasion. Of course, the pretense of virtue can be a bad thing where it is simply a tool of self-consciously manipulative ambition, where "virtue" means conformity to a reigning orthodoxy, where the pretense is unselfconscious and therefore particularly dangerous, and so on. It is not that all kinds of hypocrisy are positive in politics or that there is never the possibility of an honest political exchange, but only that some kinds of hypocrisy are both positive and necessary so that the blanket condemnation of hypocrisy must be seen as a political vice—and particularly so if what passes for honest politics is not principled politics but the frank self-interestedness of those "realists" who are, in fact, merely cynics. In sum, the paradoxical truth is that there will be more genuine virtue and integrity in politics where

4. See "Préface de *Narcisse*," where Rousseau makes this point, *O.C.*, II, 971 ff.

there is a judicious appreciation of the role of political hypocrisy than where there is a strident and wholesale condemnation of it.

A similar analysis applies to the charge that is leveled against liberal society for producing the bourgeois. The bourgeois is denounced as a hypocrite—an unselfconscious hypocrite, but a hypocrite nonetheless. But where the pretense of virtue produces civility, need we be so concerned? Where the inauthentic conformity that characterizes the bourgeois is criticized, is it really hypocrisy that is at issue? Or is it rather what hypocrisy sometimes produces: complacency toward injustice, excessive concern for reputation, and so on? In this case too, it is dangerous to reject hypocrisy wholesale—one might find that the only alternative to it is the kind of authenticity that is entirely self-concerned and knows no moral constraint.

It is not only dangerous to reject hypocrisy wholesale, in a certain sense, it is simply impossible. As a political matter, hypocrisy will always be with us; it is an inevitable byproduct of the mixture of the dependency relations of politics and the necessity of public moral principle, neither of which we could do without even if we would. The best that we can do is to judge hypocrisy, and antihypocrisy too, with a discerning eye, which requires that we keep those images of integrity that guide our judgment always within our sight.

WORKS CITED

The reader should consult the list of abbreviations for additional primary sources.

Appleby, Joyce. *Liberalism and Republicanism in the Historical Imagination.* Cambridge: Harvard University Press, 1992.

Arendt, Hannah. *On Revolution.* New York: Viking, 1965.

Aron, Raymond. *Peace and War: A Theory of International Relations.* Translated by Richard Howard and Annette Baker Fox. Garden City, N.Y.: Doubleday and Co., 1966.

Augustine, Saint. "Against Lying." In *Saint Augustine: Treatises on Various Subjects.* Edited by Roy J. Deferrari, 125–79. New York: Fathers of the Church, Inc., 1952.

Babbitt, Irving. *Rousseau and Romanticism.* Boston: Houghton Mifflin, 1919.

Baczko, Bronislaw. "Rousseau and Social Marginality." *Daedalus* (summer 1978): 27–40.

Baron, Hans. "The *Principe* and the Puzzle of the Date of the *Discorsi*." *Bibliothèque d'Humanisme et Renaissance* 18 (1956): 405–28.

Bayle, Pierre. *Dictionnaire historique et critique.* 5th ed. Amsterdam: P. Brunel, 1740.

Beitz, Charles R. *Political Theory and International Relations.* Princeton: Princeton University Press, 1979.

Berman, Marshall. *The Politics of Authenticity: Radical Individualism and the Emergence of Modern Society.* New York: Atheneum, 1970.

Blos, Peter. *On Adolescence: A Psychoanalytic Interpretation.* Glencoe, Ill.: Free Press, 1962.

Blum, Carol. *Rousseau and the Republic of Virtue: The Language of Politics in the French Revolution.* Ithaca, N.Y.: Cornell University Press, 1986.

Bok, Gisela, Quentin Skinner, and Maurizio Viroli, eds. *Machiavelli and Republicanism.* Cambridge: Cambridge University Press, 1990.

Burke, Edmund. *Reflections on the Revolution in France*. Edited by H. D. Mahoney. New York: Macmillan Publishing Co., 1955.

Carr, Edward Hallett. *The Twenty Years' Crisis, 1919–1939: An Introduction
to the Study of International Relations*. London: Macmillan and Co., Ltd.,
1940.

Cassirer, Ernst. *The Question of Jean-Jacques Rousseau*. Translated by Peter
Gay. New York: Columbia University Press, 1954.

Cavell, Stanley. "A Cover Letter to Molière's *Misanthrope*." In *Themes Out
of School: Effects and Causes*. Chicago: University of Chicago Press, 1984.

Cicero. *On Moral Obligation*. Translated by John Higginbotham. Berkeley:
University of California Press, 1967.

Cranston, Maurice. *The Noble Savage: Jean-Jacques Rousseau, 1754–1762*.
Chicago: University of Chicago Press, 1991.

Crocker, Lester G. "Julie, ou La Nouvelle Duplicité." *Annales de la Société
Jean-Jacques Rousseau* 36 (1963–1965): 105–52.

———. *Rousseau's "Social Contract": An Interpretive Essay*. Cleveland, Ohio:
Case Western Reserve University Press, 1968.

Cucchi, Paolo M. "Rousseau, Lecteur de Machiavel." In *Jean-Jacques Rousseau et son temps: Politique et litterature au XVIIIe siècle*. Edited by Michel
Launay. Paris: Librairie A. G. Nizet, 1969.

Dahl, Robert. *A Preface to Democratic Theory*. Chicago: University of Chicago
Press, 1956.

Diderot, Denis. *Encyclopédie IV*. Vol. 8 of *Oeuvres complètes de Diderot*. Edited
by John Lough and Jacques Proust. Paris: Hermann, 1976.

———. *Rameau's Nephew and D'Alembert's Dream*. Translated by Leonard
Tancock. New York: Penguin Books, 1966.

Dietz, Mary. "Trapping the Prince: Machiavelli and the Politics of Deception." *American Political Science Review* 80, no. 3 (Sept. 1986): 777–800.

Engels, Friedrich, and Karl Marx. "Manifesto of the Communist Party." In
The Marx-Engels Reader. 2d ed. Edited by Robert C. Tucker, 484–91.
New York: W. W. Norton and Co., 1978.

Erikson, Erik H. *Childhood and Society*. 2d ed. New York: W. W. Norton,
1963.

———. *Identity, Youth and Crisis*. New York: W. W. Norton, 1968.

Ferrara, Alessandro. *Modernity and Authenticity: A Study of the Social and Ethical
Thought of Jean-Jacques Rousseau*. Albany: State University of New York
Press, 1993.

Fingarette, Herbert. *Self-Deception*. London: Routledge and Kegan Paul, 1969.

Flaumenhaft, Mera J. "The Comic Remedy: Machiavelli's *Mandragola*." *Interpretation* 7, no. 2 (1978): 33–74.

Fleisher, Martin. "Trust and Deceit in Machiavelli's Comedies." *Journal of
the History of Ideas* 27, no. 3 (July 1966): 365–80.

Frederick of Prussia. *The Refutation of Machiavelli's "Prince" or Anti-Machiavel*.
Translated by Paul Sonnino. Athens: Ohio University Press, 1981.

Freud, Sigmund. *Civilization and Its Discontents*. Translated by James Strachey. New York: W. W. Norton, 1961.

Forde, Stephen. "Varieties of Realism: Thucydides and Machiavelli." *Journal of Politics* 54, no. 2 (May 1992): 372–93.

Gay, Peter. *The Party of Humanity*. New York: W. W. Norton, 1971.

Gilbert, Allan H. *Machiavelli's "Prince" and Its Forerunners*. Durham, N.C.: Duke University Press, 1938.

Gossmann, Lionel. *Men and Masks*. Baltimore: Johns Hopkins University Press, 1963.

Gourevitch, Victor. "Rousseau on Lying: A Provisional Reading of the Fourth *Rêverie*." Berkshire Review 15 (1980): 93–107.

Le Grand Robert de la langue française. 2d ed., 9 vols. Paris: Dictionnaires Le Robert, 1985.

Grant, Ruth W. *John Locke's Liberalism*. Chicago: University of Chicago Press, 1987.

———. "Locke's Political Anthropology and Lockean Individualism." *Journal of Politics* (Feb. 1988): 42–63.

Hamilton, Alexander, John Jay, and James Madison. *The Federalist Papers*. Edited by Clinton Rossiter. New York: New American Library, 1961.

Hartle, Ann. *The Modern Self in Rousseau's "Confessions": A Reply to St. Augustine*. Notre Dame, Ind.: University of Notre Dame Press, 1983.

Hobbes, Thomas. *Leviathan*. Edited by C. B. Macpherson. Harmondsworth, U.K.: Penguin, 1968.

Howarth, W. D. *Molière: A Playwright and His Audience*. Cambridge: Cambridge University Press, 1982.

Hulliung, Mark. *Citizen Machiavelli*. Princeton: Princeton University Press, 1983.

Hundert, E. J. "A Satire of Self-Disclosure: From Hegel through Rameau to the Augustans." *Journal of the History of Ideas* 27 (1986): 235–48.

Johannsen, Robert W., ed. *The Lincoln-Douglas Debates of 1858*. New York: Oxford University Press, 1965.

Kahn, Victoria. "*Virtù* and the Example of Agathocles in Machiavelli's *Prince*." In *Machiavelli and the Discourse of Literature*. Edited by Albert Russell Ascoli and Victoria Kahn. Ithaca, N.Y.: Cornell University Press, 1993.

Kant, Immanuel. *Fundamental Principles of the Metaphysics of Morals*. Translated by Thomas K. Abbott. New York: Bobbs-Merrill, 1949.

———. "On a Supposed Right to Lie from Altruistic Motives." In *Critique of Practical Reason and Other Writings in Moral Philosophy*. Edited and translated by Lewis White Beck. Chicago: University of Chicago Press, 1949.

Kateb, George. "Comments on Gourevitch." *Berkshire Review* 15 (1980): 122–28.

Kelly, Christopher. "Reading Lives: Rousseau on the Political Importance of the Hero." University of Maryland, 1990.

———. *Rousseau's Exemplary Life: The "Confessions" as Political Philosophy*. Ithaca, N.Y.: Cornell University Press, 1987.

———. " 'To Persuade without Convincing': The Language of Rousseau's Legislator." *American Journal of Political Science* 31 (May 1987): 321–35.

Lange, Lynda. "Rousseau and Modern Feminism." In *Feminist Interpretations and Political Theory*. Edited by Mary Lyndon Shanley and Carole Pateman. University Park: Pennsylvania State University Press, 1991.

LeCat, M. "Refutation of the Observations of Jean-Jacques Rousseau of Geneva." In *Collected Writings of Rousseau*. Vol. 2. Translated by Roger D. Masters and Christopher Kelly. Hanover, N.H.: University Press of New England, 1992.

Lévy, Yves. "Machiavel et Rousseau." *Le Contrat Social* 6 (1962): 169–74.

———. "Les Partis et la démocratie (I)." *Le Contrat Social* 3 (1959): 79–86.

Littré, Émile. *Dictionnaire de la langue française*. Paris: Gallimard and Hachette, 1958.

Locke, John. *Of the Conduct of the Understanding*. In *John Locke, "Some Thoughts Concerning Education" and "Of the Conduct of the Understanding."* Edited by Ruth W. Grant and Nathan Tarcov. Indianapolis: Hackett Publishing Co., 1996.

Machiavelli, Niccolò. *Mandragola*. Translated by Mera J. Flaumenhaft. Prospect Heights, Ill.: Waveland Press, 1981.

Mansfield, Jr., Harvey C. *Machiavelli's Virtue*. Chicago: University of Chicago Press, 1996.

Martin, Mike W. *Self-Deception and Morality*. Lawrence: University Press of Kansas, 1986.

———, ed. *Self-Deception and Self-Understanding: New Essays in Philosophy and Psychology*. Lawrence: University Press of Kansas, 1985.

Masciulli, Joseph. "The Armed Founder versus the Catonic Hero: Machiavelli and Rousseau on Popular Leadership." *Interpretation* 14 (1986): 265–80.

Masters, Roger D. *The Political Philosophy of Rousseau*. Princeton: Princeton University Press, 1968.

McKenzie, Lionel. "Rousseau's Debate with Machiavelli in the *Social Contract*." *Journal of the History of Ideas* 43 (April-June, 1982): 209–28.

Melzer, Arthur M.. *The Natural Goodness of Man*. Chicago: University of Chicago Press, 1990.

———. "Rousseau and the Cult of Sincerity." In *The Legacy of Jean-Jacques Rousseau*. Edited by Clifford Orwin and Nathan Tarcov. Chicago: University of Chicago Press, 1997.

Molière, Jean Baptiste Poquelin de. *"The Misanthrope" and "Tartuffe."* Translated by Richard Wilbur. New York: Harcourt, Brace and World: 1965.

Moore, W. G. *Molière: A New Criticism*. 1949. Reprint, Garden City, N.Y.: Doubleday and Co., 1962.

Morel, J. "Molière ou la dramaturgie de l'honnêteté." *L'Information Littéraire* 15 (Nov.-Dec. 1963).

Morgenthau, Hans J. *Politics among Nations: The Struggle for Power and Peace.* New York: Alfred A. Knopf, 1948.

Musa, Mark, ed. and trans. *Machiavelli's The Prince: A Bilingual Edition.* New York: St. Martin's Press, 1964.

Newman, Jay. *Fanatics and Hypocrites.* Buffalo, N.Y.: Prometheus Books, 1986.

Orwell, George. "Reflections on Gandhi." In *A Collection of Essays.* Garden City, N.Y.: Doubleday and Co., 1954.

Payot, Roger. "Jean-Jacques Rousseau et Machiavel." In *Les Études Philosophiques* 26 (1971): 209–23.

Peyré, Henri. *Literature and Sincerity.* New Haven, Conn.: Yale University Press, 1963.

Pitkin, Hanna Fenichel. *Fortune Is a Woman.* Berkeley: University of California Press, 1984.

Pocock, J. G. A. "Machiavelli, Harrington and English Political Ideologies in the Eighteenth Century." *William and Mary Quarterly* 22 (Oct. 1965): 549–83.

———. *The Machiavellian Moment: Florentine Political Thought and the Atlantic Republican Tradition.* Princeton: Princeton University Press, 1975.

———. "Political Ideas as Historical Events: Political Philosophers as Historical Actors." In *Political Theory and Political Education.* Edited by Melvin Richter. Princeton: Princeton University Press, 1980.

Reisman, David. *The Lonely Crowd.* 1950. Reprint, New Haven, Conn.: Yale University Press, 1961.

Reynolds, Noel B., and Arlene W. Saxonhouse. *Three Discourses: A Critical Modern Edition of Newly Identified Work of the Young Hobbes.* Chicago: University of Chicago Press, 1995.

Riker, William H. *The Art of Political Manipulation.* New Haven, Conn.: Yale University Press, 1986.

Riley, Patrick. "Why Rousseau Is Not Kant: The Theory of Moral Sentiments in the *Lettres Morales.*" Paper delivered at American Political Science Association annual meeting, Chicago, 1990.

Rochefoucauld, François, duc de la. *Maximes et Réflexions Diverses.* Paris: Librairie Larousse, 1972.

Romero, Laurence. "Moliére's *Morale:* Debates in Criticism." In *Molière and the Commonwealth of Letters: Patrimony and Posterity.* Edited by Roger Johnson, Jr., Edita S. Neumann, and Guy T. Trail. Jackson: University Press of Mississippi, 1975.

Rousseau, Jean-Jacques. *Correspondance complète de Jean-Jacques Rousseau.* Vol. 5. Edited by R. A. Leigh. Geneva: Institut et Musée Voltaire, 1967.

———. *Correspondance complète de Jean-Jacques Rousseau.* Edited by R. A. Leigh. Oxford: The Voltaire Foundation, 1979.

———. "Judgment on Perpetual Peace." In *A Project of Perpetual Peace.* Translated by Edith M. Nuttall. London: Richard Cobden-Sanderson, 1927.

Saxonhouse, Arlene. *Women in the History of Political Thought.* New York: Praeger, 1985.

Schwartz, Joel. *The Sexual Politics of Jean-Jacques Rousseau.* Chicago: University of Chicago Press, 1984.

Shklar, Judith N. *Men and Citizens: A Study of Rousseau's Social Theory.* Cambridge: Cambridge University Press, 1969.

————. *Ordinary Vices.* Cambridge, Mass.: Belknap Press, 1984.

Skinner, Quentin. *Foundations of Modern Political Thought.* Cambridge: Cambridge University Press, 1978.

————. *Machiavelli.* New York: Hill and Wang, 1981.

————. "Meaning and Understanding in the History of Ideas." In *History and Theory* 8, no. 1 (1969): 3–53.

Smith, Adam. *Wealth of Nations.* Edited by Edwin Cannan. Chicago: University of Chicago Press, 1976.

Spinoza, Benedict de. *A Political Treatise.* In *The Chief Works of Benedict de Spinoza: "A Theological-Political Treatise" and "A Political Treatise."* Translated by R. H. M. Elwes. New York: Dover, 1951.

Starobinski, Jean. *Blessings in Disguise; or, the Morality of Evil.* Translated by Arthur Goldhammer. Cambridge: Harvard University Press, 1993.

————. *Jean-Jacques Rousseau: Transparency and Obstruction.* Translated by Arthur Goldhammer. Chicago: University of Chicago Press, 1988.

Strauss, Leo. "Three Waves of Modernity." In *An Introduction to Political Philosophy: Ten Essays by Leo Strauss.* Edited by Hilail Gildin. Detroit: Wayne State University Press, 1989.

————. *Natural Right and History.* Chicago, University of Chicago Press, 1953.

————. *Persecution and the Art of Writing.* Chicago: University of Chicago Press, 1988.

————. Preface to American edition of *The Political Philosophy of Hobbes: Its Basis and Its Genesis.* Translated by Elsa M. Sinclair. 1936. Reprint, Chicago: University of Chicago Press, 1952.

————. *Thoughts on Machiavelli.* Chicago: University of Chicago Press, 1984.

Strong, Tracy. *The Idea of Political Theory: Reflections on the Self in Political Time and Space.* Notre Dame, Ind.: University of Notre Dame Press, 1990.

Sumberg, Theodore A. "*La Mandragola:* An Interpretation." *Journal of Politics* 23, no. 2 (May 1961): 320–40.

Talmon, J. *Origins of Totalitarian Democracy.* London: Secker and Warburg, 1952.

Tarcov, Nathan. *Locke's Education for Liberty.* Chicago: University of Chicago Press, 1984.

————. "Quentin Skinner's Method and Machiavelli's *Prince.*" *Ethics* 92 (1982): 692–709.

Taylor, Charles. *The Malaise of Modernity.* Concord, Ontario: Anansi Press, 1991.

———. *Multiculturalism and "The Politics of Recognition."* Princeton: Princeton University Press, 1992.

Thoreau, Henry David. "On the Duty of Civil Disobedience." In *"Walden" and "Civil Disobedience."* New York: New American Library, 1960.

Tocqueville, Alexis de. *Democracy in America.* Translated by George Lawrence. Edited by J.P. Mayer. Garden City, N.Y.: Doubleday and Co., 1969.

Trachtenberg, Zev M. *Making Citizens: Rousseau's Political Theory of Culture.* New York: Routledge, 1993.

Trilling, Lionel. *Sincerity and Authenticity.* Cambridge, Mass.: Harvard University Press, 1971.

Turnell, Martin. *The Classical Moment: Studies of Corneille, Molière, and Racine.* New York: New Directions, 1946.

Vernes, Paule Monique. "Nicolas Machiavel Chez Jean-Jacques Rousseau: Des leçons aux rois ou des leçons aux peuples?" *Actes du colloque franco-italien de philosophie.* Paris: École Normale d'Instituteur de Nice, 1977: 77–89.

Viroli, Maurizio. *From Politics to Reason of State:The Acquisition and Transformation of the Language of Politics 1250–1600.* Cambridge: Cambridge University Press, 1992.

———. *Jean-Jacques Rousseau and the "Well-Ordered Society."* Translated by Derek Hanson. Cambridge: Cambridge University Press: 1988.

———. "Republic and Politics in Machiavelli and Rousseau." *History of Political Thought* 10 (autumn 1989): 405–20.

Waltz, Kenneth N. *Man, the State and War: A Theoretical Analysis.* New York: Columbia University Press, 1959.

———. *Theory of International Politics.* Reading, Mass.: Addison-Wesley, 1979.

Weber, Max. "Politics as a Vocation." In *From Max Weber: Essays in Sociology.* Translated and edited by H. H. Gerth and C. Wright Mills. New York: Oxford University Press, 1958.

Wills, Garry. *Explaining America: The Federalist.* Garden City, N.Y.: Doubleday and Co., 1981.

Wingrove, Elizabeth. "Sexual Performance as Political Performance in the *Lettre à D'Alembert sur les spectacles.*" *Political Theory* 23 (1995): 585–616.

Wolin, Sheldon S. *Politics and Vision.* 1960. Reprint, London: George Allen and Unwin 1961.

Wolf, Susan. "Moral Saints." *The Journal of Philosophy* 79, no. 8 (Aug. 1982): 419–38.

Wootton, David. Introduction to *Machiavelli: Selected Political Writings.* Indianapolis: Hackett Publishing Co., 1994.

Yack, Bernard. *The Longing for Total Revolution: Philosophic Sources of Social Discontent from Rousseau to Marx and Nietzsche.* Princeton: Princeton University Press, 1986.

INDEX

evil (*continued*)
12; Rousseau on overcoming, 99;
Rousseau on pre-existing evil
versus evil acts, 109. *See also*
wickedness
existentialism, 58

fables, moral, 115, 116, 116n, 122,
122n. 32, 124
faithlessness, 24–25
fanaticism: as following from moral purity, 98–99, 109; a mean between
cynicism and, 171; the righteous fanatic, 63, 64, 65; in Rousseau, 61,
94–95, 102, 103, 109, 110, 170;
Rousseau on, 94–95
Federalist Papers, The, 36n. 27, 179n. 3
Ferdinand the Catholic, 25, 41n. 35
Ferrara, Alessandro, 59n. 6
fictions, 115, 124
Fingarette, Herbert, 67n
First Discourse (Rousseau): on arts and
letters corrupting virtue, 80n. 47,
149; on corruption, 144; on reason
causing slavishness, 138; the uncorrupted condition presented in, 142
flattery, 37, 144; in hierarchical societies, 38; *The Misanthrope* on, 69, 70,
73; the playwright having to flatter
the audience, 76, 79; by princes, 21
Fleisher, Martin, 23n, 51n, 52n
flexibility, moral. *See* compromise
force: as alternative to deception, 133;
as alternative to hypocrisy, 29; Cicero on fraud and, 25n. 10; deception as morally superior to force,
18, 48n. 44; the prince choosing between deception and, 25; and
strength, 25n. 9
foreign policy, realpolitik in, 40–41
fraud. *See* deception
Frederick of Prussia, 6, 8
freedom: as absence of personal dependence, 132–33, 138; absolute freedom as impossible for Rousseau,
133; and beneficial manipulation,
128–29, 132–39; naturalness of,
145; and perfectibility, 146–47,
146n. 7; and reason, 132, 138;
Rousseau on man as born free, 146;

and virtue obtained through deception, 138–39
Freud, 145n. 5
friendship, 20, 51, 165, 167

General Will, 164, 165
Genevans: concern for public esteem
in, 162; as ideal types for Rousseau,
80, 82; public festivals, 77, 77n. 39
goodness: doing good as element of
happy life, 169; maintaining appearance of, 2; as natural state, 96, 98,
142, 150; possible diremption between unity and, 86; Rousseau admiring qualities in men who are
not good, 86n. 60
Gourevitch, Victor, 114n, 131n. 51
Government of Poland (Rousseau): egalitarianism of *Social Contract* contra-
dicted by, 105; policy recommendations in, 104, 167; on Polish
serfdom, 105–7

Hartle, Ann, 80n. 46
Hobbes, Thomas: and *amour-propre,*
160; in intellectual tradition starting
with Machiavelli, 9; Machiavelli
and Rousseau as differing from, 12,
12n. 28, 177; on pride, 160n. 24;
and Rousseau on state of nature,
145, 145n. 6, 157; on self-interest
in politics, 40n. 32
homme du monde: Molière as, 76; Molière on, 92–93; Philinte as, 76;
Rousseauian contraries to, 170;
Rousseau on, 92, 93–94
honesty: as alternative to hypocrisy,
29–30; honest politics as beyond
reach, 16; Machiavellian critique of
honest politics, 42–53; the possibility of honest politics, 34–53. See
also *honnête homme*
honnête homme: the integrity of, 96; Molière as, 76; Molière on, 92–93;
Rousseau on, 93–94, 97–98
honor: dishonor as worse than death,
160; justice toward oneself as, 117;
as more powerful than interest,
48n. 45; as not susceptible to compromise and negotiation, 42–43, 45